SUBMERGED HISTORY

UNDERWATER ARCHAEOLOGY IN FLORIDA

ROGER C. SMITH, EDITOR

Pineapple Press, Inc.
Sarasota, Florida

Inquiries should be addressed to:

Pineapple Press, Inc.
P.O. Box 3889
Sarasota, Florida 34230

www.pineapplepress.com

Library of Congress Cataloging-in-Publication Data

Names: Smith, Roger C., 1949– editor.
Title: Submerged history : underwater archaeology in Florida / Roger C. Smith, editor.
Description: First edition. | Sarasota, Florida : Pineapple Press, Inc., [2018] | Includes bibliographical references and index.
Identifiers: LCCN 2017042456 (print) | LCCN 2017043892 (ebook) | ISBN 9781561649945 (ebook) | ISBN 9781561649921 (pbk. : alk. paper)
Subjects: LCSH: Underwater archaeology—Florida. | Coastal archaeology—Florida. | Excavations (Archaeology)—Florida. | Shipwrecks—Florida. | Florida—History.
Classification: LCC CC77.U5 (ebook) | LCC CC77.U5 S834 2018 (print) | DDC 930.1028/04—dc23
LC record available at https://lccn.loc.gov/2017042456

First Edition
10 9 8 7 6 5 4 3 2 1

Design by R. Scott Rattray, Rattray Design
Printed and bound in China

Table of Contents

Introduction

~ Roger C. Smith ~

Archaeology is the closest thing we have to a time machine. Like detectives, archaeologists look for physical evidence that people have left behind to understand what happened in the past. Much of what happened was not recorded, and if it was, it may not tell the whole story. History usually is written subjectively to spin a tale, but archaeology is the analysis of tangible pieces to a puzzle that explain what actually happened. As a subfield of anthropology—the study of humankind—archaeology deals with cultural materials (artifacts) and their relationship to each other to re-create a bygone scene or event. By contrast, artifact collectors also look for pieces of the past, but for them it is a hobby that sometimes involves trading and selling for personal profit. Salvors, treasure hunters, and looters target archaeological sites to look for items of high value that can be sold as relics in the antiquity market. Often these different activities are conflated with archaeology because each involves digging up things; collectors may consider themselves "amateur archaeologists," and salvors may claim to conduct "commercial archaeology." However, for the profession of archaeology, as Smithsonian curator David Hurst Thomas has said, "it is not what you find, it is what you find out."

"What you find out" depends on the kinds of questions that an archaeological site can answer. Aside from "where is it?", "how old is it?", and "what kinds of artifacts are here?" (the "where," "when," and "what" questions), archaeologists are interested in the "how" and "why" questions: how was the site formed, and why does the site exist at all? What can it tell us about the human activities that left behind physical evidence? (As archaeologists, we know that people do not clean up after themselves very well.) To attempt to answer these questions and others that inevitably will arise, archaeologists take lots and lots of notes, make detailed measurements and diagrams, and record their work with photography and video. They are interested in the relationships among the cultural remains within a site, which is called *context*. Initially archeologists map everything that is visible to make a preliminary site plan, which is not only a record of what is exposed but also a reference from which to create research strategies for further investigation. Next, the site is tested at predetermined intervals to determine the extent (how wide and deep) of the cultural materials and their condition (state of preservation). Archaeologists dig test pits (called *units*) or trenches to uncover evidence that can begin to answer their questions. Excavation is a destructive process that cannot be reversed, so archaeologists take more notes and measurements, and make diagrams, photos, and video recordings.

Most archaeologists will tell you that our pencils, measuring tapes, log sheets, and cameras are our most important tools. When samples are collected during testing, first their exact locations within the context are measured and recorded. Then the objects are carefully removed from their context and placed in collection bags or containers to be sent to the laboratory for study—just as detectives collect evidence at a crime scene. The decision to conduct further excavation will depend on many variables, such as institutional support and funding, laboratory and storage facilities, and staffing.

This book is about underwater archaeology, which is simply archaeology done under the water. Terrestrial (land) archaeologists use trucks and jeeps to go to work; underwater archaeologists use diving gear. The tools, techniques, and products are basically the same no matter where one works, although different environments may require adaptations to the task at hand. For example, a land archaeologist uses a trowel, shovel, wheelbarrow, and a screen; an underwater archaeologist uses a trowel and a water dredge or airlift to move sediments to a screen. Regardless of the workplace, whether in the desert, jungle, forest, river, or ocean, archaeology's goals are the same: to understand our past.

An underwater archaeologist uses the essential tools: pencil, measuring tape, and record sheet.

(Courtesy of the Florida Division of Historical Resources)

Unlike land sites, most of which have been renovated, built over, salvaged for materials, or abandoned, underwater sites tend to be singular, isolated, and undisturbed. Because underwater sites are submerged, most have been out of sight and mind, leaving them unaffected by subsequent human activity. Modern commercial and urban development have put many land sites at risk because they are in the way of building or highway construction. Increasingly, underwater sites also are becoming at risk if they are in the way of marina, bridge, pipeline, or cable construction.

Artifacts from wet sites tend to be much better preserved than those from dry sites. Waterlogged materials especially survive over time when they are covered by sediments that lack oxygen. Although metal objects corrode, especially in salt water, organic materials such as wood, bone, leather, rope, and plant remains (nuts and seeds) tend to be protected from decay compared with those buried in acidic sediments on land. However, once waterlogged objects are removed from the water, they deteriorate rapidly in the earth's highly oxygenated atmosphere. Unless they are kept wet until treated in a specialized laboratory, these archaeological resources will self-destruct as they quickly dry out.

Conducting archaeology underwater has its advantages. Many archeologists who work underwater will tell you how peaceful and focused the work is, uninterrupted by other people, cell phones, or noisy neighborhoods with traffic. We often find ourselves making friends with the creatures that live where we work. Like any wild animals, once they become accustomed to us, they often interact, especially if our digging offers them something to eat. Sometimes we give them familiar names when they hang around day after day. Although larger, potentially dangerous animals such as barracudas, sharks, and alligators sometimes are present in the vicinity, they seldom are aggressive and tend to depart once they see that we are busy doing archaeology.

Working underwater also has its challenges because it requires the life support of self-contained or surface-supplied breathing gases. Bottom time is limited to hours and minutes, which are carefully recorded to avoid decompression sickness after surfacing; the longer one stays at depth, the more time it takes to decompress and breathe off accumulated nitrogen from the bloodstream. Variable water environments also require different approaches to the work. Although the water temperature may feel inviting at first, long, motionless hours of excavation and recording rob warmth from the body unless a diving suit is worn to minimize exposure. Diving in high-energy environments such as surf zones or river channels requires a careful combination of aquatic coordination to avoid fighting against natural forces and calibrated adjustment of buoyancy to stay on the bottom and not be swept away.

Visibility in the water is a fluctuating factor of the work. Contrary to the images of divers in gin-clear water that one sees in travel advertisements, not all submerged environments offer this benefit. Visibility ranges from bright, transparent ocean and spring water to murky lake and river water, with many conditions in between. These also change with variations of wind, storms, rain, and tidal fluctuations. Some work environments have no visibility at all, especially if a diver stirs up bottom sediments; underwater archaeology students often are coached blindfolded in the training pool to learn to work by touch and feel. On sites with marginal visibility, an underwater light is standard equipment. Work in and around the water is more weather dependent than on land: bad weather quickly can present problems of exposure to heavy winds and seas, or even lightning. Inevitably, all underwater work must be supported from shore, boat, or barge, which makes all activities equipment and labor intensive. There is the constant setting up and breaking down of tools and machinery, and the inevitable maintenance and repair of diving gear, instruments, motors, and pumps.

Florida is fortunate to have a broad variety of extraordinary underwater archaeological resources. No part of the state is far from water. Except for Alaska, Florida has the longest coastline (almost 8,500 miles) in the United States, as well as more than 11,000 miles of rivers, streams, waterways, and canals. The peninsula contains as many, if not more, archaeological sites that are wet as it does sites that are dry. Consider that Florida was once twice as large as its size today. About 19,000 years ago, the world's sea levels began to rise and reached their present levels about 5,000 years ago, as the last glacial period's ice sheets melted and drained into the sea. Along Florida's coastline, many human habitation and activity areas gradually were drowned by this sea level rise. All those prehistoric coastal marinas, bait and tackle shops, waterfront restaurants, and seaside resorts are now under the waters of the Gulf of Mexico. In addition, inland sites at springs, sinkholes, near river bottoms, and in lake basins also were inundated as subterranean aquifers expanded. Most of these sites are more than 6,000 years old.

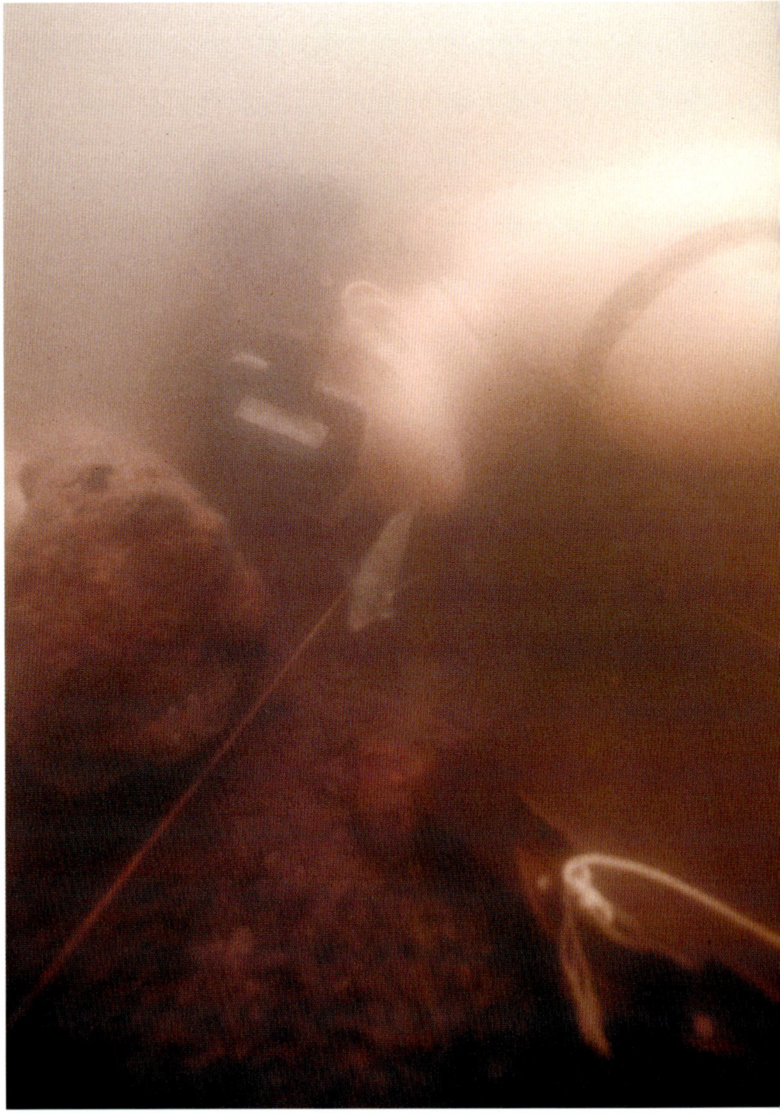

Poor visibility is normal at many underwater sites, such as this colonial English abandoned ship in Pensacola Bay.

(Courtesy of the Florida Division of Historical Resources)

Aside from drowned prehistoric terrestrial sites, many other kinds of underwater sites in Florida have been, and are being, investigated. Of course, shipwrecks come to everyone's mind because they represent elements of tragedy and romance and may contain the proverbial treasure that makes the news. Florida's location and coastal geography have made it a continual trap for navigators, leaving behind many hundreds of ruined vessels to remind us of its hazards. Shipwrecks occur along barrier reefs and islands, in and around inlets, but also offshore in deep water due to storms or leaks. Because they often contain remnants of cargo, shipboard equipment, and the personal effects of crew and passengers, shipwrecks have been called "time capsules" that resulted from a sudden catastrophic event, leaving behind the remains of a once-floating microcosm of human activity.

Florida's waters contain just as many abandoned watercraft as they do wrecks. The abandoned vessels tend to be located near or at major water arteries, anchorages, waterfront industrial complexes, river or lakeside communities, or small

The standard equipment for a small riverine test excavation includes a boat, screen barge, and floating pump platform.

(Courtesy of State Library and Archives of Florida)

bays and creeks. They include prehistoric and historic canoes, small sailing and steam crafts, and barges. Unlike automobiles hauled to junkyards, watercraft usually were left at their last port of call when their usefulness had expired, or they were pulled out of the way and scuttled at a convenient place nearby. Although they may provide us with information about construction styles, abandoned or scuttled vessels seldom contain cargo or shipboard equipment. Abandonment was a planned event that took place after the useful materials had been removed for reuse.

There also are sites constructed in water, including lighthouses and beacons, bridges, harbor jetties, wharves and dock remains, and fishing structures such as stone or wooden fish weirs (traps). Other underwater sites include refuse areas where accumulations of artifacts have been deposited over time. On land, archaeologists call these piles of trash *middens*—of interest because they represent a stratified record of human disposal over time. Underwater, they occur at anchorages, boat landings, shipping piers, and wharves. Accidentally or intentionally discarded

An archaeologist conducts a visual survey of the once-dry basin of Wakulla Springs.
(Courtesy of the Florida Division of Historical Resources)

refuse usually is associated with repeated cultural waterfront activity.

The study of wrecked or abandoned watercraft and other sites associated with coastal and riverine traffic often is called *maritime archaeology* because it deals with the history of waterborne navigation, commerce, and cultural exchange. Closely related is *nautical archaeology*, which is the study of the evolution of watercraft, emphasizing their structural and functional characteristics over time. However, nautical archaeology does not always require work underwater and might include, for example, the study of ship models, ship's figureheads, or historic ships still afloat.

Less common types of underwater sites in Florida are those that contain artifacts from upland sites that have been displaced by erosion and redeposited into the water along a riverbank, lakeshore, or beachfront. These sites do not usually have *stratigraphic integrity*—a layering over time—and they often are spread out horizontally in a random fashion. Even less common are the sites of sunken aircraft that crashed into the water and were not recovered. These tend to be found near military airfields, where the pilots learned how to fly by trial and error.

This book takes the reader on a series of tours to some of Florida's submerged archaeological sites in the company of the archaeologists who have worked on them. We begin with a visit to Warm Mineral Springs and Little Salt Spring, two submerged sinkholes that contain the well-preserved remains of prehistoric people and animals that have been studied by underwater archaeologists. Both springs are truly world-class windows into the past, and they contain

An archaeologist examines the shipwrecked remains of the Spanish galleon *Infante* in the Florida Keys.
(Courtesy of the Florida Division of Historical Resources)

the potential to revolutionize our understanding of Florida's earliest residents and the world in which they lived.

Jessi Halligan guides us into north Florida's spring-fed rivers, where her underwater research travels back in time to reconstruct the environment at the end of the last Ice Age. In particular, organic preservation in the Aucilla River helps her to determine how and when the area changed from wet to dry and back again, which plants surrounded the river, what time of year mastodons were using the water source, and what kinds of things they liked to eat. The discoveries of cut marks on a mastodon tusk and tools made of stone, shell, and animal bone point to human occupation at Florida's freshwater locations much earlier than previously recognized.

Next, we go offshore into the Gulf of Mexico with Michael Faught to look for drowned prehistoric occupation along relic riverbeds. This vast submerged continental shelf contains evidence of human activity zones that once were dry but subsequently were covered by marine sediments for thousands of years. These sites are not easy to find, but predictive modeling and modern remote sensing instruments have turned up several locations where test excavations have provided key criteria for the identification of additional archaeological sites in the future.

Florida is home to some of the oldest canoes known in North America, and more of these waterborne utility vehicles have been found in Florida than anywhere else. Ryan Wheeler tells us about the discovery of more than 101 fragmentary prehistoric canoes on the bed of Newnan's Lake in north central Florida after the water level fell during a regional drought. The makers of these watercraft used fire to hollow out large cypress or pine logs. Wheeler and his colleagues recorded many of the best preserved examples, which fell into two time periods: between 500 and 1,300 years old, and between 2,300 and 5,000 years old. They found that the canoes did not change much over time in that the oldest canoes looked remarkably like the youngest, but some of the older canoes were much longer than archaeologists had previously supposed. Study of other canoes from Florida rivers and springs have helped to build a typology that also contains historic canoes made with metal tools.

The next chapter examines Florida's role as a "ship trap." Because of its maritime location and geography, Florida always has been a natural trap for unwary mariners. Storms, barrier reefs and shoals, risky inlets, and shifting tides and currents all have taken their toll on unfortunate watercraft over the centuries. Examples of these casualties include *San Felipe*, a victim of the 1733 hurricane; *Commodore*, a gun-running steamship that sank in 1897; *Industry*, a colonial English transport that wrecked on the St. Augustine bar; *Catharine*, a Norwegian lumber carrier that ran aground at night in a gale; a small, unnamed seventeenth-century Spanish ship that struck an uncharted coral mount in deep water; and *Queen of Nassau*, a former Canadian patrol cruiser that sank under mysterious circumstances. *Maple Leaf*, a Civil War transport that struck a floating mine and sank in the St. Johns River, was the victim of a man-made rather than a natural trap. Each of these ill-fated vessels have been studied by archaeologists, who have reported their work in books, academic theses, and reports.

An unfinished wooden canoe was found abandoned in the Wakulla River. Apparently its makers found a large imperfection in the tree trunk, so they pushed it into the river.

(Courtesy of the Florida Division of Historical Resources)

The next chapter describes Florida's earliest shipwrecks, discovered by archaeologists in the shallow waters of Pensacola Bay. These well-preserved ships belonged to the fleet of Tristán

Displaced artifacts—a prehistoric ceramic pot and a modern brick—have eroded from upland sites into the Apalachicola River.
(Courtesy of the Florida Division of Historical Resources)

de Luna, who led 1,500 colonists and soldiers to settle the peninsula for the Spanish crown in 1559. Shortly after the expedition's arrival, a hurricane sank most of the ships and damaged the settlement's supplies, which doomed the colony. The underwater investigations of three of the sunken ships have stimulated academic and public archaeology in Florida and brought a forgotten chapter of Spanish American history to light.

Florida's legendary Spanish treasure galleons always take center stage in the news whenever silver bars and gold coins are found. Although these sunken watercraft represent only a small fraction of Florida's shipwreck population, they give people the impression that all shipwrecks contain treasure. Duncan Mathewson takes us to the gravesites of Spanish ships that sank along the coast during hurricanes in 1622, 1715, and 1733. He recounts his efforts to educate the small cottage industry of treasure hunters about the need to document the location of features and artifacts found on these wreck sites so that we can better understand the mechanics of wrecking and attempt to reconstruct the ships and their contents.

Next, David Moore and Corey Malcom take us to a remote corner of Florida's marine frontier, where the English slave ship *Henrietta Marie* sank in 1700 on her way from Jamaica back to England. There were no survivors, and the fate of the ship remained unknown for almost three centuries. Archaeological study of the wreck site has revealed a cross section of trade goods exchanged in the Atlantic slave market as well as the partial remains of the ship's lower wooden hull. An exhibit displaying artifacts and recounting the powerful story of this slave ship toured the United States and the Bahamas for eighteen years, and it was seen by nearly 3 million people.

St. Augustine, which was founded in 1565, shortly after the failure of the Spanish colony at Pensacola, remains the nation's oldest seaport. Chuck Meide and Sam Turner discuss how the new colony was born of storm and shipwreck, and how it continues to be a treacherous port of entry for Florida. When the potential for underwater archaeology in St. Augustine was recognized, investigations of shipwrecks began in conjunction with the St. Augustine Lighthouse and Museum. These continue today with the Lighthouse Archaeological Maritime Program, a robust archaeological team with community partnerships that continues to be one of the most active private underwater research groups in the state.

John Bratten shows us how a large part of underwater archaeology is conducted in the laboratory after the diving ends. Waterlogged artifacts must be treated and stabilized carefully to remove corrosion, salts, and the effects of years of immersion before they can be studied and displayed. As we will learn, the successful conservation of artifacts

An underwater archaeologist carefully constructs a site plan of the features of a Florida shipwreck.

(Courtesy of the Florida Division of Historical Resources)

is a specialization that requires training and experience, a well-equipped laboratory with tools and supplies, extensive contact with other scientists and laboratories, and lots of patience. Bratten shares with us the lessons he has learned and now imparts to his students about how to handle and care for a wide variety of archaeological objects.

Underwater archaeology in Florida is accompanied by strong public outreach and a number of important partnerships that encourage community participation in heritage preservation. Della Scott-Ireton describes several successful programs that are designed to educate and inform the public about underwater cultural sites. These include the Heritage Trails and Underwater Archaeological Preserves, which feature dozens of historic shipwrecks that can be visited throughout the state. She explains how underwater archaeologists have established educational courses for sport divers and dive instructors to involve them in the recording and preservation of submerged sites. These programs were made possible by formal and informal partnerships with federal agencies, local waterfront communities, amateur archaeological groups, and public and private organizations.

A final concluding chapter provides a brief review of how the submerged archaeological sites featured in this book were discovered, how they came to be managed and protected by state and federal laws, and how they can be protected for future generations.

CHAPTER 1

Secrets of the Springs: Florida's Prehistoric Time Capsules

~ Roger C. Smith ~

As nightfall darkened the skies over Sarasota County, the grounds around Warm Mineral Springs grew quiet. The daily bathers and concession staff all had gone home, and only a single light outside the bathhouse illuminated the water's edge. Larry Murphy and I donned our wetsuits and carried our diving gear into the spring. We checked our air tank pressures, breathing regulators, and buoyancy vests, just like any other dive. "Let's make sure our lights work," Larry said, and we tested our primary and secondary custom-built underwater lights, which would help us find our way under the cloudy spring waters. We both carried backup lights, because as Larry always reminded us, "One is none, and two is one." Then we submerged together and swam into the depths.

Florida is home to many freshwater springs and sinkholes, especially in the northern and central parts of the state where the Florida Aquifer is close to the land surface. The karst geology of the area is composed of honeycombed limestone, which contains underground rivers, caves, and solution features that flow in relation to periods of rainfall. Many of these clear-water springs have become the focal points of state parks, and many have been explored by a growing number of cave divers. In south central Florida, two deep, spring-fed sinkholes, Warm Mineral Springs and Little Salt Spring, have become world-renowned prehistoric archaeological sites owing to discoveries of well-preserved fossil animal remains as well as a wide range of prehistoric human remains.

A Sarasota County historic marker describing Warm Mineral Springs and Little Salt Spring.
(Courtesy of the Florida Division of Historical Resources)

Located only a few miles apart in Sarasota County, these two sites are characterized by highly mineralized, opaque water flowing from vents hundreds of feet deep. From the surface they look like circular ponds, but below the present-day water level they are distinguished by an hourglass-shaped profile, which narrows in the middle and flairs out like an inverted funnel into the depths. Thousands of years ago, these solution cavities collapsed, and their roofs fell down into the sinkholes; over the millennia this created small mountains of debris at their deepest recesses. The remarkable characteristic of both springs is that about 20 feet below the surface the water contains no dissolved oxygen, resulting in phenomenal preservation of organic remains.

With the advent of the self-contained underwater breathing apparatus (SCUBA) in the 1950s, divers began to explore both springs. They were astonished to find large dripstones (stalactites and stalagmites) along circular rock ledges, an indication that at one time the ledges had been above water. One of these divers, Bill Royal, a retired air force officer, began to dig in the sediments of a 45-foot-deep ledge at Warm Mineral Springs; he discovered several human skeletons and a number of bones from animals that have been extinct for thousands of years. Royal continued to explore, and he collected the partial remains of more than 15 humans and what appeared to be tools made from animal bones. Although he tried to attract the attention of scientists, only geologists took an interest. In 1959 he and Eugenie Clark, an ichthyologist, recovered a human skull while NBC television was filming their activities. When local physicians examined the skull, they

Bill Royal displaying a sample of prehistoric human bones that he collected in the 1950s and 1960s from Warm Mineral Springs. *(Courtesy of the Florida Division of Historical Resources)*

found it contained what appeared to be brain tissue. A radiocarbon test of nearby burned log chips dated them to be about 10,000 years old. Royal and Clark's report, published in *American Antiquity* in 1960, created a flash of excitement in the scientific community, but many remained skeptical that human remains of such antiquity could be found in Florida.

Warm Mineral Springs

Privately owned Warm Mineral Springs is Florida's only known warm water spring. The owners advertised it as Ponce de León's Fountain of Youth and developed it as a health spa, and in the 1950s and 1960s it became one of Florida's unusual roadside tourist attractions. Word of mouth eventually brought hundreds of elderly visitors, many from Eastern Europe, to soak in the soothing 87-degree waters, which were said to heal many ailments.

Surrounded by lounge chairs and beach umbrellas, bathers continue today to stroll together around the shallow periphery of the spring as loudspeakers still play easy-listening music. The center of the pond is roped off with a string of buoys to mark the central shaft of the cenote, which drops down to a cone-shaped pile of debris, 100 feet deep and 250 feet wide. The debris cone has been deposited layer by layer since the roof of the cavern first collapsed some 30,000 years ago. Preserved in the silt cone is a record of whatever has fallen into the spring over time, including skeletons of prehistoric people and animals, a turn-of-the-century wagon wheel, a 1917 Colt revolver, a Coke bottle from the 1930s, a 78-rpm phonograph record from the 1940s, modern sunglasses, Band-Aids, and a set of false teeth.

Brochure from the 1960s advertising Warm Mineral Springs as "The Real Fountain of Youth." *(Courtesy of the Florida State Archives)*

After Royal and Clark's report on their findings in Warm Mineral Springs, researchers and archaeologists continued to be unconvinced about the antiquity of human remains found there. Repeated requests to the Florida Bureau of Historic Sites and Properties by the Sarasota Historical Commission and the spa's general manager finally resulted in a January 1971 visit by Carl J. Clausen, the state's first underwater archaeologist. Royal showed him the areas from which he had collected human and animal remains. In January of the following year, Clausen spent a week excavating an undisturbed deposit on the 45-foot ledge. He recovered a human vertebra and a piece of a pelvis, thought to belong to a six-year-old child. These bones and nearby wood samples were carbon-dated to 10,000 years, corresponding to Royal and Clark's skull. Clausen noted that many of the sediments along the ledge had been disturbed by diving collectors, so he turned his attention to nearby Little Salt Spring, which also had produced human remains but appeared to be more intact.

In November 1972, W. A. "Sonny" Cockrell—who replaced Clausen as state underwater archaeologist—Royal, and hydrologist Fran Kohout spent several days surveying the ledge area of Warm Mineral Springs. They located a portion of a human mandible wedged back in a crevice; it was buried under three large boulders and associated with small animal bones, hickory nuts, acorns, and pollen. The wood found in context with the mandible was carbon-dated to between 10,240 to 11,000 years old. Cockrell recognized there were significant undisturbed areas in the springs, and he returned the following February and March, along with Ray Ruppé, his former professor at Arizona State University, and Vance Haynes of the University of Arizona. Together with Royal, they removed the three boulders and found that two stalactites were covering additional human bone deposits. The stalactites were uphill on the ledge and were wedged in place, indicating they could not have simply fallen in place. They recovered a nearly complete human skeleton including the cranium (skull), mandible (jaw) with most of the teeth, vertebrae, ribs, pelvic fragments, and phalanges (fingers and toes). A total of 18 carbon dates ranged from 9,000 to 11,000 years old.

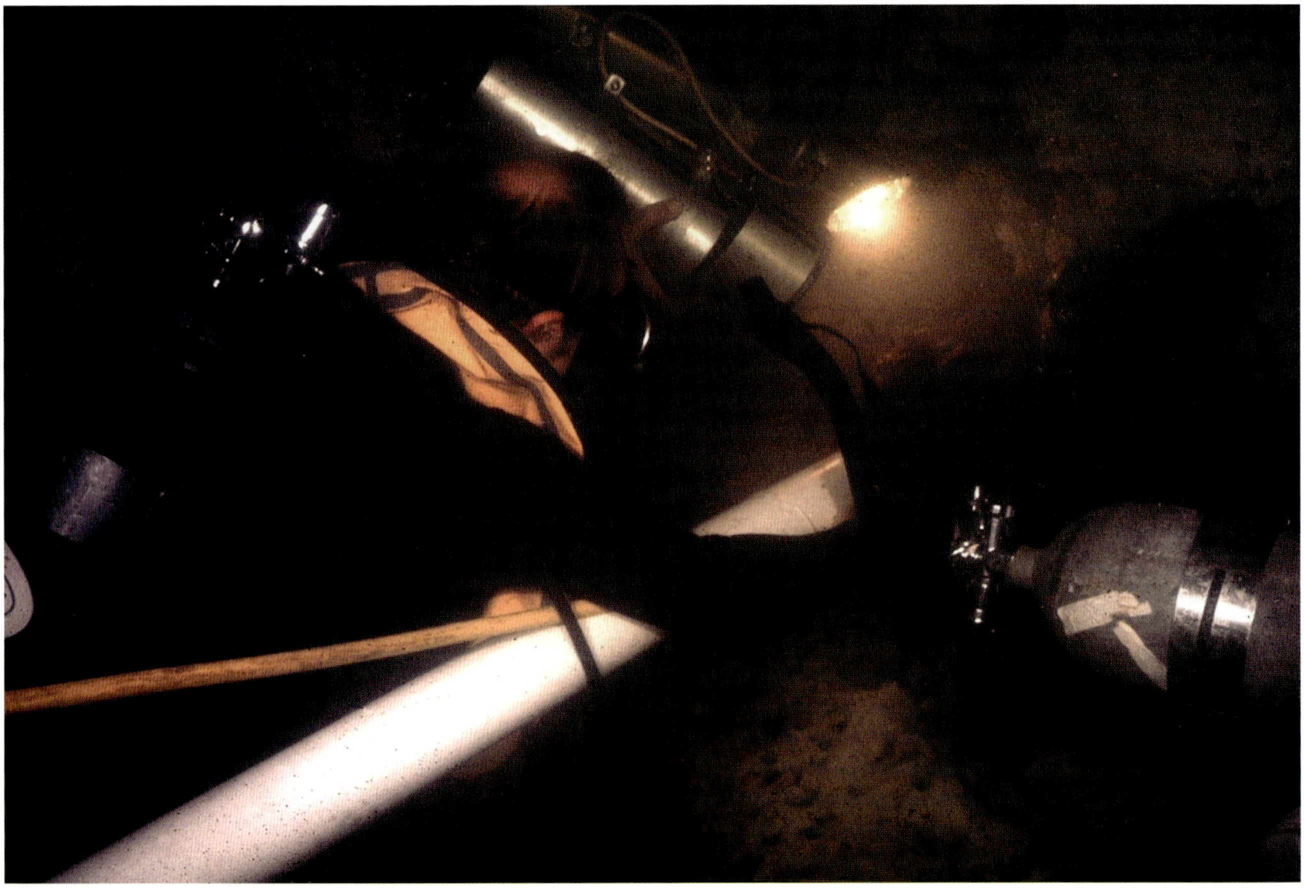

The human burial on the 30-foot ledge being excavated in 1973. *(Courtesy of the Florida Division of Historical Resources)*

Additionally, a shell artifact identified as a spear thrower (atlatl) was recovered in context with the cranium. This tool, which allowed a hunter to fling his weapon farther and with more force, was one of the most important prehistoric inventions for killing large animals from a distance. This find, along with others recovered from a rock shelter in Washington state, comprise the earliest spear thrower components in North America. Cockrell had found a nearly complete skeleton of a Paleoindian hunter—about 30 years old, 5 feet 4 inches tall, and 110 pounds—buried in a flexed position with his weapon in a crevice along what would have been the dry ledge of the spring at the time. Because most of the skeleton was found with an artifact behind wedged-in stalactites, which indicated human placement, Cockrell determined this find to be the earliest intentional burial ever discovered in North America at the time.

Sonny Cockrell examining the cranium of the Paleoindian hunter he recovered from Warm Mineral Springs in 1973.

(Courtesy of the Florida Division of Historical Resources)

Based on this discovery, state representative Robert Johnson of Sarasota, an experienced scuba diver, saw the need for positive action at the spring, and he acquired funding from the 1974 Florida state legislature. Between January and May 1975, Cockrell returned to the spring with a crew to explore the burial area further, and they discovered the in situ remains of a giant ground sloth (*Megalonyx jeffersonii*) that apparently had decomposed in a dry environment because there were clear rodent gnaw marks on its bones. In the same stratum along the ledge, he found the partial remains of a saber-toothed cat (*Smilodon floridanus*), which was the first solid evidence that these ancient animals existed at the same time and place. Near these now-extinct creatures were found parts of modern animals (panther, deer, opossum, raccoon, frog, turtle, and so on).

This history was on my mind as Larry and I descended into the spring; we stayed close together, shoulder to shoulder, and reached the 45-foot ledge. Our lights illuminated layers of dull, white carbonate crystals called "tufa," which form when minerals precipitate from the warm water and become attached to the exposed surfaces of stalactites and stalagmites. I followed Larry over the ledge to a guideline that led into the central shaft; we swam downward single file, each holding the line. Beneath the ledge, long strands of ghostlike green, red, and purple anaerobic algae hung down in sheets and threads. At 100 feet we reached the top of the silty debris cone, and Larry turned to me to give the diver "okay" signal (thumb and index finger joined to form a loop). I responded with the same signal, and we continued to follow the guideline. Diving on air, which was the only breathing gas available to us at the time, I could feel the narcosis creeping into my consciousness as exhaled bubbles echoed with each breath. At 190 feet, we entered a reverse thermocline, where the water temperature suddenly increases from 87 to 92 degrees, and the visibility cleared remarkably so that our lights began to reflect the walls of the sinkhole. At 210 feet, we felt very hot water pushing against us as it flowed from a main discharge vent at the bottom of the wall. We could see that the guideline extended into a small cave entrance that is a principal water source for Warm Mineral Springs. Larry and I paused to watch the flowing water rippling sand along the floor of the cave before we turned around and slowly made our ascent back along the guideline to the 20-foot decompression stop, where we switched to surface-supplied oxygen with a rig that Larry had built. This project was the first use of pure oxygen decompression in scientific diving. Later, as we surfaced at the darkened shore under the moonlight, I thanked him for taking me on a tour to the source of the geothermal fountain of youth for my birthday.

Our small team had arrived at Warm Mineral Springs in January 1976 to continue exploring the sediments where the human and animal remains had been found. Directed by Sonny, who I soon learned was a fiery and dedicated scientist, the state-sponsored project was the best staffed

Warm Mineral Springs at night. *(Photo courtesy of Curt Bowen)*

and equipped yet to work at the spring. One of the first things I immediately encountered was the rotten-egg smell of sulfur in the water, but as we began our daily activities around and in the spring, I became quite used to it.

Unlike the clear-water springs of northern Florida, the Warm Mineral Springs contains more than 17,000 parts per million of chloride, sodium, sulfate, magnesium, and other minerals. Some 20 million gallons surge through the cavern daily and flow out into the Myakka River at a rate of 17,000 gallons per hour. The source of this heated, mineralized water initially was thought to be ancient seawater trapped for more than 30 million years. More recently, scientists suspect that seawater from the Gulf of Mexico and the Atlantic Ocean seeps under the Florida peninsula to great depths, where it is geothermally heated and occasionally escapes upward through natural fractures in the overlying limestone such as at Warm Mineral Springs, to discharge at the surface. Numerous small springs and seeps of cooler fresh water also flow around the periphery of the sink.

Although the anaerobic nature of the water provides excellent preservation of the environmental and archaeological remains in the sink, its mineral content soon corrodes modern metal objects—such as our underwater equipment. We soon learned that after each dive we needed to carefully clean our dive tanks, regulators, cameras, and gauges. Eventually we installed a filtration system to provide freshwater to prevent the deterioration of our gear, and frequently rebuilt our diving regulators.

On one of the first dives, Cathy Tarasovic and I were asked to perform a reconnaissance dive around the 45-meter ledge. We started our circumnavigation by slowly swimming in a counterclockwise direction, trying to keep within sight of each other in the cloudy water. Then Cathy suddenly caught my attention and motioned for me to follow her to what appeared to be a human mandible lying partially buried in the sediment. We marked the location with a small flag and finished our dive. After surfacing, we located Sonny to tell him about our discovery, and he immediately

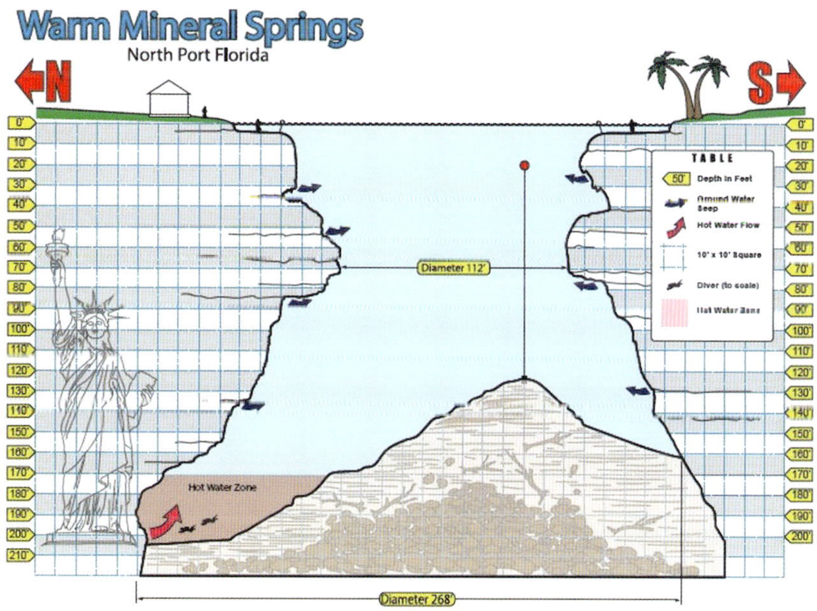

Profile of Warm Mineral Springs showing the 30-foot ledge, debris cone, and main hot-water vent.
(Drawing by Curt Bowen)

Paleontologist Greg McDonald carefully excavating the *Megalonyx* along the 30-foot ledge at Warm Mineral Springs.
(Courtesy of the Florida Division of Historical Resources)

put on his dive gear and swam to inspect the find. He determined that the mandible was an isolated find, not related to other skeletal material; it had come from a stratum directly beneath deposits containing the saber-toothed cat and ground sloth, which were previously dated 9,000 to 11,000 years before present. This, he said, was the first evidence in the Western Hemisphere of humans and saber-toothed cats existing in the same time period.

One of Sonny's technical innovations was the use of closed-circuit video to record underwater excavations. A black-and-white video camera with a light in an underwater housing was connected by cable to a television monitor and videotape recorder on the shore. Larry became the camera operator, while wearing a full-face mask with audio communication to the surface, where Melvin Kiser operated the monitor and recorder in a tent. Because the underwater camera did not have a viewfinder, Mel directed Larry where to aim it for the best recording, and Larry provided a verbal commentary about the activities being documented that was recorded on tape along with the television image.

This video system was considered to be one of the most revolutionary tools to enter the field of underwater archaeology because it offered the opportunity to involve non-diving scientists, who could monitor the progress of the work without getting wet, and it provided a permanent record of the excavation and sample collections. The video record also could be replayed afterward to recon-

Larry Murphy serving as the camera operator to record excavations with an early black-and-white, closed-circuit underwater video camera. *(Courtesy of the Florida Division of Historical Resources)*

struct the excavation sequences for the scientists who could not visit our project. The video system was used to record features, field specimens, and all excavations, including those of the ground sloth and saber-toothed cat. Sonny invited Greg McDonald, a paleontology graduate student at the University of Florida, to conduct the work, which lasted several weeks. Tom Neilson, Tom Hopkins, and I took turns assisting Larry with the camera and cable, while KC Goodyear and Nelson Comer made photographs of the exposed animal bones with underwater still cameras. Later, I used the video and photographic records to draw site plans of both sloth and cat features.

One of the things that I never quite got used to during those midwinter, early morning dive preparations was the eerie sight of the rising sun sparkling behind the steaming water surface. I could imagine how generations of ancient people would be drawn to the spring by this supernatural phenomenon.

We learned that our exhaled bubbles attracted some of the spring's bathing clients. At the 10-foot-deep decompression stop, where we spent what seemed to be hours breathing off the nitrogen that we had absorbed during a dive, we began to notice scores of kicking legs above our heads. Apparently our combined bubbles breaking the surface of the water were attracting groups of bathers who were looking for increased hydraulic stimulation or believed that the bubbles activated the minerals.

Another goal of the 1976 project was to measure profiles of the spring's basin and ledges. We accomplished this task using two different methods of measurement. Initially, we pulled measuring tapes from a central axis datum over to datum points along the walls of the spring at varying depths and points of the compass. Because the divers at the central axis often could not see the divers at the wall, a bubble level (simply a clear tube with air in it) was used to ensure the tape was straight. The diver at the center axis recorded the depth and distance to the wall at that compass bearing. This activity involved close coordination of team members and lengthy bottom times, but we finally recorded enough measurements for Ann Stanton to draw accurate profiles every 15 degrees around the spring on graph paper. The other method was an experimental use of a recording fathometer and transducer mounted on a float in the center of the spring. The transducer was lowered at 15-degree compass increments from the surface to the bottom of the spring along a measuring tape while the fathometer recorded the sonar reflections of the rock walls and ledges. We repeated the process at each of the 24 points of the compass. Once we had coordinated our rate of lowering the transducer

The author recording vertical and horizontal measurements to reconstruct profiles of the rock walls of the spring while mapping profiles. *(Courtesy of the Florida Division of Historical Resources)*

with the speed of the graph paper and stylus pen running through the fathometer, we managed to get fairly uniform readings. We made tracings of the 24 paper records, and with the graphed information we cut pieces of cardboard with the profiles to assemble a three-dimensional model of the funneled shape of the spring.

Sonny continued to work at Warm Mineral Springs until 1983. After his employment with the Florida Bureau of Historic Sites and Properties ended, he conducted subsequent investigations with legislative funding through the Florida University system, which he called "Phase II," from 1983 to 1992. He was assisted by his wife, Barbara O'Horo; Skip Wood, a Sarasota law enforcement officer; and Steve Koski, a graduate student at Arizona State University, who served as Sonny's assistant from 1986 to 1989. In 1996 and 1997, a group of diving explorers from ADM Exploration Foundation, under the direction of Curt Bowen, conducted an underwater survey of the spring using mixed gas to extend their working time and avoid nitrogen narcosis. They mapped four hot-water vents (97 to 100 degrees) and several cooler vents (76 degrees), and made extensive video records of each. During the project, a portion of Bill Royal's ashes—he died in 1997 at the age of 92—were interred in the warm water cave at the bottom of the spring.

Warm Mineral Springs was purchased on December 20, 2010, by Sarasota County and the city of North Port, putting it into public owner ship. In 2014, the city of North Port purchased Sarasota County's interest in Warm Mineral Springs and has become its sole owner.

Little Salt Spring

Located less than two miles from Warm Mineral Springs, Little Salt Spring also was discovered to be an archaeological site by Bill Royal and other divers. As early as 1960 they recovered large numbers of human bones and also found stone and wooden tools used by ancient people, and bones from a variety of animals, including deer, bison, and now-extinct species such as the giant ground sloth and mastodon.

Similar to Warm Mineral Springs, Little Salt Spring is almost perfectly circular, and is approximately 250 feet in diameter and 250 feet deep. A basin of soft sediments slopes gently to a depth of 45 feet, where a circular, near-vertical shaft, 75 feet in diameter, descends to ledges at 70 and 90 feet that are tucked back into the circular wall. At these depths, stalactites and stalagmites are present, indicating that the water level at one time was below this point. Some 14,000 years ago, this was a dry period in Florida's prehistory, before the Everglades or Lake Okeechobee existed. As the shaft continues to drop toward the bottom, it begins to flair out like an inverted funnel. At the bottom is a large cone of accumulated silt and debris, deposited over thousands of years after the roof of the solution cavity collapsed.

The spring and surrounding land were owned by Florida's largest land developer at that time, General Development Corporation (GDC). After Bill Royal showed him the site, Carl Clausen and a small team made preliminary dives in 1971. In the basin, Clausen uncovered a human skull and bones of a girl about eight years old, which were dated to at least 5,000 years old. Kelly Brooks, a professor of geology at the University of Florida, and Edward Deevey, a limnologist at the Florida State Museum in Gainesville, joined the team to study the spring's stratigraphy, structure, and aquatic ecology.

In 1974, GDC created a nonprofit foundation to investigate the site of some early human burials that were in the path of its newest housing

View of Little Salt Spring at night. (Photo by Curt Bowen)

development. Clausen was put in charge of the research, and the foundation provided several years of funding and support to maintain the spring and surrounding land as an archaeological and environmental preserve. Clausen established a research compound in 1975 and lived and worked there intermittently until 1980. His discoveries were described in the 1979 *Science* article "Little Salt Spring, Florida, a Unique Underwater Site."

In the winter of 1975, Larry Murphy and I were sent by Sonny to join Carl's team at Little Salt Spring and help them explore sediments in the basin and the deeper ledges. We met his team, which included Sheila Mathews, Steve Rogers, Nina Thanz, and Pete Farmer. Local archaeologist Marion Almy and sheriff's deputy Skip Wood also had been working with Carl. North Carolina's state underwater archaeologist Gordon Watts arrived to volunteer his time as well.

Carl asked me to help him with an ongoing excavation in the spring basin. He had found numerous small animal bones associated with what he thought was a fire pit because of the presence of charred wood fragments (dated to 10,190 years ago) in a darkened area. Associated with this, he had discovered a bone projectile point made from a deer antler, with a portion of the broken wooden shaft still lodged in the socket, and a circular piece of wood resembling a hockey puck, with a flat bottom and a shallow indented top. Carl thought the latter artifact might have been a mortar used for grinding food, possibly in conjunction with cooking, because the bottom appeared to have been burned.

Cross sectional view of Little Salt Spring, showing the research headquarters, wooden barge in center of spring, and excavation units in the basin and at the 90-foot ledge.

(Painting by Steven Daniels, courtesy of the artist)

Carl Clausen examining a deer antler projectile point with part of the wooden shaft in its socket.

(Courtesy of the Florida Division of Historical Resources)

Carl patiently showed me how to dig with a trowel, as well as label and draw measured diagrams of features in the excavation unit. I was impressed by his use of an underwater microphone attached to a clamshell helmet, into which he dictated notes while digging that were relayed to a tape recorder on the surface. Elsewhere in the spring basin, at a depth of 35 feet, Carl's team had discovered two wooden pegs, approximately 18 inches long, that had been hammered into the edge of the drop-off into the deeper area of the spring. One peg was dated at 9,700 years old, when the water level was much lower than today. The pegs may have been used as anchor points for vines or ropes to help people descend into the shaft and pull water up from the spring. Also in the now-flooded basin, they found a flat oak throwing stick, dated 9,500 years old, which was an early, non-returning boomerang used for hunting small animals. In addition, an unknown type of wooden tool was found; they called it a "putter" because it resembled a golf club, apparently one of five ever identified.

Diving took place from a small, floating barge positioned in the center of the spring. We rowed an aluminum skiff with our equipment from the shore to the barge. For decompression, a wooden picnic table had been suspended from the barge at a depth of 10 feet. We spent our decompression stops seated at the table, finishing and comparing notes or reading paperback novels and comic

The author preparing to dive at Little Salt Spring.

(Courtesy of the Florida Division of Historical Resources)

books, which (while they lasted) were attached with lanyards to the top of the table. I was glad to have a heavy wetsuit. Although the water at Little Salt Spring is a constant 73 degrees, after working stationary for several hours then waiting out a long, motionless decompression at this temperature, I became quite cold.

A unique feature of the spring, the 90-foot ledge is a horizontal crevice around the perimeter of the shaft of the sinkhole. Along the edge of the ledge, one can circumnavigate the spring by swimming in the crevice. Below the soft sediments that have accumulated along the ledge, the crevice floor is covered with a shallow layer of blue-gray clay. Carl and his team had discovered the partial remains of an extinct ground sloth, a bison, and a mastodon embedded in the clay. Of major significance, they found an extinct species of giant land tortoise with a sharpened wooden spear between the carapace and plastron (upper and lower shells). The red mulberry spear was carbon-dated to between 12,200 and 13,450 years old. The tortoise was found inverted, surrounded by fragments of fire-hardened clay, suggesting that it perhaps had been cooked upside-down in its shell. Whether it was killed on the ledge or fell into the sink, floated to the edge and became embedded in the clay, is irrelevant. The early date of the sharpened stake demonstrated a clear Paleoindian presence at Little Salt Spring.

Carl invited Larry and me to help with excavations on the 90-foot ledge, where he was working on the tortoise remains. At that depth, there is no ambient light, so each of us carried an underwater cave light and stayed close together. Hand fanning the sediments caused them to rise in suspension and cloud our visibility, even with the lights. A dive scooter with a propeller helped to wash the turbid water over the edge of the ledge and into the sink shaft away from the work area

John Gifford displaying a portion of the giant tortoise shell recovered by Carl Clausen and his team from the 90-foot ledge. *(Courtesy of the* Sarasota Herald-Tribune, *staff photo by Dan Wagner)*

to maintain clear visibility. The section that contained the tortoise remains was marked with yellow nylon line that delineated a 1- by 2.5-meter unit, which ran back to the wall of the crevice. Carl and Larry made a night dive to excavate and recover some of the tortoise material. Their dive was a lengthy one, and when Pete and I could see their lights at the decompression station under the barge, we rowed out to check on them. They transferred their recovered materials to us on the barge; these included large portions of an enormous shell with a dark brown patina.

The next day, Pete and I were asked to continue clearing the unit and to define the space by removing sediments and blocks of gray-blue clay. I began to hand fan in the area next to the tortoise and noticed what appeared to be an articulated snake skeleton, its vertebral joints and protruding ribs pointing upward and curving from head to tail in the clay. I carefully collected the bones and placed them in a collection bag. After decompression, they were cleaned, photographed, and placed in storage at the project headquarters on shore.

Aside from evidence that Little Salt Spring had been used by humans in the Paleoindian period (circa 15,000 to 11,500 years ago), Carl determined that the spring contained later human occupations from the Early and Middle Archaic periods (10,000 to 5,000 years ago). As the glaciers began to retreat, Florida became warmer and wetter as the sea level rose. With an increase in population and more water available, people found the spring a convenient water source that was more accessible after it had risen to higher levels. They began to settle at the edge of the spring and bury their dead in its submerged peat deposits. Carl and his colleagues discovered two partially articulated burials in the spring basin, one in only 6 feet of water, and another at a depth of 25 feet. Numerous disarticulated human bones also were found in the basin. In a marshy drainage slough that empties into the spring, they discovered the burial of a middle-aged woman facing east, her bones wrapped in a fragile vegetable matting. Carl estimated that this area may hold more than 1,000 burials. The bodies were extended face up on myrtle branches in graves dug into the muck, and they were pinned down into the peaty soil with wooden stakes. An oak digging stick sharpened at one end was placed with one person; another burial contained a wooden tablet with a bird carved on it. Bordering the slough was a limestone ridge with a large midden deposit, which represents an ancient village site where people lived adjacent to the spring. Carl speculated that the mortuary pond cemetery and nearby village midden constitute the well-preserved remains of a Middle Archaic population that occupied the area 6,000 to 8,000 years ago.

Little Salt Spring and 110 surrounding acres were donated by GDC to the University of Miami in 1982. Shortly thereafter, John Gifford, an associate professor at the university's Rosenstiel School of Marine and Atmospheric Science, became the principal investigator of the archaeological and ecological preserve. He worked briefly in the mid-1980s with Clausen on an excavation in the spring basin to study sediment stratigraphy and its deposition. Cores from the soft bottom sediments in 1990 determined that hard limestone rubble from the collapsed roof, which fell 15,000 to 20,000 years ago, lies below the organic material.

John Gifford, associate professor at the University of Miami's Rosenstiel School of Marine and Atmospheric Science, became the principal investigator at Little Salt Spring.

(Courtesy of John Gifford)

Steve Koski conducted research at Warm Mineral Springs and Little Salt Spring, where he was the site director for many years.

(Courtesy of Steve Koski)

Greenstone pendant, found by Steve Koski in the spring basin, made from material that is not native to Florida. *(Courtesy of John Gifford)*

Incised deer antler with 28 parallel incisions. *(Courtesy of John Gifford)*

A 1992 grant from the Florida Division of Historical Resources supported a four-month project in the spring basin for additional exploration of the 90-foot ledge. Steve Koski, who had worked with Sonny at Warm Mineral Springs, joined John at Little Salt Spring, became a research associate at the University of Miami, and served as the spring's site manager.

Work at the spring involved brief annual field sessions with graduate and undergraduate students. Excavation units in the spring basin produced several modified deer antler bones that served as projectile points, additional wooden throwing sticks, and the remains of a gourd that may have been used as a canteen about 8,000 or 9,000 years ago. One enigmatic artifact was a deer antler that had 28 parallel bands carved into it like a ruler. John suggested that it may have been a device used to keep track of time, as there are 28 days to the lunar month. He estimated the antler to be 10,000 years old. In addition, two unusual Archaic period artifacts, a greenstone pendant, one of two ever found in Florida, and another carved stone artifact that appears to be part of a spear-thrower, were estimated to be approximately 7,000 years old. On the 90-foot ledge, John and his students found additional remains of the tortoise and the slaughtered remains of a giant ground sloth.

Support for research at Little Salt Spring came from the University of Miami, the National Geographic Society, the Gulf Coast Community Foundation of Venice, Florida, the Selby Foundation of Sarasota, and the Jacarlene Foundation of Tampa. Beginning in 2005 the University of Miami began an ongoing partnership with the Florida Aquarium in Tampa to provide scientific divers to assist in exploration of the spring. Researchers from Washington State University and Pennsylvania State University also began long-term collaborative projects to study botanical remains, vertebrate paleontology, geology, and the DNA of plant, animal, and any human remains that might be found at the site.

Incredible discoveries have been made at Little Salt Spring, representing human activities that took place in the basin before it flooded and began to be used as a mortuary pond 8,500 to 9,500 years ago. Shell, bone, wood, and stone implements have been found that reflect the manufacture and technical use of tools during the late Paleoindian to Early Archaic periods by people who lived around the spring. Human burials in and around the sinkhole suggest a cultural and religious tradition that flourished in the Middle Archaic period in an environment that not only protected the deceased but also preserved them for thousands of years.

In 2013, the University of Miami announced that the research facility was closing because of shrinking budgets.

Future of the Springs

In 1989 Sonny Cockrell founded the Warm Mineral Springs/Little Salt Spring Archaeological Society at North Port, Florida. This group, under president Steve Koski, still is active at the time of this writing. They were instrumental in lobbying city and county officials to purchase and preserve Warm Mineral Springs.

Warm Mineral Springs and Little Salt Spring are unique time capsules, warehouses of environmental and archaeological material in an extremely well-preserved environment. As portals back into time, they are truly world-class sites. Studied together, they contain perhaps the lengthiest and most pristine natural and cultural record of Florida's past. Unfortunately, both sites are under severe threat from unauthorized divers and because there is no comprehensive management plan for future research development. At the time of this writing, their fate is uncertain.

Dr. Roger C. Smith served as State Underwater Archaeologist for the Florida Division of Historical Resources for three decades. He is the author of three books: *Vanguard of Empire: Ships of Exploration in the Age of Columbus* (Oxford University Press, 1993), *An Atlas of Maritime Florida* (University Press of Florida, 1997), and *The Maritime Heritage of the Cayman Islands* (University Press of Florida, 2001). He also is editor of *Florida's Lost Galleon: The Emanuel Point Shipwreck* (University Press of Florida, 2018).

For Additional Information

Warm Mineral Springs

Articles

Carl J. Clausen, H. K. Brooks, and Al B. Wesolowsky, "The Early Man Site at Warm Mineral Springs, Florida," Journal of Field Archaeology 2, no. 3 (1975): 191–213, available at https://www.researchgate.net/publication/233504695_The_Early_Man_Site_at_Warm_Mineral_Springs_Florida

Web sites

ADM Exploration Foundation and Curt Bowen, Warm Mineral Springs: The Fountain of Youth, http://www.warmmineral.com

Warm Mineral Springs/Little Salt Spring Archaeological Society (Facebook), https://www.facebook.com/wmslssas

Videos

Curt Bowen, "Warm Mineral Springs, North Port Florida," 2015, https://www.youtube.com/watch?v=LHXd6zeip2g

Sarasota County Government (Official), "Warm Mineral Springs Dive 1959," https://www.youtube.com/watch?v=eoPxF2qhRV8

Sarasota County Government (Official), "Warm Mineral Springs Dive 1992," https://www.youtube.com/watch?v=es5H-pHlh94

Little Salt Spring

Articles

George Wisner, "Diving into Paleo Florida," *Mammoth Trumpet* 23, no. 1 (2008): 8–11, available at http://www.rsmas.miami.edu/assets/pdfs/little-salt-spring/Wisner-2008.pdf.

Videos

EESI Penn State, "Penn State Science Diving: Little Salt Spring, FL," https://www.youtube.com/watch?v=23QwemDFwmc. Video from 2014 on archaeological excavations with the University of Miami.

Historic Films Stock Footage Archive, "Little Salt Spring" [Florida Archaeology—1977], https://www.youtube.com/watch?v=m-8RD216O40. Educational feature from the 1970s on Little Salt Spring underwater archaeology.

Ken Jefferson and Jarod Rogers, "Little Salt Spring," https://www.youtube.com/watch?v=Tyuutp8hTa0. ABC news report from 2013 on work at the spring and funding efforts.

University of Miami, "Little Salt Spring: 17 Meter Ledge Excavation," https://www.youtube.com/watch?v=dhJWzwFJHDY. Video of underwater work on the 90-foot ledge in July 2008, narrated by Dr. John Gifford.

WEDU (Tampa), "A Gulf Coast Journal: Ancient History," PBS Television, https://www.youtube.com/watch?v=somYPWHhJe4. Segment from 2014 on Little Salt Spring underwater archeology, including interview with Dr. John Gifford.

WINK-TV (Ft. Myers), "Little Salt Spring," https://www.youtube.com/watch?v=8R1lnhPlZNQ. CBS news report from 2012 on work at Little Salt Spring.

CHAPTER 2

Mysteries of the Ancient Aquifers: Archaeology in Florida's Rivers and Springs

~ Jessi J. Halligan ~

Sit back, close your eyes, and imagine: 14,500 years ago, a group of people crossing the upland plains of what we know today as Florida stopped at the edge of a small spring-fed pond. The pond was a bit difficult to reach, bounded by 15-foot-tall steep-edged limestone exposures on three sides with scattered limestone boulders from the semiregular rockslides, but there was a gentle slope on the northeastern side that allowed these people access. Animals also regularly used the spring, as demonstrated by the bones of bison, horse, mastodon, and llama scattered in the sediments around and within the pool. Mastodons also favored this unobtrusive reservoir for drinking, bathing, and wallowing, as evidenced by the deep deposits of mastodon dung that surround its margins. On this day, people were at the waterhole to butcher a middle-aged male mastodon lying in the waters and dung at the pond's edge. The pond was not deep—no more than 4 to 5 feet of water filled the depression. Although our band may have visited the pond previously to obtain spring water, this time the people were focused on removing the tusks of the dead behemoth from its massive skull. Made of ivory so useful for tool-making, the tusks also contained pounds of delicious fatty meat in the tusk cavity, which was precious to people who live by a strategy of food procurement rather than food production.

To harvest a tusk, someone chopped a hole through the skull below the eye socket, exposing the shiny ligament that held the tusk in place. Carefully wedged thin fragments of wood or other soft but stiff material were pushed into the tusk cavities across the ligament, severing it so that the tusk could be twisted out of the skull. After the tusks were removed, at least one was left behind in the shallow water of the small swampy pond, perhaps to be stored for later, or perhaps because it was not needed. Probably during the butchery, half a broken stone knife was abandoned on the edge of the pond, and a few stone fragments from tool sharpening were dropped and left behind as well. This knife may have been specially prepared for the butchery, since it was made of a stone commonly found within a few miles of the pond. When the mastodon had been processed to their satisfaction, the party moved on and disappeared from view.

Time passed. Water levels all over the world, including the Gulf of Mexico, were rising rapidly due to the influx of water running off the miles-thick glaciers that were melting from the poles. This led to a rise in the aquifer levels at our small pond, and at some point its stream outflow seems to have been blocked. The pond filled with both water and sediment, burying the evidence of mastodon butchery under more than 10 feet of sand, rock, mud, and wood.

Approximately 12,000 years ago, people arrived on the scene again; this time they lived on the banks of our now deeper and larger pond. People returned to the pond numerous times during the next 4,000 years, leaving behind the remains of their hearths and hunting and woodworking. These, in turn, were buried by river muds and leaf falls. By 5,000 years ago, the Gulf reached approximately its modern shoreline, and our pond became even more unobtrusive. Now it was permanently incorporated as a deep spot in the bottom of the dark waters of the Aucilla River, which flows from southern Georgia into Apalachee Bay.

This otherwise unremarkable setting continued to preserve the story of our mastodon butchers and their successors until its discovery by scuba divers and underwater archaeologists. These few pieces of evidence—a tusk with cut marks, a scarce handful of stone tools, and several tons of mastodon dung—provide a fragmentary picture of a small portion of the everyday lives of a few people who lived at the very end of the Ice Age. Butchering this mastodon could have been an event of such importance that it lived in legend, or it may have been so commonplace that it was barely noted. It could have been done by a whole family, or by a few members of a larger group, or by several groups who came together for a hunt. We do not know how long people were at the site, or how often, or whether they returned, or where they camped, or what language they spoke, or anything about their beliefs. We do not even know if they killed the mastodon or scavenged one that was already dead.

At the same time, this tiny scattering of sparse remains has revolutionized our understanding of the peopling of the Americas because it provides unmistakable evidence that people were living in the Americas more than a thousand years earlier than the Clovis people, who were long thought by archaeologists to be the original colonizers of the continent. Clovis artifacts are dated to around 13,400 to 12,600 years old in several sites across North America. Not only were people on the continent before the Clovis period, but 14,500 years ago our tiny pond would have been located more than 100 miles from the coast and more than 250 feet above sea level. The sheer remoteness and

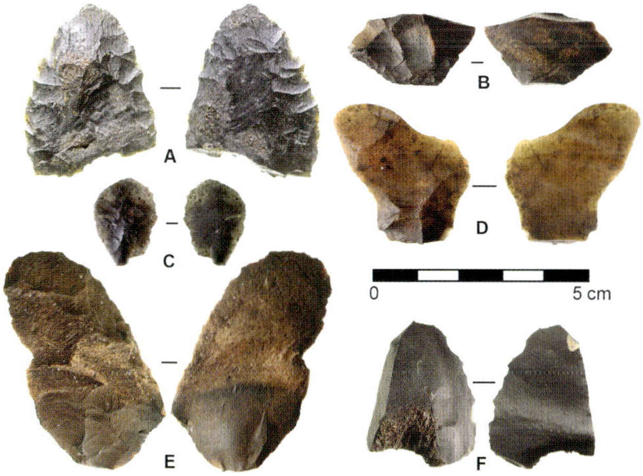

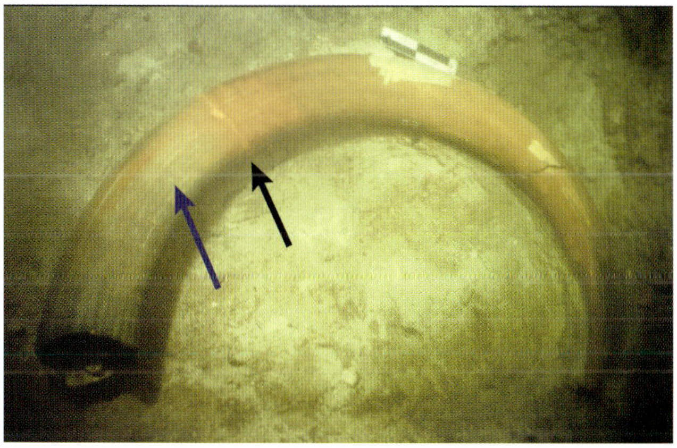

Top: Artifacts from 2013–2014 excavations at Page-Ladson. (A) A broken bifacial stone knife. (B–F) Flakes from stone tool manufacture. *Bottom:* Cut-marked tusk from the Aucilla River Prehistory Project excavations at Page-Ladson. (Original photo provided by J.S. Dunbar). The blue arrow points to cut marks. The black arrow points to a line demarcating the internal and external portions of tusk. *(Figure by the author)*

Top: Subadult mastodon radius bone from Page-Ladson during its excavation showing preservation of bone and botanical remains in bottom of site. *Bottom:* Neil Puckett bringing radius to surface to hand off to Halligan. Note that plant remains adhere to the end of bone.

(Photos by Brendan Fenerty, courtesy of the Center for the Study of the First Americans)

routineness of this area—which has been named the Page-Ladson site after its discoverer and its owner—suggests that our band of people were well familiar with the landscape and probably were not newcomers. This in turn suggests that much of the continent may have been occupied, though sparsely, by this time.

The Page-Ladson site is probably not unique. We think it is likely that the first people in the Americas left behind tangible evidence of their lives in hundreds and possibly thousands of locations across the continent. However, only a tiny percentage of these sites would have survived the twists of time over the past 14 millennia. Only a fraction of these sites would be serendipitously discovered by people who could recognize their potential importance. Even fewer sites would contain preserved organic materials that would enable us to directly date them and be sure that we are seeing evidence from very ancient sites. We only know as much as we do about Page-Ladson and other Ice Age sites in Florida because of their underwater setting. The unique geological properties of the Floridan Aquifer and the Florida

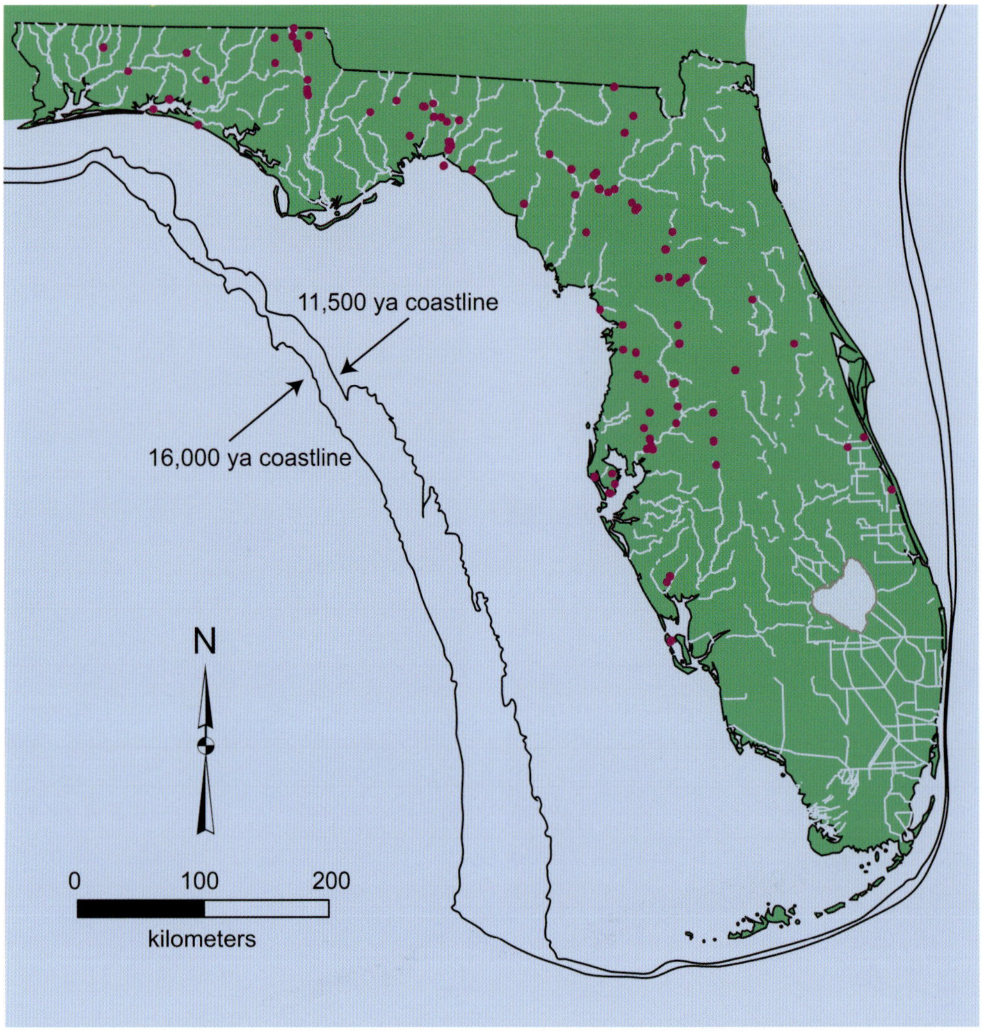

Map of Florida's modern land mass and portions of the continental shelf submerged between 16,000 and 11,500 years ago based on global sea level curves, as published by Lambeck and colleagues in 2015. The purple dots show the locations of recorded Paleoindian sites in Florida.

(Map by the author)

Coastal Plain have preserved organic materials, including the bones and mastodon dung, almost perfectly.

This organic preservation is very important for several reasons. First, organic remains can be directly dated by the radiocarbon method, which can be used to determine when anything that contains carbon died. Thus, this method cannot be used on inorganic materials like stone. Therefore, radiocarbon dating of the organic artifacts such as bones and plant materials can tell us *when* objects were made or left behind. Second, these same plant and animal remains allow us to reconstruct past environments, which is important for understanding the world the first Floridians faced. They are also important for helping us to comprehend the complexities of the environmental transitions during the end of the last Ice Age. For instance, the environmental data we obtained from sediment samples collected within the sinkhole at Page-Ladson have revealed to us how and when the environment changed from wet to dry and back again, what plants surrounded the pond and when, approximately when the pond became part of the river, what time of year mastodons were at the pond (late summer/fall), what things they liked to eat (young twigs, acacia, gourds, and grapes), and even approximately when the mastodons became extinct in the area (approximately 12,600 years ago). All this is only possible because of how well the plant and animal remains are preserved at the site.

This ability to understand the past in new and more complete ways is what originally led me to underwater archaeology. I seek the stories of the earliest human inhabitants of the New World, known now to archaeologists as Paleoindians. Although Florida probably was not the first place that people arrived in North America, Florida's fresh water rivers and streams provide a unique window into the lives of these early inhabitants. During the Paleoindian period (approximately 16,000 to 11,500 years ago), Florida was twice as large as it is now because billions of gallons of water currently in the oceans were tied up in the enormous glaciers covering most of Canada and the northern United States. As the glaciers melted, the landscape became inundated, which submerged in turn any Paleoindian sites left behind. Therefore, to find and recover that evidence we must look underwater.

My ongoing research at Page-Ladson, conducted in partnership with experts from all over the country, began in 2012, but I was far from the first researcher in the river. Our inquiries at Page-Ladson built upon decades of investigations by a number of inventive and daring folks, some of whom were trained archaeologists and geologists, but many of whom were not. Some of the earliest underwater research in the world took place in Florida, with people recording fossil finds in the crystal-clear freshwater rivers, streams, lakes, and ponds very early in the twentieth century. These intrepid explorers started using the earliest prototypes of scuba in the 1930s, and they evolved to more formal investigations in the 1940s and 1950s when buoyancy was controlled by milk jugs filled with air and regulators were attached to compressed air tanks with no pressure gauges. (People learned how to sense that they were almost out of air or learned to ascend with no air at all.) These earlier methods are considered life-threatening practices today, but the early explorers seem to have survived unscathed.

Most of the first people conducting underwater research and excavations began discovering fossils and later realized that human-made artifacts were also found in similar settings. Clarence Simpson, a Works Progress Administration archaeologist and Florida Geological Survey employee, and his family started discovering artifacts near the exposed skeletons of extinct animals underwater in the High Springs area as early as the 1920s. These finds were published in 1941 by Albert Jenks, who compared ivory rods from the Ichetucknee River to others found in New Mexico at the Clovis site associated with extinct mammoth remains. In the meantime, Simpson assisted with the removal of a mastodon from Wakulla Springs in the 1930s and continued to dive the rivers. He located several sites in the Santa Fe River and numerous sites on land after World War II, but was unable to complete the research before his untimely death in 1952.

John Goggin, the first anthropologist employed by the University of Florida, did much to shape underwater archaeology in Florida. His first dabbling in the field began in 1949, when he conducted a survey of the Ichetucknee River using glass-bottomed buckets to look for Spanish and

Seminole artifacts. Before his death in 1963, he had conducted exploratory excavations at a number of underwater sites in both fresh and salt water. In a seminal 1960 paper, he was one of the first to propose that most underwater sites in Florida's rivers were probably deflated and redeposited, which would have profound implications for the future development of archaeology in freshwater settings and Florida's policies for underwater artifact collection.

Goggin also defined underwater archaeology as systematic recovery conducted, whenever possible, by an archaeologist and not pursuing salvage or treasure hunting. Although he was more interested in more recent culture periods of Florida archaeology, he sparked extensive field investigations during his tenure at the University of Florida, and caused numerous archaeological sites, both terrestrial and underwater, to be recorded. In a rare foray into Paleoindian research, he conducted test excavations at the Butler site, located near the confluence of the Santa Fe and Suwannee Rivers, based on advice from Simpson. There he discovered several lanceolate (shaped like the head of a lance) projectile points, which he named Suwannee points, and considered them to be Paleoindian in age.

After Goggin, most river investigations in the 1960s and 1970s were conducted by hobbyists and avocational archaeologists. Professional researchers were focused on offshore and spring basin settings, possibly influenced by Goggin's thoughts on site integrity. Carl Clausen, a former student of Goggin, conducted excavations in solution sinkholes such as Warm Mineral Springs, Little Salt Spring, and Devil's Den. All three sites were of great interest because they contained human skeletal remains, some so well preserved that brain matter was still found within the skulls. Clausen's careful research, adhering to strict scientific protocols for collection of samples, allowed him and his collaborators to conclude that the human remains in Warm Mineral Springs dated to approximately 11,000 years ago, when water levels were so low that the spring would have been cenote-like, so the remains were probably from people who met with accidents or were placed there after death. The human remains at Little Salt Spring were much younger (circa 6,800–5,200 years old) and were found largely in an extensive cemetery in the adjacent spring basin, while people lived around the spring proper. There was also evidence of Paleoindian and early Archaic use of the spring from approximately 14,000 to 11,000 years ago. Research in these springs continued during the ensuing decades by archaeologists such as Sonny Cockrell, John Gifford, and Steve Koski, demonstrating that careful underwater excavation is both possible and fruitful, and that sinkholes in Florida sometimes contain important intact sites.

Although few professional archaeologists were working in the rivers in the 1960s and 1970s, there was no lack of active investigation. Hub Chason of Marianna focused on the Chipola River and discovered dozens of Clovis and younger projectile points along the scoured stream bottom; he published a book about these discoveries in the 1980s. River pioneers Ben Waller and Alvin Hendrix recovered extinct animal bones and numerous Paleoindian artifacts at the Butler site and several other locations in the Suwannee, Santa Fe, and Silver Rivers. The extensive Hendrix collection has been donated to the Silver River Museum and is available for study.

Waller was one of the first to publish his Paleoindian discoveries, bringing them to the awareness of Florida archaeologists in 1969. He noticed that Paleoindian artifacts and extinct animal bones were most commonly found in rocky shoals at the bottom of spring-fed rivers, which led him to propose that Paleoindians were ambushing animals at shallow water crossings. He also assisted with one of the few river excavations directed by a professional archaeologist in 1970s. Charles Hoffman, then at UF, conducted a season of excavation at the Guest Mammoth site in the Silver River in 1973 after diver George Guest discovered and reported the locality. This site contained the remains of two Columbian mammoths, possibly associated with stone tools and showing evidence of butchery. If so, this site would be the only evidence of mammoth butchery in the Southeast, but the site has not been widely accepted due to complexities with its stratigraphy and dating. The Guest Mammoth site currently is being reinvestigated by Morgan Smith, a doctoral candidate at Texas A&M University, so its true age and cultural affiliation may soon be understood.

Waller's "river crossing" hypothesis contrasted with the "oasis" hypothesis proposed by Wilfred Neil, manager of the Silver Springs tourist attraction, where Suwannee and Clovis Paleoindian projectile points had been discovered in stratigraphic layers below younger Archaic layers. Neil thought it likely that surface water would have been rare and hard to access during the lowered sea levels of the late Pleistocene, so people and animals would have had to cluster to the oases provided by the isolated spring heads scattered throughout the limestone bedrock of the interior of Florida—and the Page-Ladson data support this hypothesis.

The clear waters of the Silver River were known very early to contain artifacts, but Richard "Dick" Ohmes was perhaps first to dive in the black waters of the Aucilla River. Between the late 1950s and the 1970s, he discovered a number of important sites containing Clovis points and well-preserved artifacts made from the bones and ivory of now extinct mammals such as mammoths, mastodons, llamas, and horses. He reported his findings to several people, including Vance Haynes, a geoarchaeologist then with Southern Methodist University, and David Webb, then at the University of Florida. Based on Ohmes's information, two cores were collected from one site in the early 1970s. Ohmes had discovered a large number of bone and stone artifacts within this sink, including Paleoindian spear points, which eventually were donated to the Florida Museum of Natural History. Radiocarbon dates from the cores showed that there were thick deposits of sediment in the sink with very old peats (more than 40,000 years old) at the bottom of the deposits.

Don Serbousek, a Daytona native and avocational paleontologist, is probably most well-known for his 1968 recovery of the mastodon "Priscilla" from the Little River section of the Aucilla. A male mastodon, Priscilla is one of the most complete specimens ever recovered. Serbousek made a number of casts of the mastodon for display, several of which are to be found in museums, including the Brevard Museum of History and Natural Science and the Houston Museum of Natural Science. He and Ben Waller also discovered more than a dozen archaeological sites in the Aucilla River that contained Paleoindian and Early Archaic stone tools. In the early 1980s Serbousek reported these discoveries to Jim Dunbar, an underwater archaeologist for the Florida Bureau of Archaeological Research, and also donated much of his collection to the State of Florida for future research.

Webb and Dunbar became increasingly interested in the scientific possibilities of the Aucilla

The 2014 survey to relocate the Guest Mammoth Site. *Top:* Grayal Farr and Halligan on dive boat. *Bottom left:* Brendan Fenerty excavating a test trench. *Bottom right:* Halligan ascending after digging test trench. *(All photos by Morgan Smith)*

River, and by the early 1980s they obtained funding to begin investigating the river for intact archaeological and paleontological deposits. They visited locations that river divers told them about and surveyed portions of the river with teams of divers. In 1983, diver Buddy Page brought the Page-Ladson site to their attention. They were impressed by the extensive sediment sequences and the ubiquitous artifacts and extinct faunal remains in the deepest part of the site, labeled the "booger hole," and began a formal investigation. Page continued to work with Webb and Dunbar for the next several years during their extensive excavations at Page-Ladson. These excavations, which discovered the mastodon tusk mentioned earlier, were published in the 2006 book *First Floridians and Last Mastodons.*

For the next decade and a half, Webb and Dunbar directed a collaborative team, eventually named the Aucilla River Prehistory Project (ARPP). The project explored large portions of the river, recording more than 50 archaeological and paleontological sites and excavating several of them until the project's completion in 1999. The research revealed that shallow rocky shoals in the river channels often contained artifacts exposed within the cracks in the limestone bedrock, similar to the pattern noted by Waller in the eastern rivers. Drowned mid-channel sinkholes often contained artifact scatters in the deepest part of the sink. Some of these mid-channel sinks had deep sediment banks on the sides that occasionally also contained artifacts. One sinkhole site, Sloth Hole, contained all these settings, and between 1994 and 1999, C. Andrew "Andy" Hemmings, then a graduate student at UF, conducted extensive excavations of the site. Hemmings and his crew discovered that Sloth Hole contained artifacts diagnostic of Clovis and Bolen (circa 11,600–11,000 years old) cultures and extensive paleontological remains, including several mastodons in the sediment layers on the sinkhole margins. There was also evidence for extensive toolmaking scattered on and in the rocky shoals in the form of fragmented stone and ivory.

Further excavations at Ryan-Harley. *Top:* Ed Green monitoring screen deck while Morgan Smith and Brendan Fenerty fill sandbags for stabilizing the bank after excavations. *Bottom:* Diver Adam Burke recording artifact finds.

(Top photo by the author; bottom photo by Morgan Smith)

River diving brothers Ryan and Harley Means discovered in 1996 a site that was neither sinkhole nor shoal in the braided channel of the Wacissa River, a main (but clear-water, spring-fed) tributary of the Aucilla. The Ryan Harley site, which appears to be a Suwannee-aged campsite based on artifact styles and associated material culture, was located at the edge of an unobtrusive portion of the river channel on a sandy deposit in approximately 3 to 6 feet of water. Suwannee people may have been living near the edge of a water source and depositing their waste in a low spot at the edge of their campsite. Repeated efforts to directly date this and all other Suwannee sites have so far failed, so we still do not know exactly what "Suwannee-aged" means, but most of us think the Suwannee people immediately succeeded the Clovis, dating to approximately 12,800 to 12,500 years old. In 2015 and 2017, we conducted additional excavations at Ryan-Harley so that Morgan Smith could work on a further analysis of the site, and these analyses are ongoing.

I began to work in the Aucilla River in 2008. My path to underwater archaeology in Florida was far from direct, but I eventually found myself here because of its wide-ranging and unique archaeological record. For the past twenty years, I've worked on archaeological projects in more than twenty states, the Gulf of Mexico, the Great Lakes and two Canadian Provinces, but I started working in Florida's freshwater rivers and streams because these fluvial systems are one of the only places in North America where the evidence of the first Americans has been preserved. While attending college in Boston, I became increasingly interested in how the geological processes of erosion, deposition, and soil formation determine if and to what extent an archaeological site will survive after people have abandoned it. I became especially interested in how sea level change impacts our understanding of how past people used the coasts. So I learned to scuba dive, and in 2004 entered graduate school at Texas A&M University, the only American university that specializes in both geoarchaeology and underwater archaeology.

My first dive in the Aucilla River took place nearly four years later, and, without exaggeration, it was a life-changing episode. Andy Hemmings agreed to show me the river. I use "show me" in the most metaphorical way possible. We entered the extremely red water at a small boat landing and swam upstream to where Andy remembered a sinkhole in the river bed. At the time, I had one small dive light stuffed in the top of my hood for illumination, and as we descended, my view of the world was limited to a 5-inch circle of light that faded out about a foot in front of my face. We landed in a hole that was about 20 feet deep, but it could have been a hundred, as there was no way to see the surface, topography, or anything other than the twin circles of illumination from our lights. I was kneeling on a sandy slope, and I could just make out that Andy was looking closely at the bottom, picking up black things (most of the sand was kind of red). So I followed suit, pulling black objects close enough to my face to determine from the outline what they could be. I was soon thankful for my gloves because the sand was liberally littered with broken bottle glass and treble hooks since we were in the main channel near a boat landing, but I also was soon completely absorbed in the task. Down there in the dark, the world fell away. Andy was less than a yard away from me at all times, and we were talking back and forth (mostly with our hands, though Andy is surprisingly good at enunciation with a regulator in his mouth), but even he quickly became secondary to my experience. The universe consisted of red sand and things that were not red sand. Promising shapes went into a mesh bag for examination at the surface. After an hour or so, we surfaced and inspected our finds. There were numerous bones, turtle shell fragments, and flakes from stone tool manufacture, but the only thing I remember clearly was my first find: one of the small foot bones of a baby Proboscidean, probably a mastodon. After comparing our discoveries, we returned them to the river and left the small sink behind.

This was dive #102 in my cumulative dive log. I've since logged more than 500 dives, 350 of

uthor Halligan surfacing from the Aucilla River. *(Photo by Micah Mones)*

which have been in the Aucilla. The black water is not for everyone, but for those of us it hooks, it hooks hard. The promise of this sink led me to conduct my doctoral research on two underwater sites about a half-mile downstream, driving the 13 hours from College Station, Texas, to our encampment on average once every four months for the next four years. As a geoarchaeologist, I conduct earth sciences research with the goal of understanding archaeological problems. In the case of the Aucilla, I was interested in understanding how all the artifacts and bones ended up in the bottom of the river in those shoals and sinkholes, a question that remained from previous ARPP investigations in the rivers. Were they the tumbled remains of long-destroyed sites that ended up being washed into the river during long ago floods? If this were the case, these artifacts were interesting and beautiful, but could tell us nothing about people in the past beyond the fact that they made artifacts somewhere in the area. Alternately, were the artifacts and bones being discovered in places where people thousands of years ago had originally left them behind? If the latter were true, the patterns to be found by these materials would then be due to past cultural choices and therefore could be interpreted to understand Paleoindian activities.

Consequently, my research has a few combined goals. First, I want to re-create the geological history of each site, because understanding how and when sediment deposition, erosion, and stability occurred provides important clues to understanding both local environments and the opportunities available for people. Second, I need to understand which geological layers (strata) contain artifacts, and I want to figure out whether those artifacts arrived in those strata due to geological processes or cultural ones. Finally, if I find that the artifact patterns were likely the result of human activity, I need to interpret these activities to understand how people were using the sites.

To address these three goals, I've collected a number of cores, which are a quick and easy way to see the sediment layers in the bottom of the river without digging a big hole. But quick and easy are relative terms when one is working from a boat and using gasoline motors. We use these cores for my first goal, re-creating the local geological history.

To learn about the archaeology, we need to actually *find* archaeology. This means excavating

How to Collect a Core

Coring involves a crew of a least three people. Our crew varies, but usually includes myself and Ed Green, my stalwart and most steadfast volunteer (and supplier of our coring vessel and a collection of equipment that I employed—and often broke or lost). First, we place a 30-foot-long, 3-inch-diameter aluminum irrigation pipe through a hole in the center of our pontoon boat deck. Once the pipe hits the sediments on the river bottom, a vibracoring device is attached to it which when turned on vibrates the core tube rapidly, liquefying the sediments around the tube and allowing it to penetrate the river bottom. Once the tube cannot go any deeper, we cap it on the top to create a vacuum and then begin the long process of winching it up.

The coring process. *Top left*: Hooking up a vibrocorer. (Ed Green and Andy Hemmings shown.) *Top right*: Pulling down to maximize core penetration. (Ryan Duggins, Harley Means, Jim Dunbar, and Neil Puckett shown.) *Middle*: Jacking the core out of ground. (Harley Means and Jim Dunbar shown.) *Bottom left*: Diver waiting to cap the core at the bottom. (Halligan shown.) *Bottom right*: Negotiating the long pipe when the bottom cannot be capped in advance. (Rafael Fraga, Halligan, Shawn Joy, and Ben McCall shown.)

The final product. *Left:* Core from Sloth Hole immediately after splitting. *Middle:* Core segment from Page-Ladson. *Right:* Inset showing close-up of core section highlighting the areas where paleoenvironmental samples were collected.

Ultimately at some point there is a 30-foot-long metal tube filled with water and mud hanging mostly vertically above the deck of an 18-foot pontoon while the bottom of the core is sealed off. Once this delicate situation is managed, the portion of the tube filled with water is cut off and the top re-capped. This usually results in a muddy shower for whoever is holding the tube, so we make sure to rotate this duty.

After we have returned to land, these tubes filled with river muds are split longitudinally so we can look at the sediment levels and sample them. We collect organic materials to radiocarbon date, sediment samples to tell us about how they were deposited in the river, and other samples to process for microfossils such as pollen, diatoms, and spores, which tell us about past environments.

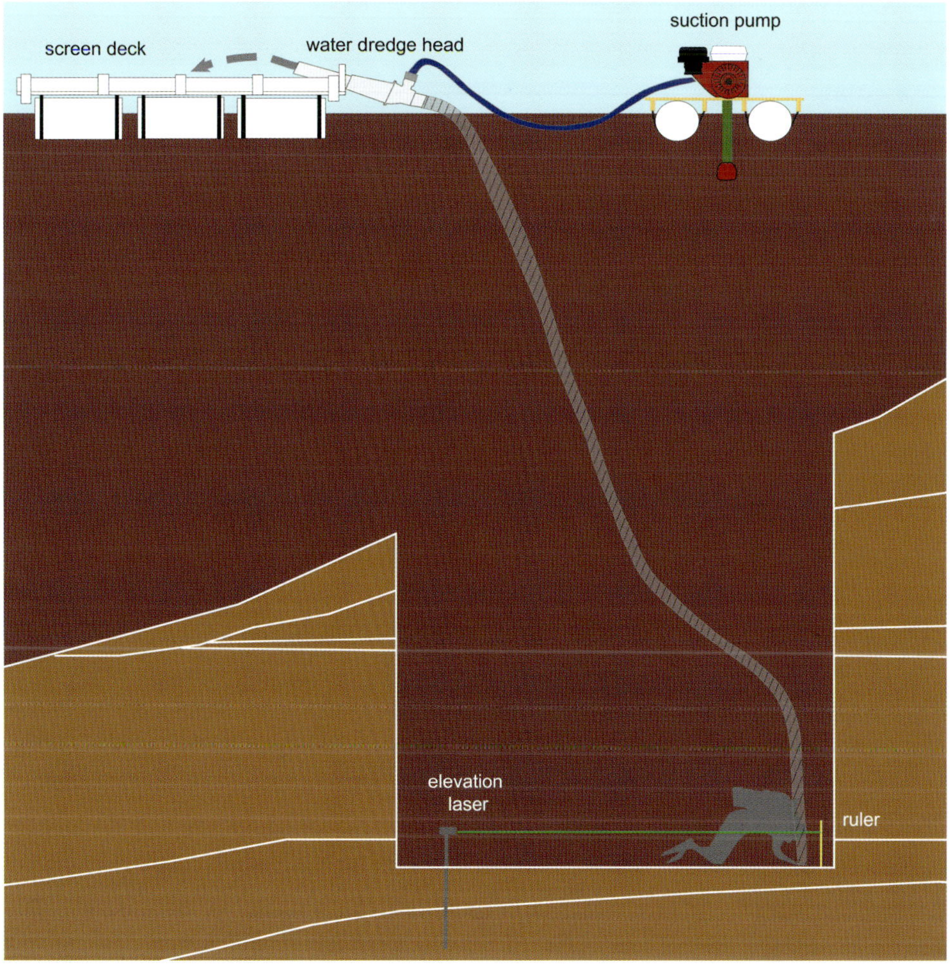

Generalized excavation schematic. The laser is used to measure depth when we dig in controlled 5- to 10-centimeter increments. The laser control mount is put at an elevation that is tied into our terrestrial grid with surveyor's equipment and a very long stadia rod. The green light of the laser shines through the black water at a constant depth elevation, allowing us to measure above and below this line. *(Figure by the author)*

bigger holes with a series of 1-×2-meter grids to look for material culture. Our excavations are placed in areas of the sites where cores have shown that the sediments were stable for so long that they had started to alter chemically and structurally into soils. Soil formation is evidence of long-term landscape stability, so it also is evidence that these sediments were dry and exposed to air at some point (most of them are 12 to 15 feet below modern river levels).

Despite wearing scuba gear, we excavate like our terrestrial colleagues in carefully controlled levels using trowels. Our dirt is sucked to the surface by a water dredge, powered by a pump attached to a hose that is carried underwater to our excavations. The pump creates a vacuum, pulling up water and dirt into screens floating on the water surface where team members can look through the dirt for artifacts. We also dig on land around the underwater sites; when trying to understand inundated landscapes, we cannot stop at the waterline. Paleoindian sites on land could have washed into the river, so we look for soils on land that correlate to those underwater to fit the terrestrial landscape into the larger geological history.

Our investigations thus far have revealed a few important clues. First, geological processes could be correlated not only between our two sites but also with three other sites that were excavated by the ARPP. The sediment layers contained clues about the local water changing from isolated ponds to a connected river system, and biomes (ecological areas) transitioning from vegetation typical of open, drier environments to the modern cypress swamps by 5,000 years ago. Before 21,000 years ago, each sink seems to have experienced its own depositional history, but by about 15,000 years ago, all five sinks were probably experiencing comparable processes, with similar sediment types deposited at parallel times. There were four major periods of sinkhole infill during the last 40,000 years, with one occurring approximately 15,000 to 11,000 years ago. This time span is very interesting because it correlates to the Paleoindian period.

The sediment layers from this depositional period were weathered into soils, which means they would have provided stable surfaces for people to live and work upon. Therefore, some of the artifacts found in these soils likely reflect human activity rather than natural processes. These activities appear to have been focused on short-term use of the area for hunting prior to 13,000 years ago, with more intensive occupation occurring sometime between 12,000 and 10,000 years ago. For instance, an Early Archaic spear point (a type called Bolen by archaeologists) was found resting on the soil at Page-Ladson, but younger layers (those above the soils) at the sites contain the remains of fishing and other aquatic activities instead of terrestrial actions.

I've continued to use the same methods to investigate other sites in the cypress swamps of the Wacissa and Aucilla Rivers, and in the Chipola, Santa Fe, Suwannee, and Silver Rivers. In general, my conclusions support my predecessors. Spring-fed rivers contain more preserved sediments than those that are not spring-fed. More sediment provides more opportunity for better archaeological preservation, so these locations are more likely to contain intact sites which can help us to more fully understand the first Americans by preserving a wider range of material culture than is found in the rest of North America and because these sites are directly dateable. The sites I am most interested in date to the Paleoindian (circa 15,000–11,500 years ago) and Early Archaic (circa 11,500–5,000 years ago) periods. This is often considered to be the period of greatest adjustment for hunting and gathering societies in the Southeast, as sea levels and floral and faunal biomes all became similar to those found in the same regions today by about 5,000 years ago. Therefore, although these early sites are underwater now, they represent the remains of activities that originally occurred on dry land (although often adjacent to water) and were submerged by rising water levels.

A notable exception are the burial ponds that have been discovered scattered throughout Florida. Most date to the Early Archaic period and are remnants of a burial practice more than 8,000 years old. For example, at the Windover site in Brevard County, more than 100 people were buried in a small pond during several centuries, showing a longstanding tradition. People were buried with fiber mats and clothing and other perishable goods, and many were staked in place by mats placed around their bodies. Because of the excellent preservation in this bog-like cemetery, many of the skeletons and their effects survived to be excavated by archaeologists when the burial pond became exposed during a modern building project. Windover demonstrated that the hunter-gatherers were very careful with the handicapped

David Thulman pointing at Early Archaic Bolen point discovered on ancient land surface at Page-Ladson in 2015.

(Photo by Shawn Joy)

members of their group: several skeletons showed severe pathologies that an individual would have lived with for years before death. This taught us that some of our models about foraging societies were completely wrong because the dominant theories when the sites were discovered stated that foragers of the early and middle Archaic were probably highly mobile and that mobile foragers would not have the ability to care for their weak and sick. Windover shows that people may have been less mobile than we thought and that they certainly took care of those who needed it. Charnel (burial) ponds have been associated with the previously discussed spring sites, and they have been found in now-offshore areas as well. Because the early Floridians were drawn to bury at least some of their dead in these watery environments, a unique view of their world has been preserved.

All of Florida's people, from ancient to modern cultures, have been reliant upon abundant fresh water. The submerged archaeological evidence of water-based activities is plentiful and spans all time periods from Paleoindian to the present day. For instance, the first thing I discovered on my earliest dive at Sloth Hole was a 50-horsepower outboard motor that apparently fell off the back of a boat that hit the rocky shoals on the downstream side of the site. Hundreds (possibly even thousands) of bone fish hooks and gorges (bone toggles that turn sideways in a fish's mouth to catch them) have been found on river bottoms in conjunction with modern steel ones, all lost in similar ways; similarly, stone and shell used to weigh down nets lie next to modern lead sinkers. The remains of numerous shellfish feasts have been discarded into rivers, lakes, and streams since time immemorial. Some of these middens, or trash deposits, can be seen in water bodies adjacent to large archaeological sites. At other sites, the shell was deposited on land to be used as construction material. Few of these have been found submerged in fresh water, but drowned shell middens have been discovered

The author and John Albertson recording the Lover's Leap canoe in Silver Springs.
(Photo by Morgan Smith)

offshore along the Gulf Coast in Florida, Louisiana, and Texas.

Waterways were used as roads as well. As Ryan Wheeler's chapter discusses in detail, more than 400 wooden dugout canoes have been recorded in Florida's lakes, rivers, and streams. We took measurements of a locally famous canoe at the bottom of Silver Springs, known as the Lover's Leap canoe. It had recently started to visibly degrade due to lowered water quality, so we made a more complete record for the state site file update in 2014. The canoe was left in place and can still be seen during glass-bottomed boat tours of the spring. It seems, from the way it was carved, to date to the Historic period. The oldest recorded canoe in Florida is more than 6,000 years old, but some date into the twentieth century. Many of these canoes have been recovered from lakes in central Florida and appear to have been deliberately submerged and cached for later use. For instance, Newnan's Lake alone contained more than 100 canoes that were exposed by receding water levels in the lake. In the Everglades, the Calusa people dug and maintained many canals for watercraft to connect settlements and ceremonial centers from approximately 1,200 to 250 years ago.

Underwater archaeology is at least 10 times as expensive as its terrestrial counterpart and at least 10 times as logistically complicated. It requires archaeologists who have not only completed training in traditional field methods but who are also comfortable with scuba diving and working in an environment where communication happens via hand signals and "wet notes" scribbled on sheets of mylar film. It requires that each item brought to the surface be carefully conserved, a painstaking and often slow process that owes as much to art as is does chemistry. It requires an excellent working knowledge of small engines and physics because troubleshooting equipment difficulties is a com-

The support setup for excavations at Page-Ladson. In the foreground, awnings are set up for divers in preparation and for note-taking. In the middle are the dive safety barges. (Left to right: Franklin H. Price, Chris Dostal, and Morgan Smith.) In the background, screen decks receive water from excavations entering the sorting area. (Left: Neil Puckett. Right: Sunshine Thomas.) *(Photo by Adam Burke)*

mon daily problem. It requires brute strength to manhandle floating screen decks into the water and the delicacy of touch to carefully lift the sediment of centuries from a preserved piece of cloth without damaging the fragile fabric. In other words, it is always time consuming and is often frustrating in the extreme. My colleagues and I fight insects and muddy swamps, hypothermia, and hyperthermia on the same day, and have lost time to thunderstorms, malfunctioning equipment, and miscommunication in the depths. At the same time, we return to these same depths year after year because it is also one of the most rewarding endeavors possible. Underwater archaeology can answer questions about human history that no other field of research can even begin to ask.

Dr. Jessi J. Halligan is an assistant professor at Florida State University in the Department of Anthropology. She has extensive field experience in prehistoric terrestrial and underwater archaeology and has worked with both professionals and volunteers.

For Additional Information

Videos

WFSU Ecology Project, "Searching for Suwannee: Underwater Excavation on the Wacissa River," 2015, https://www.youtube.com/watch?v=dbUIU0Ed_Co

Publications

Jessi J. Halligan, Michael R. Waters, Angelina Perrotti, et al., "Pre-Clovis Occupation 14,550 Years Ago at the Page-Ladson Site, Florida, and the Peopling of the Americas," *Science Advances* 2, no. 5 (2016): e1600375, http://advances.sciencemag.org/content/2/5/e1600375

Glenn Hodges, "Discovery Points to Earlier Arrival of First Americans," *National Geographic*, May 13, 2016, http://news.nationalgeographic.com/2016/05/160513-first-americans-clovis-mastodon-florida-page-ladson/

Agata Blaszczak-Boxe, "Underwater Finds Reveal Humans' Long Presence in North America," *Smithsonian.com*, May 13, 2016, http://www.smithsonianmag.com/science-nature/underwater-finds-reveal-humans-long-presence-north-america-180959103/

Emma Marris, "Underwater Archaeologists Unearth Ancient Butchering Site," *Nature*, May 13, 2016, http://www.nature.com/news/underwater-archaeologists-unearth-ancient-butchering-site-1.19913

Annalee Newitz, "Underwater Discovery Reveals 14,550 Year-Old Human Mastodon Hunters," *Ars Technica UK*, May 14, 2016, https://arstechnica.co.uk/science/2016/05/underwater-discovery-reveals-14550-year-old-florida-mastodon-hunters/

Lizzie Wade, "Ancient Stone Tools Are 'Best' Evidence Yet for Early Peopling of the Americas," Science, May 13, 2016, http://www.sciencemag.org/news/2016/05/ancient-stone-tools-are-best-evidence-yet-early-peopling-americas

CHAPTER 3

Drowned Paleolandscapes: Prehistoric Archaeology Offshore in the Gulf of Mexico

~ Michael K. Faught ~

Shipwrecks most frequently come to mind when people hear or think about underwater archaeology. And for good reason—investigating sunken vessels is the most common archaeological research done underwater, and some of the sites are spectacular. However, there is another genre in the discipline that is making rapid advancements these days, and that is paleolandscape archaeology—prehistoric archaeology on the continental shelves in places that were terrestrial during times of lower sea levels but now are submerged. This involves tracing out paleolithic river channels (paleochannels) and past landscape configurations with remote sensing, mapping where sites likely might be using terrestrial analogs, and then going there to see whether something can be found. It means excavating or sampling marine beds to look for brackish, fresh water, or terrestrial sediment layers below the marine sediments in hopes of finding evidence of past human behavior.

Of all the United States, Florida by far has the most recorded and investigated submerged prehistoric sites. They are located in rivers, lakes, cenotes in the karst geology, and offshore in the drowned karst on the continental shelf. Sites in Florida span a timeline that extends from the earliest people at the end of the last Ice Age until contact with European explorers and colonists, and that's just the prehistoric record.

Ice Age Clovis fluted points from Florida are known to have occurred between 13,000 and 12,700 calendar years ago. The flutes are indentations on either side of the base of the point for hafting of a knife handle or spear. The base of a similar point was found during the offshore research in Apalachee Bay.

(Courtesy of David Thulman with permission)

This abundance and continuity are what drew me to Florida to conduct exploratory research offshore. I organized 11 six-week summer forays, five conducted between 1986 and 1992 (phase 1, the dissertation days), and six from 1998 to 2003 (phase 2, the Florida State University days). Most of the materials and records collected during these 11 projects have been analyzed and reported in multiple venues.

In the beginning, as a graduate student in Tucson, Arizona, in 1986, I was looking for a place to test a theory in my PhD dissertation that early Clovis sites could be found offshore, and Florida turned out to be a no-brainer. During the final vestiges of the last Ice Age, Florida was more than the twice the size it is today, and people were there at that time, thus initiating a virtually continuous record of occupation over thousands of years afterward. Underwater archaeological excavations at the Page-Ladson site in the Aucilla River, less than three miles from the coast, have shown a pre-Clovis (14,000 years old), Late Paleoindian (12,500 years old), and Early Archaic (11,500 years old) sequence. This suggests that the sites of those people should continue offshore. It turns out they do.

Landscapes of the past (paleolandscapes) are drowned because of global warming at the end of the last Ice Age (Pleistocene). As glaciers in the northern latitudes melted away and exposed new landscapes there, sea levels drowned the continental shelves of the world, hiding landscapes in southern climes. These were probably times of people moving inland and readjusting to their new landscapes. The Florida peninsula was drowned over thousands of years, but especially during three major pulses of sea level rise. People occupied Florida during these later spans of time, so in addition to early Paleoindian remains there should be other, later sites underwater as well. Stated in a different way, there should be progressively younger sites in progressively shallower waters—and there are, as I will describe.

The sea levels rose in three significant stages between the western and eastern coastlines of Florida. The first meltwater pulse occurred around 14,400 calendar years before present (cal BP), the second at 11,000 cal BP, and the third at 8,000 cal BP. That last pulse has been associated with the flood in the Black Sea for which Noah was prompted to build his boat. The Clovis era coast-

Left: Late Paleoindian projectile points (12,000 years old). *Right:* Early Archaic points (11,000 years old) from the Page-Ladson site in the Aucilla River. *(Courtesy of David Thulman with permission)*

Sequence of sea level rising over the Florida Platform. *Left:* The first glacier meltwater pulse around 14,400 calendar years before present (cal BP). *Middle:* The second pulse at 11,000 cal BP. *Right:* The third pulse at 8,000 cal BP. *(Courtesy of the author)*

line of 13,000 years ago is proposed to occur about 130 feet (40 m) deep and 80 miles (130 km) offshore of the mouth of the Aucilla River. This represents a substantial coastline to survey to determine whether Clovis people had coastal activities, adaptations, or settlements.

But how far offshore do sites extend? And how old are they? What is their condition? Where are they most likely to be preserved in open-ocean continental shelf settings? In 1986, no university in the United States had a program that focused on prehistoric underwater archaeology. The programs at Texas A&M and East Carolina were focused on Euro-American history, ship building, and shipwrecks. So how does a graduate student pull together boating and diving operations from Arizona? It took the right colleagues and lots of volunteer help, and grant funding for the dissertation research. The second phase of research from 1998 to 2003 occurred while I was teaching at

Florida State University; I had funding from the Florida Division of Historical Resources (DHR) and help from numerous students. However, before I discuss the research, some background about Florida's submerged prehistoric past is warranted.

Florida's Drowned Landscapes with Prehistoric Archaeological Sites

Florida has produced more pre-contact sites underwater than any other state in the Union. This record is verified by the antiquity of its chipped stone artifacts and its preserved specimens of artifacts made of ivory and bone. In the 1930s, a nearly complete mastodon was found in Wakulla Springs near Tallahassee and was recovered by hard-hat divers. In the 1940s, Clarence Simpson found ivory foreshafts in the Ichetucknee River in north-central Florida that had been made from either mammoths or mastodons. On the assumption that the ivory needed be fresh to be worked, this indicated the contemporaneity of people and Late Pleistocene proboscideans, as well as the potential for kill sites.

With the invention and commercial production of scuba gear, early avocational collectors made significant contributions to our understanding of the past with their diving explorations. One set of findings occurred in southwest Florida by William Royal, who became known for his discoveries of human remains at Little Salt Spring and Warm Mineral Springs, where submerged prehistoric sites were found with burials in and around cenotes (see Chapter 1), and at the Venice Beach Site, a marine-inundated, ceramic-aged shell midden in a near-shore setting. After Royal showed his sites to Reynold Ruppé of Arizona State University in the 1970s, Ruppé became a vocal practitioner and proponent of doing prehistoric archaeology underwater.

Ruppé and others published the results of the offshore excavations at Venice Beach in a DHR report series that he called "Drowned Terrestrial Sites Archaeology." He also theorized on how to find older sites farther offshore near paleochannels and advocated for remote sensing with subbottom profilers. Although he did try, Ruppé did not find any sites farther offshore than at Venice Beach.

Also in the 1970s, Charles Hoffman of Northern Arizona University found artifacts with mammoth remains in the Silver River. Archaeologists from Texas A&M University recently have returned to the site and confirmed the association.

Another set of discoveries was made by river divers in the Suwannee, Santa Fe, and Aucilla Rivers. This cadre found abundant Paleoindian and Early Archaic artifacts and faunal remains in the dark, tannic, and sometimes gar- or gator-infested waters. Many shared their findings with archaeologists, especially Jim Dunbar, who was an undergraduate at the University of Florida at the time. Alvin Hendrix found and reported on multiple locations in the Silver River; Ben Waller in the Santa Fe and Suwannee Rivers; and Don Serbousek, Buddy Page, and others in the Aucilla River.

Dunbar interviewed several collectors, and he reported on the number of paleolithic projectile points they had found in a publication with Waller in 1983 and again in a landmark descriptive publication in 1991. By that time, he had inventoried 564 diagnostic artifacts (543 lithic points and 21 ivory foreshafts) recovered from 172 localities. (Many of these artifacts are in private collections, but today collecting is illegal and the law is enforced.)

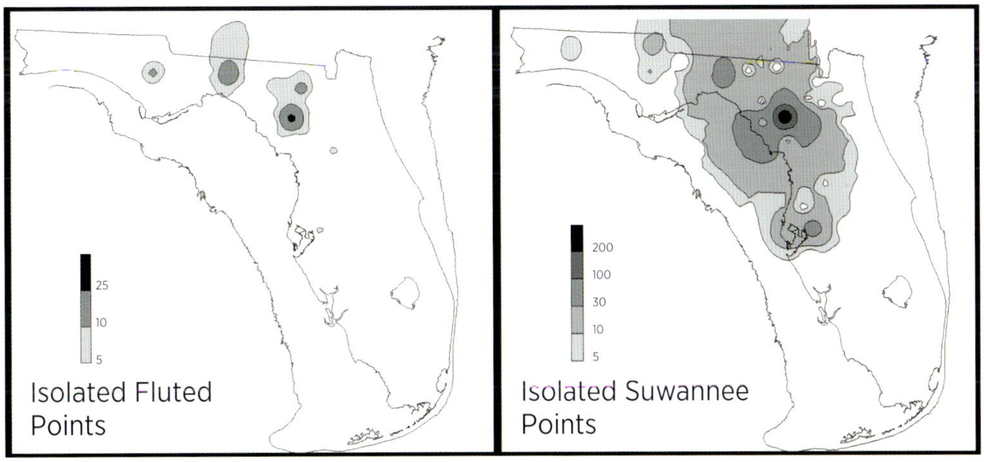

Distribution plots based on Jim Dunbar's data showing county-level estimations of artifact density. *Left:* Clovis points. *Right:* Suwannee and Simpson points. The densities of the point distributions are shown as shaded contours. This reflects the ratio of the earliest fluted points to later related unfluted lanceolate shapes of the Suwannee and Simpson points. The ratio is roughly 20 to 80 percent, no doubt because of greater population density and/or time.

(Data from Jim Dunbar, illustration by the author)

My major professor, C. Vance Haynes, became interested in the findings in Florida and dived in the Aucilla River in 1970 with collectors Dick Ohms and Don Serbousek. Haynes suggested to me the potential for underwater sites in Florida and gave me Serbousek's address; through him, I connected with Jim Dunbar, who then worked for DHR. In July 1986, Dunbar and I went offshore with state boats for three days and found six localities with artifacts—immediate success.

Forays Underwater in Apalachee Bay

Today, researchers on both sides of the Atlantic and in the Pacific are focused on prehistoric sites in offshore settings. Variously called continental shelf, prehistoric, or pre-contact underwater archaeology, the genre has been around for a while and increasingly is adding case studies. Four or five books and numerous reports now exist on the subject, coming primarily from Europe. Certain aspects of various projects are beginning to stand out as shared experiences; for example, the most frequently found and excavated sites are from the Middle Holocene (circa 6,000 years ago) and younger, and they are located in 0 to 30 feet of sea water.

When I was a graduate student in the late 1980s, there was far less institutional knowledge, so I discovered and invented how to proceed as I went along, listening to all of the advice I could get. Several useful chapters were included in the seminal book about paleolandscape archaeology, *Quaternary Coastlines and Marine Archaeology* (1983), by Masters and Flemming. In addition, federally funded studies by Woodie Gagliano's group at Coastal Environments Inc. in Baton Rouge were particularly influential and remain useful today. These include an inventory and model for submerged prehistoric sites in the Gulf of Mexico in 1977, site sampling strategies and sediment proxies for sites in 1982, and subbottom profiling and coring offshore in 1986. The 1986 research resulted in the discovery of a buried shell midden more than 9,000 years old, found by coring in a paleotributary of the Brazos River in Texas.

More importantly, I learned excavation methods at Page-Ladson and developed a network of local contacts with boats who could help. I was extremely fortunate in obtaining private funding from Dorothy C. Fitch, a friend of my mother in Arizona, who became interested in my research. I also received a National Science Foundation dissertation improvement grant in 1991 and EarthWatch volunteers and funding in 1992. The 1998–2003 FSU field school experiences were funded by the State of Florida, DHR special category grants, and boat-time support came from the Florida Institute of Oceanography. FSU offered credits to students.

I initiated and continued to use AutoCAD mapping of bathymetry from the National Oceanic and Atmospheric Administration (NOAA) navigation chart into a three-dimensional (3D) model to understand the bottom morphology and reconstruct the paleotopography. I began to read about the geology of the west coast of Florida, and I made many long-distance phone calls to obtain and organize boats, dive gear, and people. Essentially, I put together my own research program in Florida's Big Bend because of its abundant potential.

Apalachee Bay in northwestern Florida is a prime location to prospect for inundated pre-contact sites for several reasons (although, again, a survey permit from the state is required because artifact collecting is illegal). The location is logical because this area has had a significant number of archaeological sites and isolated finds indicating almost uninterrupted human presence from the Late Pleistocene through the Holocene epoch, when sea levels were lower. And some sites onshore are very early. The Page-Ladson site in the Aucilla River has unequivocal evidence of human presence beginning around 14,400 years ago, signaled by bifacially flaked artifacts in a 3-foot-thick bed of mastodon digesta (poop), which was capped by 4 or 5 feet of dense, clayey silt that accumulated from 14,000 years ago to 12,500 years ago. Artifacts in the soil that developed on this clayey silt are 12,500 years old. These artifacts include stone points along with worked wood, bone, and antler artifacts. Continued human presence in Florida is indicated by the aforementioned abundance of time-diagnostic projectile points and other artifacts. Evidence for people also continues after this, into the Holocene: Middle Archaic artifacts that are 7,000 to 4,500 years old are found offshore in 30 feet or less of water. These younger sites represent an aspect of prehistory in need of exploration and description, in addition to our need for Paleoindian data.

The Big Bend of northwest Florida is a flat, karst plain topographically, with numerous collapse and solution geologic features that are known onshore or can be mapped offshore with side-scan sonar and subbottom profilers. From Tampa

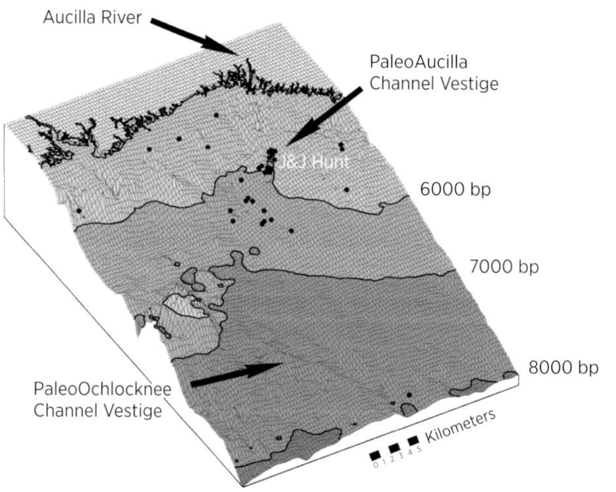

Three-dimensional image made by digitizing bathymetric data, contouring in Surfer software, and then exaggerating the vertical times 10 to emphasize any variation in what otherwise would be a flat, drowned karst landscape. This technique brought out the pathways of the Paleo-Aucilla and Paleo-Ochlocknee paleochannel vestiges. *(Illustration by the author)*

Bay to Apalachicola, several rivers flow out along the coastline, including the Suwannee, Crystal, Steinhatchee, Econfina, Aucilla, and St. Marks Rivers, and these drainages have paleochannel features offshore. Sinkholes are dispersed across the onshore landscape as isolates (cenotes) and as linear sets of solution features and fractured rock structures making up segments of the rivers such as the Aucilla. Scattered outcrops of resistant limestone and chert in various stages of decay also dot the landscape and represent the locations of past quarry activities. This is what Dunbar and I found offshore in 1986 during three days of near-shore survey—six outcrops of cherty limestone with evidence of quarrying as well as paleochannel features of the Econfina River.

Because most prehistoric archaeological sites are found in and around karst rivers and sinks onshore, these features are likely to preserve records of cultural activity and stratigraphy offshore. The pocketed karst topography drowned on the continental shelf also can act as a protective vessel for some sites. As an analog, the Page-Ladson site is an excellent example of the fact that sedimentary profiles can be preserved in these karst river channels and can reflect the Pleistocene/Holocene transition in the paleochannel sediments offshore. This was a major goal of my dissertation research, and one that remains potential today.

Another benefit of the regional geology in terms of research is the fact that the sediment overburden on the continental shelf immediately

During a 2001 field school, Kimberly Kasper measuring depths as wood items are exposed in a unit being excavated by induction dredge. *(Photo credit Norma Garcia)*

offshore is minimal, and it often consists of a thin, sandy, biogenic (shell hash) cover. The lack of significant sediments from the local rivers is due to the drainage characteristics of the onshore karst limestone bedrock. Finally, the somewhat protected position of Apalachee Bay within the Gulf of Mexico contributes to a comparatively mild marine environment, so sites are not as affected as they might be in a different environment such as the Atlantic Coast. Nonetheless, transgressing and surging seas are effective, depending on local conditions and the strength of particular storms.

During my field research, I found artifacts indicating Paleoindian and Early Archaic occupation when the sea levels were rising and the coastline was coming in from 100 to 40 miles away (at today's depths of 40 m to 20 m). My forays also found later Middle Archaic (circa 6,000 to 4,000 cal BP) artifacts and shell middens, which indicated that the coast was nearby but still encroaching. These are at the same place, although humans experienced significantly different environments—inland uplands earlier in time, and coastal or near coastal later in time. Features that might occur in the drowned karst from this Middle Holocene near-shore context include fish weirs, canoes, and possibly residence features (such as houses built on posts).

Searching for Drowned Landscapes

So how do you go about searching drowned landscapes for prehistoric sites? In the grand scheme of things, a drowned prehistoric site is a small thing to find in a big body of water. What you see from the boat is monotonous and massive. When you descend to the depths, the visibility can be minimal, and sediments, bottom relief, and marine growths often conceal past terrestrial characteristics. So the search is challenging but frustrating as well. Perhaps the best additions to the research have been remote sensing, with acoustic underwater images delivered by side-scan sonar and subbottom profilers.

Most of my initial research forays (1986–1992) were in small boats in shallow water—studying navigation charts, towing divers along, and sampling at new discoveries. Although it was effective at the time, towing divers has its perils, and acquiring boats of sufficient size or number was a major issue during my phase 1 research. We spent a lot time in transit, loading boats at ramps, and heading out to sea—only to be chased home by afternoon thunderstorms. During my phase 2 research, we had access to large vessels that we could anchor offshore, with smaller boats used for lightering.

In order to write proposals, give presentations, and determine diving targets, I needed maps that conveyed the paleotopographic potential. Using a NOAA navigation chart at first and subbottom profiling records to refine them, I digitized the data to AutoCAD with a State Plane geodesy and then constructed a 3D mesh bathymetric graphic to show the paths of the modern rivers as they continue in troughs offshore—as paleochannels.

Positioning of the three sites found during the 1986–1992 research was achieved with Loran-C devices, having about 100-foot (30 m) accuracy or precision. These sites, and those found during the 1998–2003 research, were positioned with satellite Global Positioning System (GPS). I cannot overstate the fact that archaeology for submerged landscapes would not be possible without GPS, not only for mapping with remote sensing devices but also for returning to a site for additional research.

In terms of how we identified sites early on, I have mentioned that we towed divers around areas that looked promising on the NOAA chart. In a creative methodology, Buddy Page found two sites by watching the fathometer closely while motoring slowly and then investigating areas that reflected a rocky bottom. Likewise, a simple fathometer can be used to map the bottom with ±1-foot precision, and it can be used to distinguish sandy, low-reflection areas from high-reflection channel fill with fine-grained, organic-rich sediments. However, the most useful means of reconstructing paleolandscapes and identifying places where sites are likely to be is to use modern acoustic underwater sonar and seismic remote-sensing devices. There are several ways to use acoustic underwater imagery to understand the bottom and sediment beds or bedrock morphology below it. Furthermore, boats with these devices can cover far more area than towing a diver in the same amount of time.

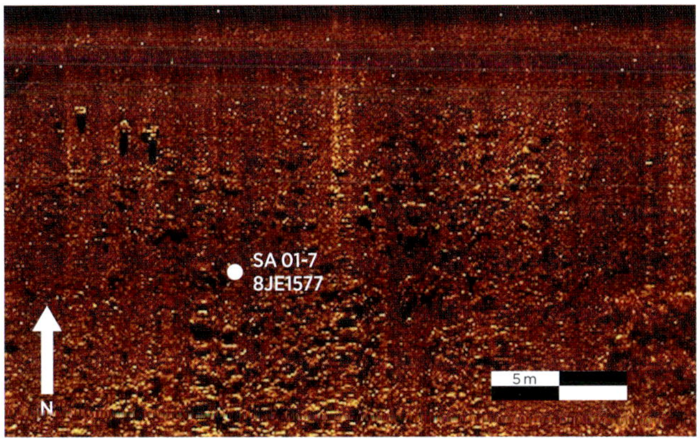

The starboard half of a 600-kHz side-scan sonar image showing a rocky area of interest. The boat is going left to right, and the sea floor bottom is at the top. Rocks are showing "shadows" from the propagation and reflection of sound underwater.

(Courtesy of the author)

Jim Dunbar in 1988 offshore along the Paleo-Econfina River with a dredge pump and floating screen deck rig.

(Photo by Joe Latvis)

Lower sound frequency subbottom profilers are used to image stratigraphy, mid-range frequency fish finders and multibeam devices are used to reconstruct bathymetry, and high-frequency side-scan sonars create photograph-like images of the bottom and objects in or on it. Today, all of these devices have GPS data embedded to allow for geographic information system (GIS) mapping. Side-scan images can map swaths of bottom that are 100 to 150 feet (30 to 40 m) wide, while surveying at 3 to 4 nautical miles per hour. Subbottom profilers have a narrow beam, so coverage is possible with survey vessels going 4 knots, for instance, but the slice is narrower, penetrating the bottom and pinging back contrasting strata. These data then can be reviewed to find targets and be used for publications and presentations.

I conducted remote sensing with a "boomer" subbottom profiler during Phase 1 to identify sinkholes that may have contained sediments similar to Page-Ladson. I crisscrossed where we thought the paleochannel was and then plotted a centerline, or what is called a thalweg ("valley way," along the natural direction of a watercourse), and surveyed "up river" along that. The result was a line of about eleven depressions or sinkhole features that define a portion of the PaleoAucilla. One of these sinkholes was excavated in 1992 to a depth of 3 meters. Unlike Page-Ladson, it didn't have ancient sediments; rather, only sediments dated to 7,000 years and younger.

The author pounding a 3-inch pipe into a sediment bed offshore to recover a sample of the stratigraphy. *(Photo by Norma Garcia)*

The author and Joseph Latvis cutting open a 3-inch aluminum core tube full of sediments from the Paleo-Aucilla offshore. *(Photo by Ryan Pendleton)*

I had the benefit of both side scan and sub-bottom profiling during the phase 2 PaleoAucilla prehistory project. Data from these tools, particularly the side-scan, were used to identify "targets" of potential rocky areas, and 80 percent of the time when we dived to ground-truth a target we found artifacts.

Much of the sampling and testing was done with Loran-C and later with GPS along predetermined transects marked with datum pins. Collections were controlled by hand fanning at regular intervals and by collecting sediment samples and any fauna or artifacts.

A second method of sampling included the use of hydraulic dredges. Also known as couple jets or water dredges, they also are used by placer gold prospectors. With this tool, we could excavate test pit units 1×1 meters or larger with floating screen decks. This type of underwater excavation is equivalent to terrestrial archaeological methods, just done underwater.

We conducted some coring by pounding in 3-inch aluminum pipes or vibrating them down with gasoline engine vibrators. While these "vibracores" were useful, the sediment depth is unpredictable in the rocky karst without first conducting remote sensing to acquire imagery and positioning. After recovering these cores, they were cut open in the laboratory and photographed. Then samples were taken to examine the sediment texture and radiocarbon ages.

What Do the Sites Look Like, and How Have They Fared?

Unlike shipwrecks, archaeological sites offshore that have been underwater for thousands of years are not immediately recognizable or easily located. The ocean floor is covered with sandy, shelly sediments of varying thicknesses, and finding and studying sites with stratigraphic integrity in sinkholes or maybe caves presents a challenge. Rocky outcrops often are covered with corals and other live bottom organisms. Moreover, most of the terrestrial soil cover was removed and reworked, as in a plow zone, when the sea levels rose and then stabilized; this transgression and marine reworking has occurred across most of the paleolandscape. The working environment is complicated if visibility is poor, as it is in Apalachee Bay. Nevertheless, detailed analysis can identify different site functions, and the deeper sediment beds remain intact. We found several intact tree stumps that indicated minimum depths of reworking in certain conditions.

Conclusion

What sites have yet to be discovered? Sites of the earliest Paleoindians and their Early Archaic progeny could extend out as far as the continental shelf break, at 100-meter depths, but do they? In the past few years, James Adovasio and Andy Hemmings have made a few forays out that far funded by NOAA; although they encountered paleochannels and rock outcrops, no specific sites or artifacts were located. Beyond the scientific objectives and academic research designs, discoveries such as this have been useful to garner sufficient attention and additional funding to proceed farther out on the shelf and deeper into the sediments.

The objective is to target the highest probability landscape settings and work from the known to the unknown. In that light, Ryan Duggins of Florida's Bureau of Archaeological Research made GIS models for his dissertation that show the likely locations of paleochannels and springs offshore that could be a template for identifying project areas. However, later sites also are important for reconstructing Florida's prehistory, particularly the sites that bridge the Late Archaic to Early Woodland transition between 5,000 and 3,000 cal BP.

Here are a few take-home messages. Florida has abundant, early, and robust evidence for occupations by Paleoindians and their Early Holocene to Early Archaic descendants when the sea levels were lower, so there must be submerged sites on the continental shelf. And they actually are there—at least out to about 10 miles offshore in 20 feet of water. Theoretically, only the oldest sites can be found at the extreme deepest places, if they exist out there. Although these earliest people can be represented in shallower water as well, so can additional culture groups. The sea levels rose from 14,000 years ago to about 3,000 years ago, so lots of human behaviors could be involved.

The author holding a bifacially flaked artifact found on the seafloor surface near the Paleo-Aucilla relict river channel. *(Photo by KC Smith)*

My specific interest in the Big Bend was the discovery and excavation of an inundated sinkhole exhibiting Late Pleistocene and Early Holocene sediments analogous to the important sediment bed in the Aucilla River at Page-Ladson. However, what I found was a terrific challenge to inventory, describe, analyze, and interpret *whatever* geomorphic features and inundated archaeological sites were encountered. From my perspective as a geoarchaeologist, the task at hand was to reconstruct the path of the paleodrainage system and other sedimentary details of the offshore environment, to inventory the past human settlement patterns (sites) as they evolved before full inundation, and to determine the chronology and impact of transgressing seas afterward. To date I have conducted 11 sessions offshore toward that goal, but Florida's continental shelf remains an enormous *terra incognita subaqueous.*

Dr. Michael K. Faught is vice president and treasurer of the Archaeological Research Cooperative, a courtesy assistant professor at the University of Florida, and a geoarchaeological specialist for SEARCH Inc. He established Florida State University's program in underwater archaeology and is a pioneer in the field of submerged offshore prehistoric archaeology.

For Additional Information

Websites

Appalachicola River Valley Archaeology, http://apalacharchaeology.blog.usf.edu/?page_id=8

Michael Faught, PhD, RPA, http://www.mfaught.org/

"Research: Florida's First People," Florida State University, http://www.rinr.fsu.edu/winter2002/index.html

Publications

Michael Faught, "Finding Submerged Paleoindian and Archaic Archaeological Sites: Experiences from Karstic NW Florida," poster presentation, http://www.mfaught.org/wp-content/uploads/2015/11/Faught-2006-GSA-Poster.pdf

CHAPTER 4

Paddling into the Past: Archaeology of Florida Canoes

Ryan J. Wheeler

Lake Pithlachoco has helped rewrite the story of Florida's dugout canoes. For me, the story of the Lake Pithlachoco canoe find began on April 25, 2000, with a phone call and email message from Scott Mitchell. Scott and I knew each other from our time as graduate students at the University of Florida (UF). He was now working at the Florida Museum of Natural History in Gainesville, and I was working for the state archaeologist's office in Tallahassee. Scott was relaying information from someone who had walked the shoreline of Newnan's Lake near Gainesville and observed what appeared to be several dugout canoes. The lake levels had fallen significantly over the winter and spring during a regional drought, and a photo accompanying the email showed a historic watercraft—a small skiff or rowboat—buried up to its gunwales. I was busy with work on the recently discovered Miami Circle and my own project near Lake Okeechobee, so I tentatively planned to visit the area as time allowed.

In the meantime, Barbara Purdy and Ray McGee heard the same stories about dugout canoes and decided to check it out. I knew Barbara and Ray well from my time at UF. She had chaired my master's committee before she retired in 1992, and the three of us had worked on excavations of a Middle to Late Archaic site at Lake Monroe near Sanford. Barbara and Ray also had introduced me to Florida's dugout canoes as part of their research to document the interesting features of these watercraft. At that time (in the early 1990s), very few people were interested in dugout canoes, and those who

A dugout canoe from Mariner Lake in Putnam County documented by Barbara Purdy and her students in 1990 as part of the Florida Canoe Project. *(Courtesy of the Florida Division of Historical Resources)*

thought about them often considered them more of a nuisance than a resource. A decade earlier, as dugout canoes were collected and stored at the Florida Museum of Natural History, one suggestion to reduce storage space was to simply cut off and keep the ends, which were considered to be the most diagnostic part. Another plan—which was put into practice—was to submerge a bunch of the surplus dugouts in a central Florida spring.

Barbara, who was interested in wet site resources—primarily the preservation of organic materials in an anaerobic environment, found the dugout canoes to be an important part of that story. Following on the master's thesis research of Ray McGee, Barbara began a canoe-recording project that included responding to discoveries, obtaining radiocarbon dates, recording basic dimensions and making sketches, and identifying the wood of each new find. With droughts occurring locally and regionally every 7 to 10 years, it was easy to amass a database of canoe finds. Some were from the recent past and bore traces of construction by metal tools, but others were ancient. In at least one case a group of 20 or more canoes had been preserved in a peat bog, prefiguring the discovery at Pithlachoco in 2000.

Out on the Lake

Barbara and Ray visited Lake Pithlachoco—also called Newnan's Lake—at the end of April 2000. They never did locate that historic skiff, but they did find dugout canoes preserved in the dried lake bed. Local high school teacher Steve Everett

The author excavating a dugout canoe at Lake Pithlachoco, June 2000. Note the ominous clouds in the background and the deteriorated nature of the canoe, probably reflecting periods of wetting and drying that accelerated decay.

(Courtesy of the Florida Division of Historical Resources)

and his environmental science students had been studying the 11.75-square-mile lake, and they too were finding canoes—a lot of canoes. These discoveries were reported to the state archaeologist's office, and Melissa Memory, who was staffing the Gainesville field office at the time, confirmed the canoes' discovery. Together with State Archaeologist Jim Miller, we formulated a relatively simple plan for investigating the watercraft. Steve and his students were good at locating the canoes; often, only the ends protruded slightly above the sandy lakebed. They would mark them with flags and stakes, then our team of archaeologists and volunteers would traverse the lakebed, excavating carefully around the fragile canoes to expose what usually were the remains of the bottom and ends.

Often the canoes were so deteriorated that it was difficult to distinguish the surrounding soil from the wood. Using some simple forms that I had developed, we recorded basic information about the dimensions and shape of the canoe, including drawings from above and the side. Donna Ruhl, an archaeobotanist at the Florida Museum of Natural History, helped to take samples for wood identification and radiocarbon dating. We found other artifacts and features as well, including evidence of an ancient fish trap or weir, large nodules of chert, and one carved wooden paddle.

Working on the lake was not without its challenges. One was the weather. We accessed the north side of the lake—where many of the dugout canoes had been found—through the Gum Root Swamp preserve, tromping through the cypress swamp that bore traces of nineteenth-century logging. Once out on the lakebed, we headed to the east where many of the canoes had been flagged by the high school students. High nutrient levels in the lake had encouraged the growth of weedy plants, which were beginning to obscure the sandy bottom. After a long hike, we settled in to begin excavating and recording the vessels; teams of two or three usually tackled one canoe. In the afternoon we often saw violent electrical storms building and coming our way from the south and west. We hustled to complete our work and rebury the canoes, but sometimes the storms overtook us. On more than one occasion, we found ourselves running back through the swamp toward the safety of our vehicles as lightning struck around us, the smell of ozone filling the air.

Economic and bureaucratic forces also were working against us and the canoes. The state's

Ancient canoe paddles and poles are even rarer than dugout canoes. This paddle, dating to about 200 to 300 years ago, was found intact on the desiccated bed of Lake Pithlachoco by archaeologist Ray McGee. It is incredibly long and likely was used as both pole and paddle. *(Photo by Ray McGee)*

Department of Environmental Protection had issued leases for the recovery of so-called "deadhead" logs—old logs cut in the nineteenth century but lost in the lake. Submerged for a hundred years or more, these logs had taken on distinctive patterns and, when cut, were highly prized for flooring and other woodworking projects. In the case of Lake Pithlachoco, the archaeologists investigating the canoes quickly found themselves at odds with deadhead loggers and residents who claimed ownership of the submerged lands where the canoes (and valuable deadhead logs) were found. Ultimately, these intrigues paled in comparison to what we discovered about the canoes.

Back in the Office

Despite the challenges, discovery of the canoes was fascinating on several counts. The high school students ultimately located 101 canoes on the exposed lakebed. This raised several initial questions—most notably, why were so many canoes found in the bottom of one lake? And why were they mostly on the northern side of the lake? We hoped that analysis of the data that we had collected might provide some answers, but this also was an opportunity to revisit the Florida Canoe Project files that had been amassed by Barbara Purdy and her UF students during droughts in 1976–1977, 1981, and 1990. After her retirement, Barbara had sent her files to the state archaeologist's office because most of the canoes that she recorded were from submerged lands, usually claimed by the State of Florida. Statutorily, the canoes from these bottomlands were under the jurisdiction of the state archaeologist. The range of information was impressive and included data on some of the oldest canoes known in North America, as well as craft made by Seminole Indians, Anglo Americans, and others who were moving to Florida. The historic-period dugouts were the most varied; some were made of several logs pinned together, others had mast steps carved into their decks, and all had been made with metal tools.

I decided that the canoes should be recorded as sites in the Florida Master Site File, the state's official database of recorded archaeological and architectural sites. This was a significant turning point in our approach to dugout canoes. Prior to this, most canoes had not been recorded as sites but were considered isolated discoveries, perhaps akin to pop-tops tossed along the roadside that reflect nothing more than discard or loss. However, my motivation for recording them as sites was simple; it allowed us to plot their locations using the site file's Geographic Information Systems (GIS). In addition, putting the canoes in a database allowed us to look for other patterns beyond geographic distribution. Some of this information already had been synthesized by Barbara and her students and by archaeologist Mark Hartmann, who used the data for his 1996 dissertation on dugout canoes in the southeastern United States. However, the discovery of the Lake Pithlachoco project and our subsequent findings fundamentally changed the way we think about dugout canoes. Today, when canoes are found they always are recorded in the Master Site File—once reserved for historic houses, village deposits, and burial mounds. We also always try to identify wood species and obtain a radiocarbon date.

Making a Canoe

The use of fire to hollow a log was the most common technique for making canoes across much of the Southeast. Mud dams probably were used to control the charring, and shell and stone tools were used to scrape away the burned areas. Robin Brown, who experimented with making his own dugout canoe using the char and scrape technique, remarked to me that it was best to work on the canoe at night when the burning embers could be easily traced in the dark—too much charring could ruin a boat! Felling an appropriate log of pine or cypress may have involved fire, as shown in the background of de Bry's engraving. Selecting, felling, and transporting a log, as well as manufacturing the canoe itself, likely were a community activity that involved many people.

A sixteenth-century engraving by Theodor de Bry based on John White's watercolor drawing showing how the native inhabitants of the Carolinas made canoes.

(Collection of the author)

What Lake Pithlachoco Taught Us

We learned a lot from the dugout canoes at Lake Pithlachoco. We ultimately recorded detailed information on 55 canoes, and radiocarbon dating was conducted at the Beta Analytic laboratory in Miami. We suspected that all of the canoes had been made by Native Americans before the arrival of Europeans, as was indicated by the method of manufacture—essentially using fire to hollow out a large cypress or pine log. However, we were surprised by the results. The canoes fell into two groups: 13 were between 500 and 1,300 years old, and 41 were between 2,300 and 5,000 years old. The latter group was most interesting because these were some of the oldest canoes in North America and dated to the Late Archaic period. Finding canoes from this era was not unexpected because this was when the Everglades and most major river systems known today were formed. Shifting through the data from Barbara Purdy's canoe project, we found that, until the Lake Pithlachoco discovery, very few watercraft were known from this time period.

When comparing all the canoe data, we also found that few chronological markers were known for dugout canoes. In other words, canoes did not change much through time, and the oldest canoes looked remarkably like the youngest. The accepted wisdom was that the oldest examples

A dugout canoe from Magnolia Lake in Clay County with a charred spot on the deck. Native paddlers regularly carried fire in their canoes, and this likely is evidence of this flammable cargo. *(Courtesy of the Florida Division of Historical Resources)*

An almost intact canoe from Lake Pierce that required transporting with a front-end loader, which shows how heavy some of these waterlogged boats can be. This one was stored in a lake in Tallahassee before preservation treatment and could still float. *(Courtesy of the Florida Division of Historical Resources)*

The overhanging platform bow of a canoe found at Lake Munson in Tallahassee, November 2010. Most ancient canoes lack gunwales (sides), which is not surprising when one considers how thin and finely made they are, as shown on this canoe. Radiocarbon dating indicates that this watercraft was made 530 to 340 years ago. It may have been paddled by those traveling from Tallahassee to the coast. *(Photo by Ryan Wheeler)*

would be short, crude, and stumpy looking, while more recent craft would be longer, more carefully built, and more elegant in appearance. One of the few chronological hallmarks that archaeologists had recognized among Florida dugout canoes supported this idea. Around AD 1,200 a new vessel design appeared; this new style—perhaps an innovation—is best described as a canoe with overhanging platform ends. Why this feature appeared at this time remains unknown, but similar craft are known from other parts of the world. The platform ends are a perfect place to stand and to pole through shallow water or from which to fish.

What we found at Lake Pithlachoco was that the oldest canoes were anything but short and crude. In fact, one that we excavated was more than 30 feet long! This was well above the average for all known canoes and held the record for longest prehistoric canoe until the documentation of the Weedon Island canoe in 2015, which measures more than 40 feet in length! However, we were able to distinguish one trait that characterized these ancient canoes.

Many of the oldest canoes, at Lake Pithlachoco and elsewhere in Florida, had small raised ridges near the end or center of the craft. These usually were a few inches wide and only an inch or so tall and ran athwart the canoes. So we called the ridges thwarts. Whether these served a purpose or were a relic of carving the canoe is unknown. We do know that Seminole and Miccosukee canoe makers in the twentieth century hewed out their logs in sections, leaving partitions that were removed just before finishing their boat. These served to limit warping. Underwater archaeologists from Florida's Bureau of Archaeological Research recorded an unfinished dugout canoe in the Wakulla River just south of Tallahassee that was made with metal tools but also exhibited these "bulkheads" or thwarts, apparently an artifact of the manufacture process. The archaeologists also documented a fascinating aspect of canoe making, noting that nearly 30 feet of the canoe had been hewn carefully with an axe, but that an imperfection of the tree in the section on the other side of the bulkhead caused the project to be abandoned. Florida's oldest known canoe, from DeLeon Springs in Volusia County, is around 7,000 years old and exhibits these thwarts. It is unclear whether the similarities in construction techniques really represent a continuous technology or convergent evolution, but it is fascinating to consider that similar details of manufacture are present in the most ancient and most recent dugout canoes. We also recognized another chronological trend—namely, that a few of the older canoes were made of cypress, while the majority were made of pine. Both of these represent the longest, straightest trees available in Florida, and these were the trees targeted by loggers in the nineteenth century. Interestingly, Seminole canoes are more frequently made of cypress.

In 1990, paleoethnobotanist Lee Ann Newsom, working with her former professor Barbara Purdy, synthesized all the known information about Florida's dugout canoes. They developed a typology of canoe styles that incorporated aspects of form, manufacture, and chronology. Three of the types characterized canoes that were made before European contact. Type 1 represented the earliest style, blocky and rough-hewn and averaging about 12 feet in length. Type 2 canoes were similar but better made and with slightly beveled

An example of a "thwart" on one of the Lake Pithlachoco canoes. The feature may be evidence of manufacture or may have served as a foothold for use during poling in shallow water. *(Photo by Ryan Wheeler)*

ends, averaging 18 feet in length. Type 3 boats have the overhanging platform ends, as described earlier; radiocarbon dates indicate that this feature was introduced around AD 1,200 and persisted into the period of European contact. Additional styles defined by Newsom and Purdy represent historic watercraft, including Seminole dugout canoes.

The Lake Pithlachoco canoes provided an interesting test case for this typology and chronology. The oldest Lake Pithlachoco boats consistently were longer and wider than the Type 1 and Type 2 canoes defined by Newsom and Purdy, and the chronological distinctions between the two types were not observed in the Pithlachoco samples. In our study of the Lake Pithlachoco canoes we concluded that, for the most part, dugout canoe design characteristics already were well-developed during the Archaic period and persisted with few innovations throughout the ensuing 7,000 or 8,000 years. This may have been in response to sea level changes during this early time period, when modern water bodies came into being, including many of Florida's rivers and lakes, Lake Okeechobee, and the Everglades. Long, narrow watercraft were excellent for use in shallow fresh-water environments such as these, and what they lacked in stability was compensated for by speed and maneuverability.

The Seminoles and Lake Pithlachoco

Perhaps one of the most fascinating parts of the Lake Pithlachoco canoe story is the interest and involvement of the Seminole Tribe of Florida. You already may have wondered about the name of the lake—Pithlachoco. If you look at a modern map, you won't find this name; the lake, located on the east side of Gainesville, is quite large and typically is marked as Newnan's Lake. However, older maps use its earlier name, Lake Pithlachoco, which predated Daniel Newnan's incursion into Spanish Florida in 1812 and his skirmish with the natives living in the area now known as Gainesville and Alachua County. Pithlachoco is itself a fascinating word, especially in light of the canoe discovery. In the language spoken by many Seminoles, it means something like "boathouse" or "place of long boats." Did the Seminoles of the eighteenth and early nineteenth century know about all those ancient canoes submerged in the lake? We simply don't know, but there certainly were Seminole settlements in the area, and these were some of the natives the botanist and explorer William Bartram met in the eighteenth century. Seminoles of the nineteenth century developed their own distinctive style of canoe, with a prominent cutwater at the bow, which gave them dominion over the Florida Everglades, their refuge from the wars of Indian removal. A mast step carved in the deck allowed for the canoes to transform into small craft for coastal sailing.

We all were surprised by the Seminole reaction to the discovery of the Lake Pithlachoco canoes and the subsequent issues with a deadhead logger who had damaged one or more of the canoes

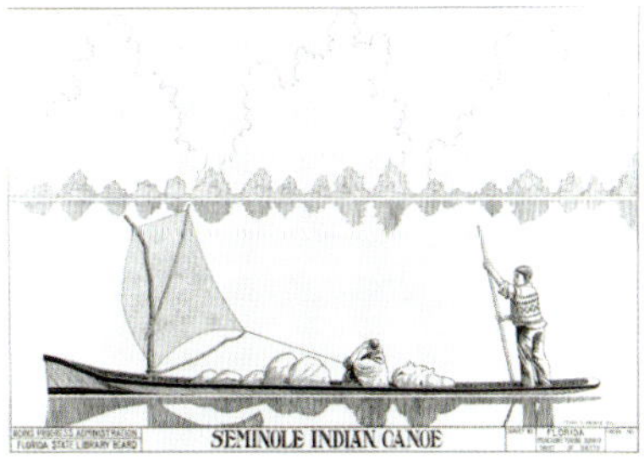

Frank S. Browne's drawing of a Seminole sailing canoe, made as part of the Works Progress Administration's Historic American Merchant Marine survey in 1936–1937.

(Courtesy of the State Archives of Florida, Florida Memory Project)

The "Minorcan Freighter," also known as "The Louis" and "Lord Nelson," is a log boat used in nineteenth-century St. Augustine and Jacksonville. The vessel is known from historical records and apparently was built by Native Americans under the direction of a Minorcan named Hudnel. Note the blend of traditional dugout canoe manufacture and the use of frames on the interior.

(Courtesy of the Florida Museum of History)

during his log removal work. The Seminoles of Oklahoma—descendants of those removed during the Indian Wars of the early nineteenth century—were interested in the discovery as well. At one point, Chief James Billie of the Seminole Tribe of Florida flew in his helicopter to visit the site with then Florida Secretary of State Katherine Harris. At the time, I thought that the Seminoles' reaction was not unlike the reaction that we sometimes saw when a native burial site was disturbed or desecrated. Burials and many other archaeological sites are protected under state and federal law, but sometimes construction work causes a disturbance, or unscrupulous individuals dig up sites to steal grave goods for sale on the antiquities market. If they are on state or federal lands, including submerged lands, canoes also are protected.

However, since working with the Pithlachoco canoes in 2000, I've read a lot more about dugout canoes throughout the world and found many instances in which indigenous cultures recognize that canoes are living, breathing beings imbued with human souls just like the rest of us. For example, the Yurok of northern California carve kidneys, a heart, and a nose on each dugout because they are considered to be living beings. Anthropologists use the expression "canoe culture" to describe societies in which canoe building and use is not just central to the economy, but also is at the very heart of how people think about themselves. A great example is found in the Pacific Northwest, where traditional dugout canoe building and the associated fishing technologies were largely abandoned until a recent interest in building and using canoes. The tribal elders recognized that canoe building wasn't just an important part of their culture—it was critical for cultural survival.

Segment of the Ortona Canal, west of Lake Okeechobee and north of the Caloosahatchee River, which still held water when the author visited in 1996. *(Photo by Ryan Wheeler)*

Water World

In 2003, we published our findings on the Lake Pithlachoco canoes in the scientific journal *American Antiquity*. We emphasized that Native Florida was a world in which water travel was primary and that canoes, as pointed out by canoeist and educator Chuck Blanchard, served as pack animal, portable work bench, and more. My introduction to Florida's dugout canoes while a student of Barbara Purdy had well prepared me for research on the Lake Pithlachoco project and also intersected with my interest in Florida's prehistoric canoe canals. During the 1990s, my friend George Luer had encouraged me to join him in research on these unusual features found in southern Florida. I first investigated a system of canals associated with the Ortona site on the west side of Lake Okeechobee. The site's inhabitants had constructed two canals that allowed travelers to bypass rapids on the Caloosahatchee River, a major east-west connection between the interior wetlands and the coast. Paddlers were routed through the Ortona site, which was situated to the north of the river.

Aerial photo of the Mud Lake Canal at Cape Sable in the Florida Everglades. The canal allowed paddlers to bypass the treacherous waters of Florida Bay as they traveled around the Ten Thousand Islands, Florida Keys, and the Everglades. This photo was made during a 1966 archaeological survey by William Sears and Wm. J. Kennedy from Florida Atlantic University. *(Courtesy of the Department of Anthropology, Florida Atlantic University)*

Study of the hydraulic characteristics of the canals shows that they were carefully constructed to take advantage of natural changes in the topography and that their flow was designed to mimic that of natural water bodies in the area. Similar canal systems, also known on Pine Island, at Florida Bay in the Everglades, in Naples, and even in the Florida panhandle, seem to be unique to Florida and confirm the significance of canoes in prehistoric times. Ancient Floridians had the know-how and desire to construct long-distance canoe canals that provided safe passage and routed travelers through important villages. Extensive exchange networks on local and regional levels made use of these linked waterways to transport goods such as shark teeth, shells, pottery, food stuffs, and even exotic materials from farther afield. We also suggested in the 2003 article that water was central to the lives of people and communities in ancient Florida in ways that were difficult for us to understand and access. However, by thinking of their world as an inverse of ours—where water is an element at the heart of culture, rather than a nuisance to be exploited, controlled, and drained away—might provide some insight into the lives of these people.

More Canoes

Dugout canoes are known from a whopping 242 archaeological sites in Florida; many were recorded by Barbara Purdy and her students, while others have been found more recently. There are too many wonderful finds to discuss in these few pages! However, a few more examples are worth mentioning because they demonstrate the most interesting aspects of dugout canoes.

In May 2006, while I served as Florida's state archaeologist, I received a call from the Apalachicola office of the Florida Fish & Wildlife Conservation Commission to report the discovery of an extraordinarily long dugout canoe. Hauled from the Apalachicola River by deadhead loggers, the canoe was being stored—and exhibited for a price—at the logger's sawmill. Clearly made with metal tools, the watercraft measured more than 50 feet in length. After a bit of legal sparring with the Conservation Commission and the finder, we recruited the Florida Division of Forestry to help us move the canoe so it could be conserved and, ultimately, displayed at the Apalachicola Center for History, Art and Culture. A semi-tractor trailer and two truck-mounted cranes were used to gently lift and transport the massive canoe. In an article in the journal *Historical Archaeology*, archaeologist Kevin Porter concluded that the canoe combines features of Native American and European construction techniques to create a hybrid—perhaps made quickly to serve some specific purpose—that could be best described as

Transport of the Apalachicola Traders' Canoe required the help of the Florida Division of Forestry. At more than 50 feet in length, this was the largest dugout canoe that we ever heard of.
(Photo by Ryan Wheeler)

a cargo or pack vessel designed for ease of movement and directional stability. The Apalachicola Trader's Canoe demonstrates the range and specialization that dugout craft have undergone in the centuries since European contact and conquest.

Perhaps even more extraordinary is the prehistoric canoe found at the Weedon Island Preserve near St. Petersburg. Measuring more than 40 feet in length, this canoe is the longest prehistoric canoe known in Florida and perhaps the entire Southeast. It also is unusual because it was found in a saltwater environment. Although its length and location suggest that it may have been an oceangoing canoe, it is similar to other Florida canoes in most respects. Fragments of a pole were found with the canoe, and both the boat and the pole date to 1,100 years ago. In 2011, the Friends of Weedon Island and the Alliance for Weedon Island Archaeological Research and Education partnered to excavate and conserve the canoe, a lengthy and expensive process that involved the gradual impregnation of the boat with polyethylene glycol. Three-dimensional laser scanning helped in the creation of a cradle, and the canoe is now on exhibit at the Weedon Island Preserve Cultural and Natural History Center.

These two examples of extremes—incredibly long dugout canoes—demonstrate some of the range and skill possessed by Florida's past inhabitants. Dugout canoes were a part of everyday life and likely were ubiquitous on waterways throughout the state in ancient and more recent times. In all these cases, the high-profile discovery of the canoes at Lake Pithlachoco encouraged public and professional interest in the vessel type and helped other investigators recognize that each find has much to contribute to Florida's canoe history.

The incredibly long Weedon Island Canoe on exhibit at the Weedon Island Preserve Cultural and Natural History Center. Note the special cradle that was made using three-dimensional scans of the canoe. *(Photo by Ryan Wheeler)*

✳ ✳ ✳

As a bit of an epilogue to this story, an article in the fall 2016 issue of *American Archaeology* magazine reported on the discovery of human footprints on Calvert Island in Canada that date to 13,000 years ago. People needed boats to travel to the island, making this one of the earliest indications that Paleoindian people were making and using watercraft. Paleoindians represent the earliest human presence in the Americas and may date well before this Canadian find. We don't know whether the boats in question were dugout canoes or other small craft made from hides and skins, but this bolsters the idea that the first settlers in the New World were traveling via boats along the Pacific coastline from Asia. This is one of the reasons that it is so important to record data and obtain dates on all of Florida's dugout canoes. As noted previously, the canoe form does not change much through time. Each new canoe discovered could be the oldest and provide clues about the earliest occupation of the state.

Dr. Ryan J. Wheeler, the director of the R. S. Peabody Museum of Archaeology at Phillips Academy, served for several years as Florida's state archaeologist, which gave him the opportunity to study a number of unique prehistoric and historic canoes. He is the author of *Treasure of the Calusa: The Johnson/Willcox Collection from Mound Key, Florida* (Rose, 2000).

For Additional Information

Websites

"Archaeology: Canoes: Prehistoric Canoes in Florida," Florida Division of Historical Resources, http://dos.myflorida.com/historical/archaeology/projects/canoes/. Information on dugout canoes, including what to do if you find a canoe.

Florida Memory: State Library & Archives of Florida, https://www.floridamemory.com/. Site to search for photos of Florida's dugout canoes, especially Seminole canoes and canoe making.

"What to Do If You Find a Dugout Canoe," Florida Museum of Natural History, University of Florida, https://www.flmnh.ufl.edu/flarch/what-do-if-you-find-dugout-canoe/. Information on dugout canoes, links to more information, exhibition links to Paddling Through the Americas, and a brief documentary video on the Lake Pithlachoco excavations.

Publications

Mark Hartmann, "The Development of Watercraft in the Southeastern United States," PhD dissertation, Texas A&M University, 1996, http://anthropology.tamu.edu/wp-content/uploads/sites/11/2016/07/Hartmann-PhD1996.pdf

Elizabeth Lowman, "Canoe Building: A Journey from History to the Present," June 8, 2011, Seminole Tribe of Florida, Ah-Tah-Thi-Ki Museum Blog, https://ahtahthiki.wordpress.com/2011/06/08/canoe-building-a-journey-from-history-to-the-present/

"Prehistoric Canoe Found at Weedon Island Preserve," Weedon Island Preserve, http://www.weedonislandpreserve.org/prehistoric-canoe.htm

CHAPTER 5

Ship Trap: Florida's Unique Collection of Shipwrecks

ROGER C. SMITH

What comes to mind when you hear the word "trap"? Perhaps a mouse trap or a booby trap? These traps involve elements of surprise and capture. What about a trap door for concealment or a sand trap at the golf course as an artificial hazard? Each of these devices are intentional man-made constructs designed to hold an object for a purpose. Under the water, the fish weir was an ancient tool to direct the passage of fish in tidal waters or rivers into a holding area for collection; today, the trawl net is dragged along the sea bottom to collect fish. Aside from these purposeful traps, there are natural phenomena that unintentionally entrap the unwary human who happens to be in the wrong place at the right time—quicksand or the sudden onset of a sandstorm or avalanche can be natural traps. Water also can serve to catch the unsuspecting—for example, a flash flood in a narrow, dry canyon. The Sargasso Sea, the eddy of surface water between major North Atlantic ocean currents, becalmed sailing ships before mariners learned to avoid it. Perhaps the best definition of a trap that applies to marine archaeology is "something by which one is caught or stopped unawares; also, a position or situation from which it is difficult or impossible to escape." Every captain who commands a ship at sea is keenly on the lookout for such unknown perils that might lie ahead.

Florida has thousands of miles of coastline, tidal inlets, bays, and waterways, all of which require careful maritime navigation to avoid calamity. The long peninsula protrudes from the North American mainland into the Caribbean Basin, separating the Atlantic Ocean and the Gulf of Mexico. Of the numerous natural factors that affect nautical activities, none is more powerful than a hurricane. Although the season extends from June to November, the most frequent and strongest hurricanes occur during the months of September and October. Florida is exposed on the Atlantic side to storms that develop far out to sea, build strength in warm Caribbean waters, and come ashore along the low-lying coastline. Along the Gulf coast, hurricanes develop from tropical depressions in the Gulf of Mexico that increase intensity in the warm shallow water, then come ashore with devastating results. Modern technology for weather prediction and communication can provide early warning and accurate hurricane tracking so ships can avoid or prepare for these storms. However, as late as the beginning of the twentieth century, the only warning of a potentially disastrous storm was the weather change recognized by experienced mariners. Hurricanes were the cause of several Spanish fleet disasters in Florida waters that occurred in 1559, 1622, 1715, and 1733.

San Felipe (aka *El Lerri, Terri*)

The Florida Keys in the summer of 1977 was a good time to explore shipwrecks. Jim Dunbar and I, field agents for the Florida Division of Archives, History and Records Management (now Division of Historical Resources), were stationed in the Lower Keys and decided to try to locate and record sites of the Spanish merchant fleet that had wrecked there in the summer of 1733. The fleet had departed Havana for Spain on July 13, consisting of four armed galleons, 18 merchant *naos*, and smaller ships carrying the products of

Spanish fleet in the 1733 hurricane. *(Painting by William Trotter)*

Mexico. The next day, when the vessels sighted the Florida Keys, the captain-general sensed an approaching hurricane and ordered his captains to turn back to Havana. Already it was too late. Part of the fleet struck the outer reefs; some vessels were swept over the reefs and sank behind them, and others were carried toward channels between the islands before they ran aground. By nightfall, most of the ships had been scattered 80 miles up and down the Keys, sunk and swamped, their survivors gathering in small groups throughout the low islands (see Chapter 7).

I had a dog-eared copy of *Diving to a Flash of Gold* (1971) by Martin Meylach, which contained a chart with numbered circles showing shipwrecks he had explored, a short description of each, and running ranges of features on shore to line up for each wreck location. In August the sea was flat calm; the water between the islands and the reef was so transparent that we easily could see the brown patch reefs, dark green grass beds, and white sand pockets from the boat. Jim and I began to look systematically for the 1733 wreck sites featured in Meylach's book by approaching each general area of the chart and trying to match his running ranges. Before the age of hyperbolic-

Jim Dunbar and the author relocating the 1733 shipwrecks from running ranges. *(Photo by KC Smith)*

radio-based long-range navigation (LORAN) or satellite-based Global Positioning System (GPS), these ranges were a set of two or more drawings showing tall trees or telephone poles in front of prominent buildings or landmarks that would line up as the boat moved toward the wreck location. We needed binoculars, calm water, and patience for the ranges to fall into place; then we put our trusty waterglass over the side of the boat. The three-foot-long conical box had an open port at the top and a glass pane at the bottom through which we could observe the seabed. We looked for telltale mounds of egg-shaped ballast stones, which ships had carried deep in their holds to counterbalance the force of winds through the rigging.

Fortunately, the midsummer weather remained calm, and we located eight of the 1733 merchant shipwrecks. We discovered that each contained a distinct microcosm of marine life, both sedentary and pelagic, that called the wreck site home. These creatures were the latest generation of inhabitants that lived and died among some of Florida's oldest artificial reefs, created almost 250 years earlier. Jim and I made diagrams of each shipwreck and collected samples of small ballast stones and ceramic sherds that we tagged and bagged. One day, as I was hand-fanning the sediments between ballast stones, I came across a simple gold ring that gleamed brightly in the underwater sunlight. Excitedly, I swam over to Jim to show him my discovery. He looked at me, then at the ring in my hand, and resumed what he was doing, seemingly uninterested. I approached him again, grabbed his arm, and held the ring up to his facemask so that he could not miss it. He looked at me again and shook his head, pointing to my left hand, which no longer had my recently acquired wedding band on it. Sheepishly, I put on my ring and thought about how lucky I was to have found it at all.

Soon after the wrecking, Spaniards had salvaged the vessels they were unable to refloat. Years later, the wreck sites were rediscovered by fishermen and skin divers in the shallow, clear water of the Keys. Scuba divers began to dig through the ballast piles looking for sunken treasure and collecting souvenirs. Unfortunately, numerous iron anchors and cannons were removed from the sites; many turned up in front of local marinas and restaurants, where they eventually crumbled in the sun without the benefit of conservation treatment. The sites Jim and I recorded that summer all showed signs of modern disturbance—ballast stones had been displaced, lower hull timbers exposed, and in some cases digging tools left behind. However, one site appeared to be relatively undisturbed compared with the others—the shipwreck known as *El Lerri*.

Spanish documents listed this ship by several names: *El Lerri*, *El Tyrri*, and *Navio de Terry*. The nicknames reflected her owner, Guillermo Terry, the Marques of Canada, whose family shipped sherry wine between Cádiz and England. Her formal name was *San Felipe*, and she was one of six English-built ships of 400- to 500-ton capacity that sailed in the 1733 fleet. Her cargo was mainly organic, consisting of cochineal (a red dye), *anil* (blue indigo dye), chocolate, molasses, snuff, purgative herbs, vanilla beans, and fruit relish. Stationed near the center of the convoy, *San Felipe* was pushed by the storm over the reefs, where her hull opened up and she bilged close to shore in 18 feet of water. All of her people were saved.

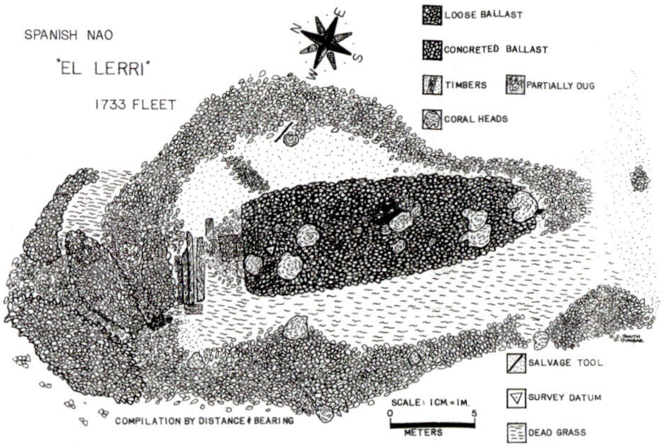

1977 site plan of *El Lerri*. *(Drawing by Roger Smith and Jim Dunbar)*

We found *San Felipe* on the inner edge of Hawk Channel, in a pocket of sand and silt where underwater visibility is reduced. Her prominent loaf-shaped mound of cemented ballast stones created an oasis of marine life in an otherwise monotonous, grassy plain. The ballast pile had been picked apart along its outer edges sometime in the past, and a few central timbers of the lower hull were exposed. Large coral heads, thriving in the channel currents, had made their home on top of the ballast, and we noted the usual communities of grouper, snapper, grunts, blennies, wrasses, damselfish, angelfish, and hogfish. In a concavity at one end of the mound, a large green moray eel was stationed like a tail gunner. None of the fish

Recording of San Felipe's lower hull timbers. *(Photo courtesy of Indiana University)*

seemed alarmed by our presence, but their curiosity suggested that the shipwreck had not been visited by divers for some time. After exploring eight of the 1733 shipwrecks, Jim and I wrote up our notes, drafted site plans, developed underwater photographs, created new running ranges, and submitted a formal report to our Tallahassee office.

Eleven years later, Charlie Becker and I led a joint Indiana University/Florida State University field school back to the 1733 fleet sites. Our objective was to evaluate them for their potential to became a second State Underwater Archaeological Preserve. Eleven sites were relocated (this time using LORAN) by students, who recorded cultural and biological features and compared criteria such as water condition, accessibility, aquatic life, archaeological integrity, and research potential. We ranked each site for its promise as a destination for heritage, as well as recreational and ecological tourism. The results of this 1988 fieldwork were circulated among the Keys waterfront community, and a consensus indicated that *San Pedro*, a picturesque shipwreck off Islamorada, was the most likely candidate due to its proximity to marinas and Indian Key State Park. *San Felipe* had been ranked highest in research potential because of its relatively undisturbed condition, but ranked lower for water conditions and accessibility.

In 1992 and 1993, Indiana University returned to *San Felipe* to conduct a multidisciplinary field school with professors and students to address specific research questions about the vessel's identity, history, construction materials, and site dynamics. Overseen by professionals with backgrounds in biology, geology, archaeology, and archival research, the study was one of the most comprehensive examinations of an early eighteenth-century shipwreck in Florida. *San Felipe* subsequently was listed on the National Register of Historic Places in Washington, DC.

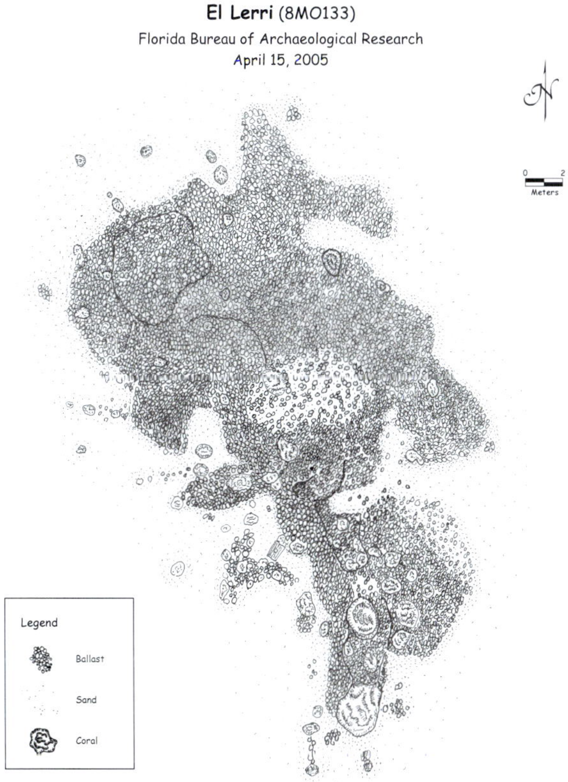

2005 site plan of *El Lerri*.

(Drawing by Roger Smith, Della Scott-Ireton, Jennifer McKinnon, and Jason Raupp)

In 2004, the State Underwater Archaeology Team returned to the Keys to create a Spanish Galleon Trail to guide visitors to the 13 known 1733 shipwreck sites. Each of the sites was reassessed for new site plans and biological inventories, resulting in a colorful guide booklet and an Internet website providing GPS coordinates for visitors to follow (see Chapters 7 and 11). As with *San Felipe*, each of these sites is now listed on the National Register.

Barrier islands and related landforms fringe most of Florida's coastline. Almost all the state's sandy beaches are on coastal barriers, which serve as buffers between the mainland and the open ocean. The islands on the Atlantic coast and along the Panhandle are longer than those along the west coast, and many are unstable and shift with tides, currents, and sea level changes. Consequently, coastal navigation near shore is hazardous due to shallow water and changing sandbars.

Commodore

When *Commodore*, a steamship running guns to Cuba, began to sink off Ponce Inlet in 1897, journalist Stephen Crane declined to board either of the two lifeboats, but stayed behind to assist with their launching. Crane then joined the captain and two other crew members in a 10-foot dinghy as *Commodore* sank beneath the sea. Little did they know that they would spend the next 30 hours aboard the frail craft at the mercy of wind and waves. Crane, author of *The Red Badge of Courage*, later wrote about his escape from the sinking ship in a short story titled "The Open Boat."

Commodore, which was owned by wealthy Cuban expatriates, had twice carried a cargo of rifles, ammunition, gunpowder, medicines, and revolutionaries to the island to fight for independence from Spain. Hired by a New York newspaper as a war correspondent, Crane boarded the filibustering steamship in Jacksonville on New Year's Eve, 1896. The voyage was doomed from the beginning. Heading up the St. Johns River in dense fog toward Mayport and the open sea, *Commodore* struck a sandbar and damaged her hull. Towed off the next day, she steamed southeast to Cuba into a fierce nor'easter, where heavy pounding from the waves further weakened the hull, causing her to spring a leak. The captain ordered the crew and the Cuban passengers to form a bucket brigade and the engineer to stoke the engine with everything he could to build up enough steam to make for Mosquito Inlet (present day Ponce Inlet) 18 miles away. However, the incoming water soon drowned the furnace, and the order was given to abandon ship. Two lifeboats made it to shore, but eight men were lost the night of the wrecking. Meanwhile in the dinghy, the captain, cook, oiler, and Crane were tossing in heavy waves and wind. Rising on one swell, they could see the tiny lighthouse at Mosquito Inlet far away on the horizon and tried to head for it. Once they were close to shore, they were exhausted and were reluctant to breech the breakers. Finally, the next day they made an attempt, swamping the dinghy but struggling ashore nevertheless in the cold January water. The oiler was injured during the capsizing and did not survive.

The filibuster steamship *Commodore*. *(Painting by William Trotter)*

The sinking of *Commodore* immediately received sensational yellow press coverage, with speculations of sabotage at a time when the start of the Spanish-American War was still 16 months away. Crane published an eyewitness account of the episode for the *New York Times* while recovering in Jacksonville. Later this account formed the basis for "The Open Boat," a symbolic tale of human mortality in the face of nature.

In 1986, Elizabeth Friedmann, a professor of English at Jacksonville University, became inter-

The only known photograph of *Commodore*, circa 1896.
(Courtesy of the Ponce Inlet Lighthouse and Museum)

ested in the whereabouts of the *Commodore* shipwreck, a topic that came up when teaching about Stephen Crane. She contacted veteran Ormond Beach diver Don Serbousek, who by coincidence had been exploring a shipwreck that contained numerous rifles, bullets, and a pulley with the date 1885 stamped on it. As an avocational archaeologist, Serbousek had been carefully mapping the site and the locations of artifacts he found and recovered. He suspected that the wreck was *Commodore* and believed that it needed protection from other divers. By the late 1990s, he stopped diving, and much of his collection came to be housed by the Ponce Inlet Lighthouse Preservation Association (PILPA). A federal court in 1998 awarded PILPA and Serbousek title to the wreck, which is outside state waters, based on their belief that it was *Commodore*.

Seeking to establish a firm identity for the wreck as *Commodore*, PILPA partnered with the not-for-profit Cambrian Foundation, which asked archaeologist Kimberly Eslinger to supervise investigations from 2002 to 2004. This fieldwork included detailed mapping the site and its features, artifact analysis and recording, and recommendations for artifact conservation. Meanwhile, historical documents and contemporary accounts of the ship and its sinking were gathered to compare with the archaeological data. The wreck site is situated in 70 to 82 feet of water about 12 miles from Ponce Inlet on a shell and sand bottom. Although most of the vessel's wooden hull has deteriorated over time, more durable features such as the steam engine, propeller and its shaft, a small boiler, fire tubes from the main boiler, ammunition boxes, windlass, and an anchor stretch across a field 110 feet long by 50 feet wide. The orientation of these features suggests that the vessel sank stern first, rolled to her starboard side, and at some point, the bow separated from the hull.

Detailed measurements of the engine closely matched the 26-inch bore and 30-inch stroke specifications for *Commodore*'s engine as listed in the *American Shipmaster's Record Association 1884 Registry*. The four-bladed propeller at the site matches a Philadelphia flywheel, which was designed to balance a steam-driven shaft inside a wooden boat. According to documents, *Commodore*

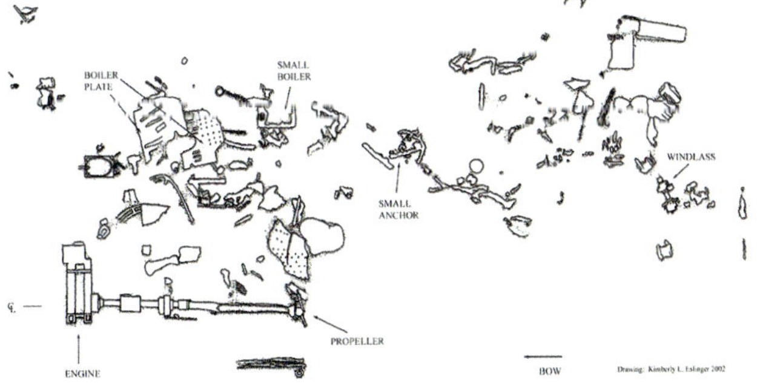

Site plan of *Commodore*. *(Drawing by Kimberly Eslinger)*

Engine and propeller shaft of *Commodore*.
(Photo by Cindy Burnham, Lucky Shot Productions. Courtesy of Nautilus Productions)

had a single boiler with its engine, and boiler-plate remains litter the site, suggesting that it exploded when cold winter water overwhelmed the pumps. Discovery on the site of two intact wooden crates of ammunition with .43-caliber shot, along with pieces and parts from .43-caliber Remington rolling-block rifles, matches the cargo list printed in the newspapers after *Commodore's* sinking. An ironstone plate recovered from the site is inscribed with the registered trademark of an English potter from 1875 to 1897. The plate and bronze pulley with an 1885 stamp mark helped to narrow the wreck's date and support the contention that the site certainly is *Commodore*, lost on January 2, 1897.

Today, the Ponce Inlet Lighthouse serves as a storage and conservation facility for *Commodore*'s artifacts and maintains a permanent public display about the shipwreck.

* * *

The submerged coastline of Florida has a steep slope on the Atlantic side and a shallow slope along the Gulf side. Although both these shorelines can present navigational hazards, they are primary destinations for shipping. Inlets from the open sea provide access to protected inland bays, harbors, and rivers, but they often are extremely risky to traverse because of shallow sandbars that form barriers to the entrances. Moreover, they are notoriously unstable—tidal erosion and accretion can cause some to shift location in a very short time. Before inlets were improved by dredging, reinforced by jetties, and marked by aids to navigation, crossing the bar often was accomplished only with assistance from a local pilot who was familiar with the depths, tides, currents, and wind conditions. Historically, the most hazardous inlets during the colonial period were at Florida's earliest settlements, St. Augustine and Pensacola.

Industry

St. Augustine's harbor entrance has caused many maritime casualties over the years. The shifting sands offshore create a sandbar, which has changed gradually over time; although modern dredging is used to keep the inlet open, mariners still treat

Four-bladed propeller of *Commodore*.

(Photo by Cindy Burnham, Lucky Shot Productions. Courtesy of Nautilus Productions)

the channel with great respect. St. Augustine, the nation's oldest continuously occupied port, was settled as a Spanish colony in the mid-sixteenth century to support and defend maritime fleets sailing from Havana through the Florida Straits back to Spain. After Florida was acquired by Britain in 1763, a new colony was created, with Pensacola as the capital of West Florida and St. Augustine as the capital of East Florida. A second Spanish occupation followed (1784–1821) before Florida became a U.S. territory, and then a state in 1845.

Having worked in the early 1990s for the Pensacola Shipwreck Survey, archaeologists Marianne Franklin and John W. Morris III established Southern Oceans Archaeological Research (SOAR), a not-for-profit Florida corporation, and set their sights on St. Augustine. They designed a comprehensive project in 1995 to conduct archival research on how the inlet and shoreline had shifted over the centuries in order to select areas for electronic survey to locate potentially significant shipwrecks. The St. Augustine Shipwreck Survey received a research permit and grant funding from the state Division of Historical Resources to conduct the work. Historic colonial charts and maps were consulted to compare with modern aerial photographs, thus documenting the dramatically changing landscapes and seascapes along the coast. Two offshore areas were selected for a magnetometer survey, which produced a number of magnetic targets: two turned out to be an eighteenth-century shipwreck in 20 feet of water.

Diving on the two targets from the research vessel, the archaeologists discovered that their boat anchor had snagged on an exposed iron ring attached to a large, buried colonial anchor. Test excavations revealed three anchors, eight cannons, and a number of other artifacts, all of which appeared to be part of the cargo of a ship that ran aground on the bar outside the historic channel.

Although no hull structure was uncovered, the artifact assemblage reflected their stowed position in the hold of the wrecked vessel. One of the cannons was recovered in 1998; when cleaned of concretion, it was identified as a British six-pounder, incised with a broad arrow (signifying government property), a crest of George II (1727–1760), and a raised letter "A" on one of the cannon's trunnions, a mark of the Ashburnham foundry in Sussex, England.

Further archival research focused on the East Florida Papers and correspondence of General Thomas Gage, commander of the British army in New York between 1763 and 1765. Study of these documents pointed to a candidate for the shipwreck—the sloop *Industry*, an army transport vessel that wrecked while attempting to enter St. Augustine harbor on May 6, 1764. *Industry* was carrying six-pound cannons, ammunition, and tools to supply the East Florida garrison after the British acquired the colony under terms of the Treaty of Paris in 1763. The location of the wreckage and its cargo fit the description of *Industry*, one of four transport vessels sent from New York to St. Augustine in 1764.

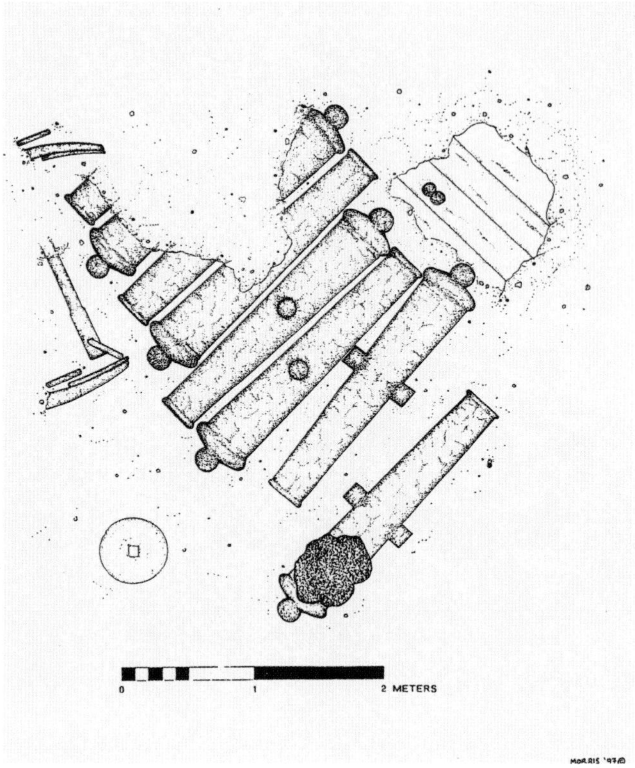

Preliminary site plan of *Industry*, 1997. (Drawing by J. W. Morris III)

The recovered cannon was placed in a tank on the grounds of the St. Augustine Lighthouse and Museum, where it underwent treatment for nearly four years while on public display. In 1999, archaeologists discovered that looters had stolen two of the other cannons from the site. A prop-wash deflector had been used to blast away sand, washing other artifacts from the hole it created. Despite news coverage, public outrage, and law enforcement investigations, the looters escaped apprehension, and the cannons have not been found. Continued research on the *Industry* site was conducted by the new Lighthouse Archaeological Maritime Program (LAMP), which was formalized in 1999. An iron swivel gun, crates of cannon shot, lead musket balls, iron bar stock, and a wide variety of tools intended for the garrison were discovered. The tools included iron axe heads, shovel blades, a bundled parcel of iron files, drawknives, hand saws, a whetstone, and a millstone. A cast iron cooking pot and a brass teakettle may have been part of the ship's culinary equipment. Most of these artifacts were recovered and transported to Texas A&M University's Conservation Research Laboratory, where they were cleaned and stabilized for study.

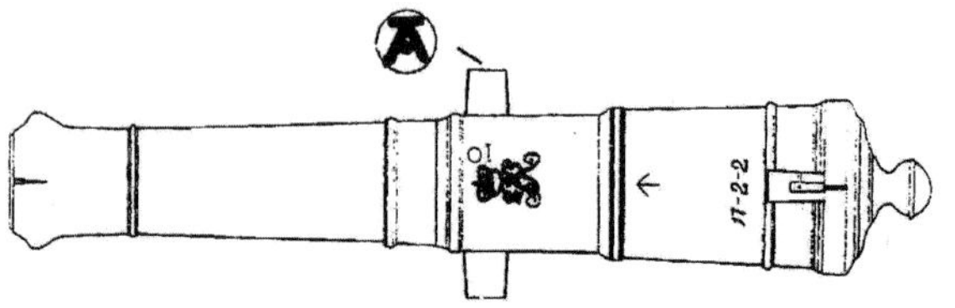

Cast iron six-pounder cannon with the crest of George II. (Drawing by J. W. Morris III)

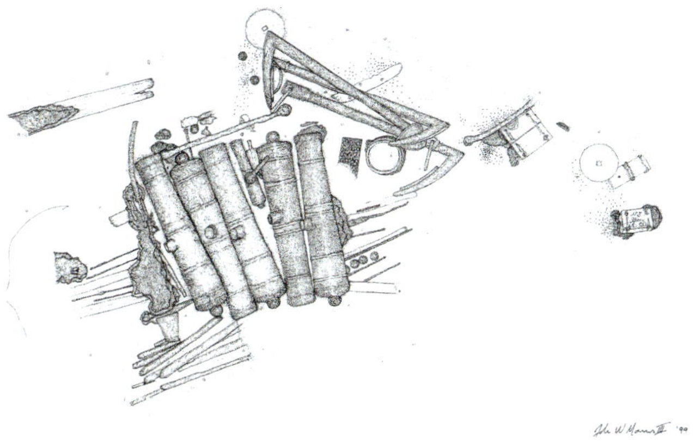

Final site plan of *Industry*, 1999. (Drawing by J. W. Morris III)

As property of the State of Florida, they were returned after conservation to be accessioned, then loaned to the St. Augustine Lighthouse Museum for display in a special exhibit about *Industry*.

Although navigators became familiar with Florida's inlets, in the absence of lighthouses, illuminated channel markers, and ranges, passage was extremely hazardous at night, especially in bad weather.

Catharine

Stroll along the white sands of Santa Rosa Island on Florida's Panhandle, gaze out to the clear emerald waters of the Gulf of Mexico, then close your eyes and imagine the following scene: at daybreak the storm has abated, but heavy seas still pound the beach. A full-rigged sailing ship lies stranded barely 300 yards from shore, rolling precariously in the troughs of waves that repeatedly break over her hull. As the sky gets lighter, several groups of tiny figures can be seen huddled together in the ship's rigging, seeking refuge from seas crashing on deck below. This was the scene that greeted Life Saving Station keeper Robert Broadbent on the morning of August 7, 1894. With the help of his teenage daughters and a volunteer crew, he managed to rescue the vessel's 18 crew members, but the ship *Catharine* could not be refloated. Eventually, a second storm broke her hulk into pieces that disappeared beneath the water. Struck from shipping lists, *Catharine* became another forgotten casualty of Florida's coastline.

Christened *Eliza* in 1870, the newly built ship sailed from St. John, New Brunswick, to Liverpool, England, where she was sold to British owners and renamed *Carnarvonshire*. Historical documents show that the ship served more than two decades in the British Merchant Marine and eventually was sold to Norwegian owners, who named her *Catharine*. A veteran of late nineteenth-century global maritime trade, she repaid her Canadian, British, and Norwegian owners many times over by carrying a variety of cargos between far-flung ports for 24 years, in a time when the average working life of wooden merchant vessels was just 18 years. Repaired at least five times during her career, *Catharine* was one of many old wooden sailing ships that Norwegian merchants purchased cheaply at the end of their working lives to carry bulk cargos such as coal, timber, and guano. Drawn to Pensacola by its growing lumber industry, the ship attempted to enter the bay at night during a gale, but grounded instead on a sandbar east of the pass.

For more than a century, *Catharine*'s remains served as an occasional nursery for marine life, alternately becoming exposed on the seabed, then buried by sand during episodic tempests like the one that drove her ashore. Ultimately, *Catharine* assumed yet another life—as an archaeological site and underwater classroom. During a 1992

Catharine aground off Santa Rosa Island. (Courtesy of the University of West Florida Historic Trust)

survey of Pensacola shipwrecks, archaeologists found the site to be completely buried in sand; however, in 1995, Hurricanes Erin and Opal and subsequent winter storms in 1996 and 1997 uncovered significant portions of the sunken vessel. Located in the Gulf Islands National Seashore, the wreck site was visited by sport divers who alerted Park Service personnel about the presence of exposed artifacts, such as a compass binnacle, porthole, and glass deck lights. The Park Service requested assistance from the University of West Florida (UWF) Archaeology Institute to document the site and provide conservation treatment for artifacts given to the park by divers.

In 1998, a UWF field school mapped and recorded the visible hull remains, rigging, and associated ballast stones. The hull remains consisted mainly of framing and inner ceiling planking of the vessel's starboard side, with some outer hull planking and yellow metal sheathing around the perimeter. The sheathing, patented as Muntz metal in 1846, ultimately became common on late nineteenth-century merchant ships to protect wooden hulls from shipworm damage. Internal iron rider knees, which reinforced the hull and saved cargo space, were scattered along the inner planking. A portion of the ship's iron mast and spars also were found on the site, as were wire rope and anchor chain.

The following year, a second field school continued to map the remains of *Catharine*. Representative samples of wood, iron, and bronze fasteners were recovered, photographed, and sketched. Larger examples of ship's hardware, such as the compass binnacle, nameplate, porthole, and lantern were taken to UWF's conservation laboratory for cleaning and stabilization. Examples of deck lights (glass prisms inserted into holes in the deck to illuminate the hold) also were cleaned

Catharine during her Norwegian shipping life. *(Courtesy of the Norwegian Maritime Museum)*

and conserved. A small collection of ceramic and glass fragments represents simple utilitarian wares common on board the ship. A small brass teaspoon found on the site may reflect the presence of a captain's wife and children on board, which was not uncommon on merchant ships.

Shipwrecks and their contents offer more than a diving adventure and the collection of trophies. When they are allowed to tell their own particular story, they offer unique clues to the cultural systems of yesterday. In this case, Jason Burns, a UWF graduate who participated in the field schools, discovered that *Catharine* has many stories to tell: the rise of Canadian shipbuilding, the global trade network of Victorian England, the Norwegian reliance on sailing ships in the age of steam, and the intimate Norwegian connection with Pensacola's timber industry. Burns published these stories in a synthesis of archaeology and history titled *The Life and Times of a Merchant Sailor: Archaeology and History of the Norwegian Ship* Catharine.

As if strategically situated to trap ships, the Florida Straits are a notorious shipping passage. Bordered by hidden coral reefs, subject to erratic and often violent weather conditions, and swept by the flow of the Gulf Stream, the Straits were, and still are, a major avenue to be treated with respect by mariners. In the narrow waterway between the Florida Keys and the shallow Bahama banks lies the Florida Reef, one of the most dangerous snares for shipping along North America's Atlantic coast. Five to seven miles offshore, shoals covered with living corals run parallel to the Florida Keys and are impossible to see at night or in bad weather. Over the centuries, hundreds of vessels have run aground on the Florida Reef, and

Archaeology students map *Catharine*'s hull remains. *(Courtesy of the Florida Bureau of Archaeological Research)*

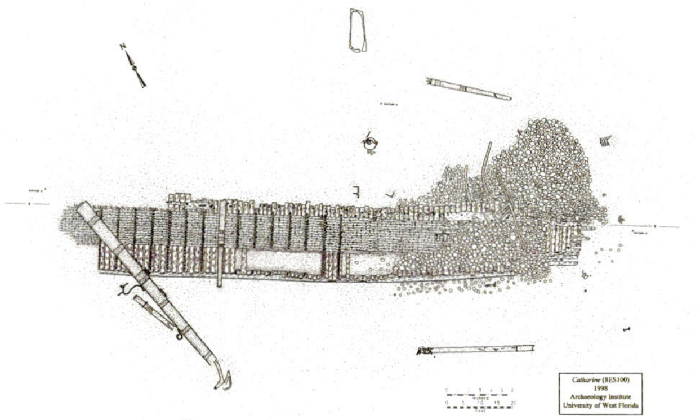

Site plan of exposed wreckage of *Catharine*. *(Courtesy of Jason Burns)*

salvage of these ships' cargos offered a profitable pastime for small groups of determined "wreckers," who waited near dangerous sections of the reef for ships to become stranded. Vessels that could not be refloated or salvaged slowly became entombed in sand and coral. Between the outer reef and the island chain, Hawk Channel provides a waterway the length of the Keys that can be reached via numerous passages through the reef. However, this channel also has shoals and flats that can trap unwary mariners.

Mystery Wreck

Sometime during the seventeenth century, a small Spanish ship was sailing along the remote islands of the Florida Keys when it strayed from the deep water of Hawk Channel and ran hard aground on an isolated coral mound. Because she was damaged and stuck fast by the bow, her crew was unable to get her off the reef, and she was stripped and abandoned. As the ship slowly dete-

Remains of *Catherine*

Catharine's binnacle housed the ship's compass in a bowl with gimbals to keep it upright with respect to the horizon, despite the ship's pitching and rolling. The bowl had a top that could be closed over the compass when not in use and side lanterns to illuminate the compass at night. The binnacle has three ornate legs in the shape of dolphin-like fish with scales. A large bolt passes through each fish head to connect a plate that attaches the binnacle to the deck near the ship's helm.

Catharine's solid brass nameplate.

(Photo courtesy of the University of West Florida Archaeology Institute. Drawing by James W. Hunter III)

Catharine's binnacle, which housed the ship's compass.

(Photo courtesy of the University of West Florida Archaeology Institute)

The ship's solid brass nameplate also was found, and it contains the following inscription:

CARNARVONSHIRE
1871
BARNES FLETCHER & CO.
MAKERS
LIVERPOOL

Normally affixed to the deckhouse, the nameplate reflects the new name given to the ship by her British owners. These artifacts are on exhibit in the UWF Archaeology Institute.

riorated, her ballast stones concreted together into a solid mass. Wooden timbers not covered by sediments were consumed by marine organisms and destroyed by waves and currents. The surrounding reef community eventually engulfed the wreck, and marine life colonized the ballast, helping to protect the ship's remains over the centuries.

During the summer of 2004, the Underwater Archaeology Team of the Florida Bureau of Archaeological Research was recording 13 of the shipwrecks of the 1733 Spanish Plate Fleet in the Florida Keys (see Chapters 4 and 6). During this fieldwork, local informant Dave McCampbell offered to show us additional sites that needed recording. One of these was simply called the "Mystery Wreck," located on top of a coral pinnacle that rises from the 30-foot-deep sandy floor of Hawk Channel to within eight feet of the water's surface, about two miles seaward of Vaca Key. We decided to partner with staff of the Florida Keys National Marine Sanctuary to explore and record the site's archaeological and biological features.

According to the bureau's files, the site had been worked under a state salvage contract granted to amateur salvors in 1972 for a period of one year. It is unclear who first discovered the shipwreck, but it was thought at the time that it might be *San Ignacio* of the 1733 fleet. The con-

Mystery Wreck ballast pile. *(Photo by Jeff Anderson. Courtesy of the Florida Keys National Marine Sanctuary)*

tractors worked for only 20 days, digging around the perimeter of the ballast pile, hoping to find valuable materials. On the last day, a 13-foot-long anchor was raised. Encrusted iron objects, pottery sherds, cannon balls, and lead shot were turned over to the state, and the contract was not renewed in the absence of treasure. The artifacts were typical of the colonial period; comparison of the Spanish olive jar rim sherds with others from closely dated shipwrecks suggested that the Mystery Wreck is a Spanish ship that wrecked in the seventeenth century.

Two weeks of fieldwork in June 2005 allowed our combined team to study, map, and record the shipwreck and its contents. The large concreted ballast mound had been picked at by salvors, who removed loose stones along its outer edges, exposing some of the lower hull structure. This created a surprising and interesting visual experience. The wreck appeared to be resting on its keel, with the lower hull planking removed. As we shone a light into the void between frames, we saw sections of the keel, as well as groupers, lobsters, and a large green moray eel living in the space. Portions of the eroded hull included stern and bow timbers; amidships, exposed by past salvage activities, were sections of the vessel's framing. We had begun to record these elements of the ship's architecture and to take small samples of wood for identification when we realized that most of the tail and bow frames—and all the framing in the starboard edge of the ballast mound—were not made of wood at all. Rather, they were composed of a concrete-like substance. We later learned from archival shipbuilding contracts that a mixture of lime, sand, and gravel sometimes was poured into the hull as permanent ballast, thus protecting the floors and lower frames from damage due to shifting cargo. This was the first time that we had seen an example of this practice on a shipwreck. What we first thought were wooden frames actually was the cement ballast that filled the spaces between the frames, giving us a "negative image" of the original lower hull timbers, which had deteriorated over time.

We discovered a long, pole-shaped log of wood wedged under the forward most bow frame. At first we thought it might be a gunner's wedge or other tool used to try to heave the ship off the

Anchor recovered in 1972 on exhibit at the HistoryMiami Museum. *(Courtesy of the Florida Division of Historical Resources)*

Diagnostic shape of Spanish olive jar rims date the Mystery Wreck to the 1600s.

(Courtesy of the Florida Division of Historical Resources)

reef, but we learned that the five-foot-long log with one chopped end was *lignum vitae* wood and probably part of the ship's cargo. This ironwood, collected from the Caribbean for its dense, hard quality, was used in making sheaves and pulleys, and our specimen had resisted shipworms and erosion on the shipwreck site for centuries.

The identity of the "Mystery Wreck" remains a mystery. Among potential candidates are the following ship losses reported in documents housed at the Archivo General de Indias (AGI) in Seville, Spain:

Year 1630——Two galleons were sent to carry supplies to St. Augustine from Havana, but both were wrecked at the head of the Florida

The ship's lower wooden hull is visible beneath the ballast stones.

(Courtesy of the Florida Division of Historical Resources)

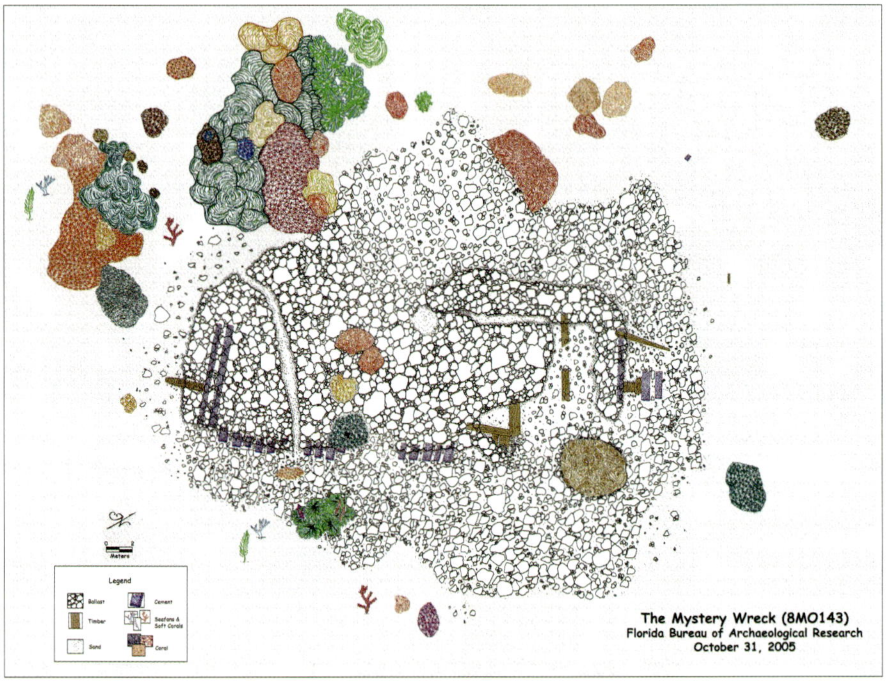

Mystery Wreck site plan.

(Drawing by Roger Smith, Della Scott-Ireton, Jennifer McKinnon, and Jason Raupp)

Keys. All the men on both wrecks were saved, and the 56 bronze and iron cannons on the two wrecks also were recovered and taken to Havana, where they were distributed for use in the various forts of that port. [AGI, *Indiferente General*, legajo 1154]

Year 1665——The Spanish merchant ship *Santa Ana María* was wrecked on Key Largo on February 15, and there is no mention of what she carried or whether she was salvaged. [AGI, *Santo Domingo*, legajo 150]

Year 1688——Brief mention exists of an unidentified merchant *nao* that was lost in the Florida Keys this year. [AGI, *Santo Domingo*, legajo 168]

The "Mystery Wreck" has become part of a new Heritage Awareness Diving Seminar, conducted annually by the bureau in conjunction with the marine sanctuary and the Florida Public Archaeology Network. The seminar offers national dive training organizations a curriculum of lessons about underwater historic preservation for dive instructors to deliver to their students (see Chapter 6).

Life at sea is rough on ships, which need above all to float, endure constant strain and stress even under normal sailing conditions, withstand unusual or extreme weather conditions, and continue earning their keep. Many oceangoing vessels paid for themselves several times over, carrying lucrative cargos over long distances without mishap. Many were overdue for maintenance and overhaul, which were postponed as long as profitable passages were possible. Nautical archaeologists have a scenario called "one more voyage," which accounts for ships that did not make port due to equipment failure, disability, or advanced age.

Queen of Nassau

A favorite fishing spot for local charter boats in the Florida Keys off Islamorada was known by word of mouth as the "220 Wreck" because it rests at that depth of water. Unmarked on nautical charts, the shipwreck was investigated briefly by local divers in the 1990s, who found it to be of modern vintage and not a Spanish galleon. Relocated by technical divers in 2001, the large, intact wreck sitting upright on the sandy bottom was unusual for its long thin hull and pronounced ram bow. Because it is located in the Florida Keys National Marine Sanctuary, the divers reported the site to sanctuary officials, who made plans to survey and record the wreck.

National Oceanic and Atmospheric Agency (NOAA) archaeologist Tane Casserley was asked to lead the investigation with scientific divers from East Carolina University, the National Undersea Research Center of the University of North Carolina, the Association of Underwater Explorers, and NOAA's Maritime Archaeology Center. For several days in October 2001, the team measured and recorded the intact ship's hull with digital video and still photography. The vessel's narrow dimensions (10:1 length-to-beam ratio), jutting ram bow below the waterline, and riveted rather than welded construction suggested an early steel warship. Abundant, well-preserved artifacts were noted throughout the site, although divers did not penetrate the hull because of the fine sediments that could reduce visibility to an unsafe level. However, they recovered a broken ceramic plate and a small ceramic pitcher with maker's marks that dated them to around 1923. Based on the survey results, Casserley concluded that, due to the undamaged hull and intact artifact assemblage, the vessel was historically significant, but

A NOAA diver documenting the ram bow of the "220 Wreck."

(Photo by Doug Kesling/NOAA)

further research would be necessary to identify it and determine what it was doing when it sank.

With these few clues—including the fact that the diagnostic ceramics had come from Ohio potters—Casserley began combing through reference books such as *Jane's Fighting Ships* and sources on U.S. Revenue Cutters. However, no single vessel matched the hull features of the sunken ship. Beginning with the American Civil War, the diagnostic ram bow had been added to steam warships for ramming into enemy vessels, but it also was found to create a hollow in its wake, thus providing much less resistance through the water, especially at higher speeds. These bulbous ram bows ultimately evolved into the forms that are used today on both naval and commercial ships.

Casserley found that the shape of the shipwreck's ram bow most closely resembled the bow

A NOAA diver swimming past the bridge wing on the *Queen of Nassau*. (Photo Tane Casserley/NOAA)

of HMS *Triumph*, a Royal Navy cruiser built in 1903. Focusing on warships built under the British Admiralty's oversight, he discovered that one vessel in particular, Her Majesty's Canadian Ship (HMCS) *Canada*, had very similar dimensions, but the historic photographs of this ship did not match the wreck's profile. Further research in Canadian archives revealed that *Canada*'s profile had been changed in 1912 with the addition of a forecastle. Along with a photograph of the ship, documents reported that it was sold for commercial purposes in 1924, but was lost near Miami in 1926. This lead failed to turn up a ship named *Canada* listed in *Lloyd's Register* as being lost off Florida between 1924 and 1930.

Casserley then researched every vessel listed in the *Register* that had sunk off the east coast of Florida from 1925 onward. Using this tactic, he discovered that a steamer named *Queen of Nassau* (ex-*Canada*) was listed as sinking 50 miles south of Miami on July 2, 1926. A search in the photographic collections of the Mariners' Museum in Newport News, Virginia, produced a photograph of *Queen of Nassau* from 1925 that was nearly identical to the image of HMCS *Canada* in 1918, except that the hull was painted white. Casserley had found a potential match.

CGS (Canadian Government Ship) *Canada* was built in an English shipyard for the Canadian government in 1904. On delivery, she became the flagship of the Canadian Fisheries Protection Services and was Canada's first armed, steel-hulled cruiser. She played a key role in the establishment of the Royal Canadian Navy in 1910 and was

HMCS *Canada* in 1918. *(Courtesy of Canadian Department of National Defence)*

The first-class passenger steamer *Queen of Nassau* at anchor in 1925.
(Courtesy of the Mariners' Museum)

commissioned as HMCS *Canada* in 1915 during World War I. After five years of service, she resumed her duty as a fisheries patrol vessel but was decommissioned in 1919 and put on the auction block. In 1924, she was purchased by Barron Gift Collier, a wealthy Florida advertising entrepreneur and landowner, who renamed the ship *Queen of Nassau* and converted her into a first-class passenger steamer to run between Nassau and Miami.

After less than six weeks of service, *Queen of Nassau* could not compete with two other larger passenger steamers along the same route and was replaced by another ship, *Collier County*, also owned by Baron Collier. *Queen of Nassau* remained anchored at Miami in Biscayne Bay for 18 months, until it was reported that she was being sold to Mexican interests to run between Tampico and New Orleans. Plans were made to send the vessel to Tampa where she could be dry-docked for final inspection before sale. *Queen of Nassau* departed Miami on July 1, 1926, but the next day she began to take on water in the ship's lower compartments. After the crew tried desperately for an hour and a half to pump out the increasing influx of water, the captain ordered everyone to abandon ship. Watching from the safety of the lifeboat, he reported that the vessel's bow rose up, the boilers exploded, and the hull crumpled like an eggshell. Eight minutes after the crew abandoned ship, *Queen of Nassau* disappeared into the sea.

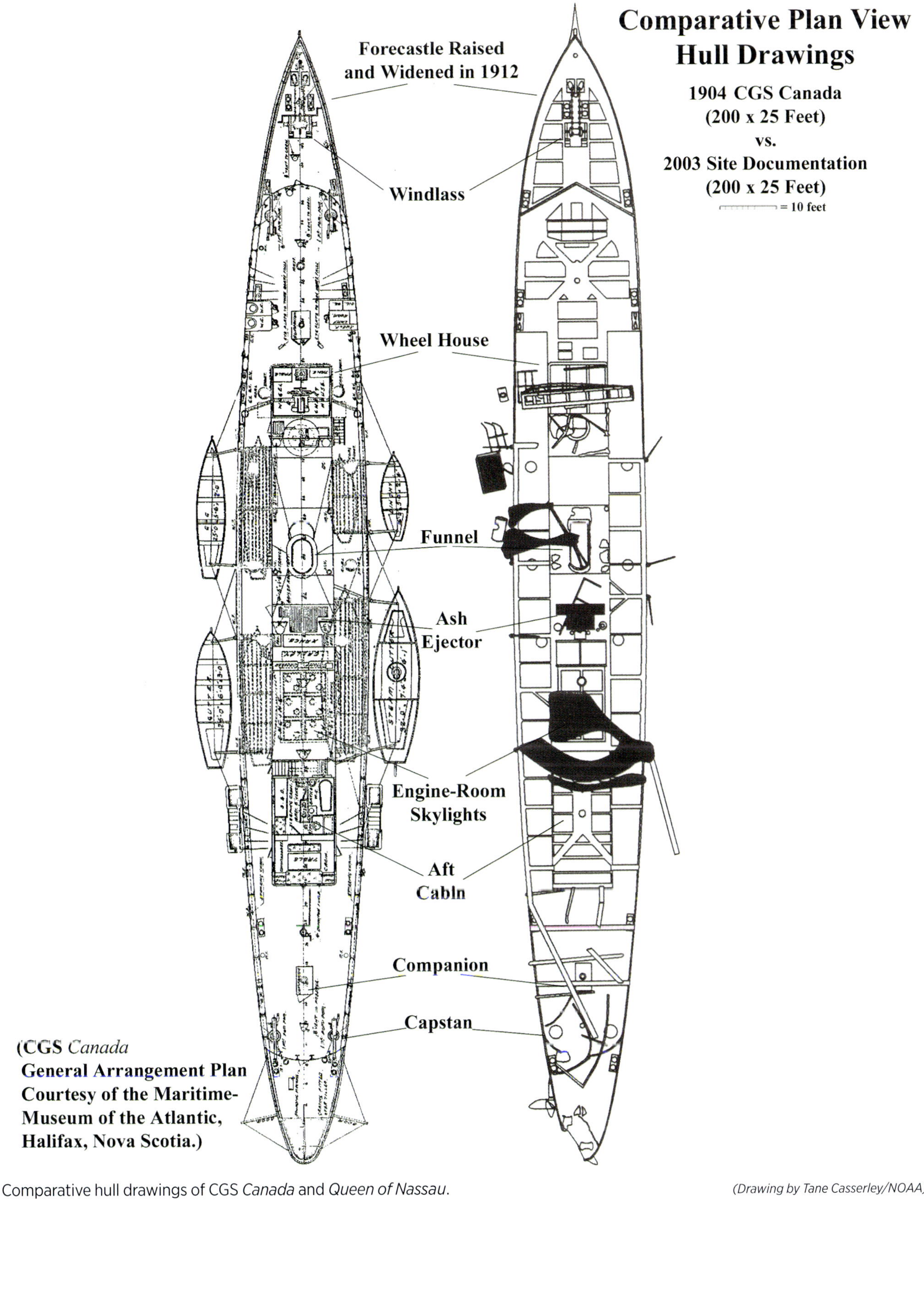

Comparative hull drawings of CGS *Canada* and *Queen of Nassau*. *(Drawing by Tane Casserley/NOAA)*

A second NOAA survey was organized in 2002 to continue documenting the shipwreck with a detailed site plan and additional video and photo recording of the hull and diagnostic features. The team found that the hull was structurally sound and covered in several areas by fishing nets. While historical data on *Canada*'s construction matched the features and dimensions of the wreck, and modifications noted to the hull were consistent with a warship's conversion to a passenger steamer, the team found no evidence of separation of hull plates or any break in the hull, except in the stern where the vessel impacted the bottom as it sank. Several structural features, such as the ship's funnel and ventilator cowlings, were missing. Since underwater visibility often was less than 20 feet, the team decided it would be unsafe to send divers beyond visual range in 230 feet of water to search for debris around the wreck site. Consequently, side scan sonar was used to create an acoustical image of the wreck and its surroundings, but it detected no significant debris within a large radius around the upright, intact sunken vessel.

A third survey was conducted in 2003 to recover more data that might confirm the shipwreck's identity and the cause of its sinking. Examination of the boiler room, which was filled with fine sediment, was accomplished by lowering a video camera into the compartment and rotating it 360 degrees at varying heights. No evidence of a catastrophic explosion, as described by the captain, was found. A plan-view overhead video mosaic of the entire wreck produced more evidence that it was indeed *Canada/Queen of Nassau*. Despite the accumulation of detailed data about the wreck's features, the surveys could not determine whether the ship sank due to the failure of hull plates or some other event. A much more probable reason for her sinking was a missing starboard propeller shaft, which apparently slid out of the stern at some point allowing a large amount of water to enter the hull in a short time.

Today, *Queen of Nassau* has a new life as a federally protected cultural resource open to qualified diving visitors and as a historical site reflecting the role of North American fisheries, the origins of the Royal Canadian Navy, and the eager commercial development of Florida tourism in the early twentieth century.

* * *

In addition to natural hazards, Florida had occasional man-made traps that caused marine casualties. For example, the Civil War left a number of sunken vessels from both sides of the conflict in southern rivers and harbors. Explosive mines placed in the water to damage or destroy enemy ships became both an offensive and defensive device used extensively by the Confederates against the federal navy. In December 1862, the ironclad USS *Cairo* was destroyed by a mine (then commonly called a "torpedo") in the Yazoo River in Mississippi. The submarine *H.L. Hunley* used a "spar torpedo" (a mine attached to a long pole) to sink USS *Housatonic* in Charleston harbor in February 1864. In August of the same year, Admiral David Farragut led a naval attack into Mobile Bay, Alabama. When the Union monitor *Tecumseh* suddenly struck a mine, he ordered "Damn the torpedoes, full speed ahead!" *Harvest Moon*, flagship of Rear Admiral John Dahlgren assigned to the Union blockading squadron, struck a mine and sank in Winyah Bay, South Carolina, in March 1865. These "torpedoes" typically consisted of a wooden keg or container packed with fine-grain gunpowder, into which a contact fuse and detonator were fixed. They were moored just below the surface of the water so that they were difficult to detect. Contact with a ship's hull ignited the black powder, creating an underwater explosion.

Maple Leaf

On the night of March 30, 1864, Captain E. P. Bryan, a Confederate operator from Charleston, and five soldiers installed a dozen contact mines in the St. Johns River off Mandarin Point, 12 miles south of Jacksonville, Florida. The St. Johns River system was an important waterway to the Florida interior. The steamboat *Maple Leaf*, loaded with Union troops and their baggage, had arrived from South Carolina at Jacksonville earlier that same day but was ordered upriver to Palatka. On the return trip, the steamer was traveling at night to avoid Confederate artillery along the river banks. At four o'clock on the morning of April 1, 1864, *Maple Leaf* struck a mine in the narrow pass at Mandarin Point and quickly sank to the muddy bottom of the river, leaving only the upper deck above water. The mine had exploded near the keel, about 30 feet from the bow of the ship, killing four crew members sleeping on the foredeck. The remaining 58 passengers and crew escaped into lifeboats and were saved.

The steamer was carrying the equipment and personal belongings of officers and men from a federal army brigade headquarters and three infantry regiments, as well as inventories of sutlers (civilian merchants who sold provisions to the army). The 181-foot sidewheel steamer and its contents were declared a total loss. In 1882, the U.S. Army Corps of Engineers contracted for the wreck to be removed to a depth of 18 feet because it was a hazard to navigation. Although its location continued to appear on charts of the river, the sunken steamer slowly became covered with mud and sediments.

In 1984, a group of Jacksonville residents interested in maritime history located a wreck in the St. Johns River that they believed to be *Maple Leaf*. Led by scuba-diving dentist Keith Holland, they compared modern satellite imagery with historical charts to define a small search area off Mandarin Point. Towing a large metal detector through the water, they located the steamer's buried wreckage on the fourth day of searching. Divers probing the bottom encountered a wooden structure approximately 50 feet long and 25 feet wide under five feet of mud. They formed St. Johns Archaeological Expeditions Inc. (SJAEI) and received an exploration contract from the Florida Division of Historical Resources to conduct remote sensing and diver verification of targets. Questions of legal ownership and jurisdiction were resolved in 1986 with a court settlement that assigned ownership to the U.S. Army and exclusive salvage rights to SJAEI. By 1988, with all state and federal permitting requirements completed, exploratory excavations were conducted to confirm its identity. Meanwhile, SJAEI had contacted several professional archaeologists, historians, and conservators for advice and guidance.

Underwater visibility at the site was extremely poor, and any disturbance of the sediments reduced it to zero. Divers received surface-supplied air and had the benefit of hard-wired communications with each other and the dive boat. Hoping to find artifacts that could identify *Maple Leaf*, they searched by feel in the stern area and cut a hole in the deck to access the cargo hold. Under the mud, they could feel boxes, barrels, and trunks. A few boxes were bought to the surface and carefully opened. Identification markings on the outside of boxes packed with personal belongings and camp equipment

Maple Leaf steaming at night along the St. Johns River.
(Painting by William Trotter)

corresponded with regiments whose baggage *Maple Leaf* was known to be carrying, which confirmed the wreck's identity. The recovered materials had been remarkably well preserved in the cool, oxygen-free mud at the bottom of the river.

In 1990, the Florida Division of Historical Resources provided funding through the Jacksonville Museum of Science and History to conduct further research and produce educational materials. The following year a second grant was awarded to the Jacksonville Historical Society. Funding also was provided by the Department of Defense. These funds helped SJAEI to establish a conservation laboratory to document, study, and preserve *Maple Leaf* artifacts. Commercial diver Lee Manley became the project director and supervisor of the laboratory. In addition, a three-year cooperative agreement was initiated between SJAEI and East Carolina University's Program in Maritime History and Nautical Archaeology. The university assigned Frank Cantelas to oversee three summer field schools dedicated to documenting the shipwreck.

Exploration of the sunken steamer continued by feel, and a preliminary site plan of its features and extent was created. A silt barrier was erected around portions of the hull to divert currents and sediments, affording divers some visibility using underwater lights. As recoveries from each part of the wreck were meticulously recorded, an understanding of the scope and magnitude of the ship's contents began to emerge. Soldiers had packed their possessions in wooden boxes, barrels, and trunks marked with their names; some boxes contained the possessions of several soldiers. Baggage of each army unit appeared to have been stowed together, with camp equipment placed on top or between stacks of trunks and boxes to serve as dunnage or packing material. The camp equipment included tent and shelter assemblies, stoves, lanterns, tools, and field desks. The military mess equipment included pans and pails, cutlery, plates, tin cups, and coffee pots. Medical supplies and surgical equipment also were packed aboard the steamer.

As wooden boxes containing soldiers' personal belongings were recovered from *Maple Leaf*'s cargo holds, excavators found that many had their owner's name and regiment painted on the lid. Inside were the types of things that any soldier might pack to take to war. Necessities included spare shoes and socks, buttons and buckles, sewing kits, candles and candlesticks, pens and pencils, ink and inkwells, and smoking pipes and tobacco. Personal hygiene items included toothbrushes, hair brushes, combs, razors, shaving paste, mirrors, and shoe polish. Small personal treasures and comforts of home included early photographs (daguerreotypes, ambrotypes, and tintypes) of family members, brass rings and other jewelry, musical instruments (flutes, fifes, a violin, a clarinet), and gaming pieces (dominoes and checkers). The excavators were surprised to find fine china, fancy door knobs, ornate cutlery, and even window panes, apparently looted from plantation homes

Civil War artifacts recovered from *Maple Leaf*. From top left clockwise: China plate, aromatic stomach bitters bottle, infantry and calvary buttons, wooden military fife (small flute), ink bottle, minié ball (muzzle-loading shot), sword belt plate, talon-design pipe bowl, army belt buckle, sword guard with grip.
(Courtesy of the Florida Division of Historical Resources)

during the army's forays into South Carolina. Sea shells also had been collected by the soldiers from the Carolina beaches. Each container represented an intimate time capsule lost for almost 130 years.

A world-class archaeological site, *Maple Leaf* contains the largest known collection of Civil War material culture, entombed and perfectly preserved in the riverbed. The ship was carrying an estimated 400 tons of military equipment and the personal possessions of more than a thousand soldiers. By 1992, more than 3,000 individual artifacts had been recovered from the ship's hold, only a fraction of its contents. After conservation treatment, a well-preserved collection of items was put on exhibit at the Jacksonville Museum of Science and History, and a traveling exhibit was developed by the Museum of Florida History in Tallahassee. In 1993, SJAEI published a book on the excavation, *The* Maple Leaf: *An Extraordinary American Civil War Shipwreck*, and several videos have been produced about the sunken ship and its contents. *Maple Leaf* was designated as a National Historic Landmark in 1994, and the following year artifacts recovered by SJAEI were donated to the State of Florida. A portion of that collection designated to the federal government was transferred in 2015 to the National Museum of the U.S. Army at Fort Belvoir, Virginia. Additional artifacts are on display at the Mandarin Museum, located on the river bank near where the steamer sank.

Maple Leaf is an outstanding example of a government-supported, nationally significant effort that involved a nonprofit organization, a volunteer base, university cooperation, museum exhibits, a video, a book, and other publications, with no sale of artifacts for commercial gain.

Dr. Roger C. Smith served as State Underwater Archaeologist for the Florida Division of Historical Resources for three decades. He is the author of three books: *Vanguard of Empire: Ships of Exploration in the Age of Columbus* (Oxford University Press, 1993), *An Atlas of Maritime Florida* (University Press of Florida, 1997), and *The Maritime Heritage of the Cayman Islands* (University Press of Florida, 2001). He also is editor of *Florida's Lost Galleon: The Emanuel Point Shipwreck* (University Press of Florida, 2018).

For Additional Information

San Felipe

Publications

Bill Belleville, "Diving into History after Fighting Off a Challenge by Treasure Hunters, Indiana University Scientists Are Unlocking Clues to the Past by Studying Two Spanish Ships That Went

Down in the Florida Keys 260 Years Ago," *Sun Sentinel* [Deerfield Beach, Fla.], April 11, 1993, http://articles.sun-sentinel.com/1993-04-11/features/9302050414_1_treasure-salvors-ballast-wrecks

Susie Mills, "El Lerri Sank during the 1733 Hurricane That Hit the Florida Keys," *N the Florida Keys,* http://www.n-the-florida-keys.com/El-Lerri.html

Videos

James White, "Snorkel on El Lerri," June 7, 2014, https://www.youtube.com/watch?v=L2Itns8fzlo

Commodore

Publications

Robin Benedick, "Diver Hopes Theory on Ship Holds Water," *Orlando Sentinel*, November 29, 1986, http://articles.orlandosentinel.com/1986-11-29/news/0270400237_1_serbousek-stephen-crane-ponce-inlet

Stephen Crane, "Stephen Crane's Own Story: He Tells How the Commodore Was Wrecked and How He Escaped," reprint courtesy Town of Ponce Inlet, Florida, http://ponceinlet.org/images/content/openboatnewspaper.pdf

Kimberly Eslinger, "'. . . And All the Men Knew the Colors of the Sea . . .': Historical and Archaeological Investigation of the SS *Commodore*'s Remains, Ponce Inlet, Florida," PhD diss., East Carolina University, http://thescholarship.ecu.edu/bitstream/handle/10342/1113/Commodore%20FinalThesis%20_KimberlyEslinger_01.pdf

Lighthouse Archaeological Maritime Program, "The Shipwreck, Discovery, and Investigation of the SS *Commodore*," http://www.staugustinelighthouse.org/LAMP/Research/SS_Commodore

Marine Science Center, "Diving Volusia County's Artificial Reefs," http://marinesciencecenter.com/DivingArtificialReefs.pdf. Presentation on the county's artificially created reefs, which includes the earliest: SS *Commodore.*

Ponce de Leon Lighthouse and Museum, "Stephen Crane, 1871—1900, http://ponceinlet.org/stephen-crane

Videos

Nautilus Productions, "SS *Commodore* Shipwreck Project," January 27, 2015, http://nautilusproductions.com/archaeology. Dive footage of mapping the underwater archaeology site.

Industry

Publications

Marianne Franklin, "Site 8SJ3478, Possibly the *Industry*: A British 18th-Century Shipwreck," Conservation Research Laboratory Report 10, Texas A&M University, 2000, http://nautarch.tamu.edu/CRL/Report10/introduction.html

Museum of Underwater Archaeology, "*Industry* Methodology," http://mua.apps.uri.edu/IndustryMeth/IndustryMethIndex.shtml

St. Augustine Lighthouse Archaeological Maritime Program, "British Sloop *Industry*," http://www.staugustinelighthouse.org/LAMP/Research/british_ship

Catharine

Publications

Jason M. Burns, "The Life and Times of a Merchant Sailor: History and Archaeology of the Norwegian Ship *Catharine*," PhD diss., University of West Florida, 1996, https://secure.uwf.edu/cassh/departments/anthropology-and-archaeology/research/graduate-theses/burns/

Jason M. Burns, *The Life and Times of a Merchant Sailor: The Archaeology and History of the Norwegian Ship* Catharine (New York: Kluwer Academic/Plenum, 2003), http://link.springer.com/book/10.1007/978-1-4615-0209-8

Mystery Wreck

Publications

Jennifer F. Mckinnon and Della A. Scott-Ireton, "Florida's Mystery Wreck," *International Journal of Nautical Archaeology* 35, no. 2 (2006):

187–194, https://www.researchgate.net/publication/229738182_Florida's_Mystery_Wreck

National Oceanic and Atmospheric Administration, "Mystery Wreck! Archaeologists Hunt for Clues into Identity of a Centuries Old Florida Keys Shipwreck," *National Marine Sanctuaries News & Events*, updated July 31, 2017, http://sanctuaries.noaa.gov/news/features/mystery.html

Roger C. Smith, Della Scott-Ireton, Jennifer McKinnon, et al., "Archaeological and Biological Examination of 'The Mystery Wreck' (8MO143) off Vaca Key, Monroe County, Florida," Florida Bureau of Archaeological Research, Florida Keys National Marine Sanctuary Report, January 2006, http://dos.myflorida.com/media/30887/mystery_wreck_final_report.pdf

Queen of Nassau

Publications

Michael C. Barnette, "The *Queen of Nassau*: How One of Canada's First Warships Ended Up off the Florida Keys," reprinted from *Divers,* November–December 2002, Association of Underwater Explorers, http://web.archive.org/web/20040907231541/http://uwex.us/qonarticle.html

Randy Boswell, "Canada's First Warship to be Preserved—near Florida Keys," Canwest News Service, May 2, 2010, http://bodwell.edu/r_smith/Images/CGS%20Canada%20Randy%20Boswell.pdf

Tane R. Casserley, "CGS *Canada:* A Canadian Warship in the Florida Keys," M.A. thesis, East Carolina University, 2005, http://www.ecu.edu/cs-cas/maritime/Maritime-Studies-Program-Grads-Tane-Renata-Casserley.cfm

"HMCS *Canada*," Wikipedia, revised September 24, 2017, https://en.wikipedia.org/wiki/HMCS_Canada

Websites

National Oceanic and Atmospheric Administration, "Maritime Heritage: *Queen of Nassau*," National Marine Sanctuaries, revised July 31, 2017, http://sanctuaries.noaa.gov/maritime/expeditions/qon.html

Maple Leaf

Publications

Thomas M. Flemming, "The Maple Leaf Adventure: A Florida Civil War Shipwreck Reveals Civilian and Soldier Life in the Mid-19th Century," *Military History Online,* February 25, 2007, http://www.militaryhistoryonline.com/civilwar/articles/mapleleaf.aspx

Websites

Keith Holland, *Maple Leaf* Shipwreck: An Extraordinary American Civil War Shipwreck, http://www.mapleleafshipwreck.com/index.htm

Maple Leaf: Time Capsule of the Civil War, National Museum of the United States Army, http://thenmusa.org/maple-leaf.php

Videos

Florida Humanities Council, "The *Maple Leaf:* A Civil War Shipwreck," https://www.youtube.com/watch?v=bbQw6eJg59o

GENESIS

CHAPTER 6

The Old Spaniards: Florida's Earliest European Shipwrecks

Roger C. Smith and Gregory D. Cook

The First Emanuel Point Ship (Roger C. Smith)

The oldest shipwrecks to be discovered in Florida are located in the shallow waters of Pensacola Bay, one of the state's most sheltered natural harbors. The well-preserved remains of three Spanish ships were part of the ill-fated fleet of Tristán de Luna, who commanded the first royal attempt to colonize Florida for the Crown. Investigation of these shipwrecks has opened a long-forgotten chapter in early Spanish American history and has galvanized the world of public archaeology in Florida.

We began our underwater survey of Pensacola Bay in 1990, based on references to shipwrecks in historical documents and the reports of fishermen and divers who had encountered wreckage on the bottom of the bay. During the first year, we located and recorded 45 sites of wrecked vessels from several periods of Florida history. We used a magnetometer to find magnetic anomalies caused by the presence of iron and sonar to detect solid objects that protruded from the bottom sediments. While these instruments helped us to discover submerged historic sites, they also led us to anchorage trash piles, modern construction debris, and "midnight reefs," consisting of old cars, boats, and appliances deposited by fishermen to attract fish. Our team included Jim Spirek, Della Scott, Chuck Hughson, Amy Mitchell,

A small mound of ballast stones conceals the remains of one of Florida's earliest shipwrecks.

(Courtesy of the Florida Division of Historical Resources)

and Jeff Lockwood; we quickly learned to work well together at our headquarters in the historic district, on our survey boat, and under the murky waters of the bay.

Late in 1992, we discovered a small mound of oyster-encrusted ballast stones on a shallow sandbar off a small bluff called Emanuel Point, near the mouth of a fresh water bayou. Below the stones, we began to find fragments of leather shoes, butchered animal bones, and bits of rope and packing material among the articulated timbers of an old sailing ship. When sherds of colonial Spanish olive jars turned up, we realized the antiquity of the site, which we began to call "the old Spaniard."

The Old Spaniard

It was my turn to dive after lunch. We had opened a test pit in the central part of the ballast mound, which exposed the ship's mainmast step and two pump wells, one on each side of the keel. The mast and the pump shafts no longer were part of the assembly, but the remains of a wooden box that had protected the pump wells from stones and bilge trash were recognizable in the sediments. After suiting up and checking my air supply, I jumped from the barge into the water. This immersion ritual, the abrupt transition from air to liquid, is the way in which underwater archaeologists commute to their workplace. However, in this case it took just a few seconds because the site is only 12 feet deep. Although the sun was bright, as I approached my work station, visibility decreased in the tea-colored water. Armed with a trowel and paintbrush, I began to gently explore the layers of silt covering the ship's lower hull. As I fanned the area with my hand, it attracted small resident fish hoping that I would uncover something tasty for them to eat. Archaeologists who work underwater learn to tolerate the companionship of marine life, except when excavation accelerates the food chain and our new friends impatiently nip our fingers to encourage us to work faster. As I swept away the silt, small carpenter's scraps with adze scars littered the area around the pump wells.

Suddenly, there appeared a wooden scrap that looked quite different from the others. I picked it up and, looking closely in the dim light, could see that it been carved in the shape of a ship silhouette. The small, thin piece of waterlogged wood had been fashioned with classic features of a sixteenth-century galleon—the heavy overhanging beak at the bow, high forecastle and sterncastle, and the balconied gallery at the stern. Whoever had worked this simple sliver of wood had faithfully captured the characteristics of a ship just like the one we were investigating. Initially, I thought this carving might be a child's toy that became lost in the bilge, but then I realized that it probably had been left behind by the carpenters who constructed the pump well box. As I held the unique, orphaned artifact in my hand, I thought about how many miles and years it had traveled between the ship's launching and my afternoon shift at the bottom of Pensacola Bay.

The magnetic anomaly that had led us to this shipwreck was found to be an iron anchor, embedded in the bottom at one end of the ballast pile. Its size and shape were quite similar to anchors found on the Spanish ships that wrecked on Padre Island, Texas, in 1554. Comparison of the olive jar sherds we were finding with those from other dateable sites suggested that the ship off Emanuel Point sank during the sixteenth century. A test trench running perpendicular to the mast step revealed that one side of the ship had broken away after pounding violently on the sandbar, as though during a powerful storm. We began to wonder whether this shipwreck might be associated with the expedition of Tristán de Luna y Arellano and his attempt to colonize Florida.

Found among carpenters' scraps near the ship's pump, a small carving features the classic shape of a sixteenth-century galleon. *(Courtesy of the Florida Division of Historical Resources)*

The Luna Expedition

They came by sea. After a two-month voyage across the Gulf of Mexico, the first modern boat people to reach Florida entered the Bay of Ochuse (modern Pensacola Bay) and thanked God for a safe passage that had brought them to their new home. The date was August 15, 1559. Among the more than 1,500 people who prepared to come ashore, no one imagined that their ambitious settlement scheme would end in calamity, confusion, starvation, and mutiny.

By the middle of the sixteenth century, Spanish navigators had become familiar with the coasts of Florida. The two explorations of Ponce de León and other mariners, and the gold-hunting expeditions of Pánfilo de Narváez and Hernando de Soto, revealed a northern frontier of Spanish America that remained outside the control of the Crown. This territory, known as *La Florida*, stretched from modern-day Texas to the North Atlantic seaboard. Aware that other European nations shared an interest in this strategic region, King Philip II ordered the Viceroy of Mexico, Luís de Velasco, to establish a fortified settlement on the Gulf and the Atlantic coast.

Painting by Herbert Rudeen (1888–1985) shows Tristán de Luna's landing in Pensacola Bay.

(Courtesy of the Pensacola Historical Trust)

Tristán de Luna was chosen to lead the project. Luna was an experienced conquistador who first came to the New World in 1530 in company with the soon-to-be conqueror of Mexico, Hernán Cortés. Luna became a captain in the cavalry and served as *maestre de campo* (second in command) for Francisco Vázquez de Coronado on the march to find the Seven Cities of Gold (1540–1542). The viceroy instructed Luna to build regular Spanish towns in *La Florida*, the first of which at Ochuse was to have a fortress, inns, storehouses, jails, and slaughterhouses. Preparations for the colony took months as people and supplies were assembled at the Mexican port of Veracruz. Twelve ships were loaded with food supplies, arms, and tools for construction and agriculture. When the fleet departed for Florida on June 11, 1559, it carried 540 soldiers, 240 horses, and more than 1,000 colonists, including women and children, servants, Aztec mercenaries, and Tlazcalan farmers. Compared to those who embarked before them on the ships of León, Narvaéz, and Soto, Tristán de Luna and his people left with certain knowledge of where they were going and what they were supposed to do.

After a lengthy voyage, the armada finally anchored in Pensacola Bay, and the colonists went ashore to find a suitable place to build a town. Equipment and tools were unloaded, but much of the food supplies were left aboard the ships anchored nearby. Five weeks after they landed, a fierce hurricane struck Ochuse, sinking all but three ships. Many people lost their lives, and the supplies on shore were damaged by heavy rains. Although four relief voyages were sent from Mexico and Cuba, the disaster doomed the new colony. Luna fell ill, and discontent grew among the hungry immigrants. Although Luna was replaced by another governor, the enterprise was beyond salvation, and its survivors eventually trickled back to Mexico.

The Luna expedition became a forgotten chapter in Florida's history, overshadowed by the successful establishment of St. Augustine a few years later by Pedro Menéndez de Avilés. However, discovery of the Emanuel Point Ship rekindled the story of Luna's lost colony and opened a new chapter in shipwreck archaeology.

The First Campaign

As we began to investigate the shipwreck, we were surprised by the preservation of its lower wooden hull and contents, lying in shallow water exposed to waves and currents. Over time, the ballast stones had provided a substratum for generations of oysters, clams, and mussels that lived and died on the remains of the ship. They left countless shells bound in compacted silt and sand that formed a calcium carbonate cap and protected the site for centuries from erosion and dispersal.

To pursue our investigations, we devised a strategy of cooperative partnerships for the development and management of the site toward academic research and public benefit. We decided to invite the University of West Florida (UWF) to become a partner in the project, not only for the shipwreck's obvious research potential for students but also because of UWF's record of public-oriented archaeology in Pensacola. This partnership resulted in both undergraduate and graduate courses, field schools, internships for students from other universities, and several master's theses focused on the shipwreck.

The Historic Pensacola Preservation Board (now called Historic Pensacola Trust), located in the waterfront historic district, also became a partner in the Emanuel Point project. Given its public mission and central role in historic preservation and interpretation, the board sponsored the establishment of a conservation laboratory for waterlogged artifacts in the T. T. Wentworth Jr. State Museum and the construction of a museum exhibit for the shipwreck in the Earl J. Bowden Building. John Bratten joined the team to assemble the laboratory and exhibit; his scholarly research helped to identify and conserve each of the recovered artifacts and field specimens. Soon both the laboratory and exhibit became popular destinations for hundreds of visitors and school children.

Our first campaign of excavations focused on the stern area of the shipwreck, where we found stone cannonballs and smaller lead and iron ammunition, indicating that the ship probably had carried batteries of heavy and light artillery for defense at sea and fortification of the new colony. The ship's rudder had become detached; we found it nearby, surrounded by remnants of lead sheathing torn from the hull. Ships built in the sixteenth century rarely lasted more than a dozen years, especially if they frequented tropical waters where shipworms infested and ate their wooden hulls. To keep the marine mollusks at bay, planking below the waterline often was covered with lead strips. Repairs to the hull and lead patching reflected years of service delivering goods and products to the Spanish colonies; our ship must have been a veteran of the transatlantic trade.

During one voyage she apparently carried a cargo of mercury, some of which escaped into the bilge. We collected more than seven pounds of the liquid, which was exported to Mexico under royal monopoly from 1556 onward for the amalgamation of silver from ore. On another voyage, the ship carried New World products back to Spain, possibly cowhides from the growing number of cattle farms. Evidently the shipment was accompanied by hungry hide beetles that fed on the stored leather goods because we found their wing covers deep in the bilge. Sherds of distinctive mid-sixteenth-century Aztec pottery from central Mexico provided more clues to confirm the shipwreck's association with the fleet of Tristán de Luna.

Discovery of an iron breastplate near the rudder and copper crossbow bolt heads suggests that the settlers were prepared for close combat. Unwelcome stowaways also came to *La Florida* aboard the ship. Cockroach eggs, perhaps borne in hampers of sea biscuits, would have hatched in the darkness of the bread locker below deck. The

Distinctively molded sherds of red-burnished, hand-painted Aztec pottery helped to support the shipwreck's connection to Mexico.
(Courtesy of the Florida Division of Historical Resources)

insects multiplied in the dim and humid recesses of the hold, probably taking over the galley at night after the cookstove was extinguished. We found their egg cases and body parts among other organic deposits in the bilge. Competing with the cockroaches for sustenance at sea were larger stowaways; black wharf rats colonized the vessel's lower deck and gnawed on foodstuffs in the ship's stores. Aside from being a nuisance, the rats also carried disease, and they were hunted down periodically by the crew for this reason. Rat bones that we collected show evidence of rickets, poor dental health, and cannibalism. Remains of the common house mice (or, in this case, "sea mice") also were found in the bilge; they had developed their own

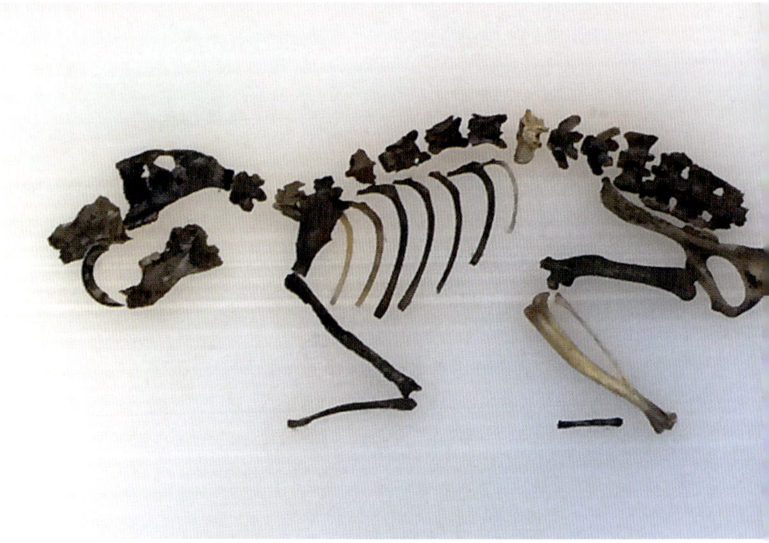

The remains of 21 black rats found in the bilge of the ship probably represented only a few of the stowaways on board.
(Courtesy of the Florida Division of Historical Resources)

niche in the floating ecosystem despite the more numerous rat population.

The Second Campaign

The second campaign of excavations focused on the bow area of the shipwreck, where we hoped to find the ship's galley and to complete our measurements of the ship's lower hull. In addition to John Bratten, our team members included Joe "Coz" Cozzi, Keith Plaskett, and David Pugh. The small volume of ballast in relation to the original size of the ship suggested to us that the vessel was heavily laden on her last voyage. However, the lack of primary cargo items on the site, such as expedition stores, tools, and artillery, indicated that the ship probably was salvaged by survivors soon after the hurricane. Nonetheless, what we recovered has provided tantalizing clues to the material culture of Florida's first Hispanic immigrants.

Evidence of their shipboard diet turned up with the discovery of butchered bones of domestic pigs, cows, and sheep or goats. Traditional Mediterranean foods, including olives, plums or prunes, cherries, and hazelnuts, also are represented. Other fruits such as papaya and sapote and nuts such as coconut, hickory, and acorn reflect foods available in the Caribbean tropics and the Gulf of Mexico. In the ship's forward galley space, we found the utensils that were used to prepare meals at sea: copper cauldrons, a metal pitcher for heating water and wine, a skillet, a saucepan, a copper funnel, and a bronze mortar and pestle. Fibrous matting woven in a crisscrossed fashion also was recovered from the galley, which may have served as packing material for provisions.

We discovered that the starboard bow of the ship, along with the anchor, had collapsed outward, either during the wrecking process or shortly thereafter. Surprisingly, as we raised the anchor from the site we found an intact dinner plate directly under the crown, where the two arms join the shank. Nearby, two gun-port covers that had been hinged to the side of the ship remained well preserved in place. After completing our measurements of the main architectural dimensions of the lower hull, we estimated that the Emanuel Point Ship was more than 100 feet long, with a cargo capacity of more than 400 tons, and apparently was one of the principal ships in Luna's fleet.

Throughout two campaigns of excavation, the project developed a highly public profile in Pensacola, which is a region known for its active participation in and promotion of history and archaeology. The Emanuel Point Ship became a favorite media and print topic; local television coverage of the ongoing investigations in the bay allowed residents to view the wreck site from their living rooms. On one occasion, a live underwater broadcast was made via satellite on national cable television. In response to continuous requests, public lectures by the project's staff to civic groups and schools generated enthusiastic volunteers and sponsors eager to assist with everything, including artifact analysis, exhibit construction, and fund raising.

As a publicly owned resource, the shipwreck and its contents were adopted by a close-knit and caring community cognizant of its role in the management and interpretation of Tristán de Luna's legacy. Situated off Emanuel Point, close to the busy commuter bridge into Pensacola, the site also has demonstrated the remarkable role that public interest, support, and involvement can play in shipwreck research and management. To that end, the shipwreck was listed on the National Register of

A large copper cauldron was discovered in the galley area of the ship, along with several other cooking utensils.

(Courtesy of the Florida Division of Historical Resources)

An artist's rendering shows the Emanuel Point Ship and the excavation of its remains. *(Painting by John LoCastro)*

Historic Places, in recognition of its importance to American history.

The Second and Third Emanuel Point Ships (Gregory D. Cook)

The discovery of the Emanuel Point Ship in the 1990s proved to be a milestone for Florida archaeology in several ways. It brought to light the oldest wreck in Florida (in U.S. waters only the 1554 Padre Island wrecks in Texas were older), provided insights into early Spanish colonization in northern Florida, and also served as a springboard for the development of maritime archaeology as a specialization at the University of West Florida.

The fact that such an amazing site was preserved in murky Pensacola Bay captivated locals and visitors alike, and this soon led to investigations of other submerged sites. Some were wrecks already known to locals; others resulted from searches and surveys conducted by UWF archaeologists and students or through cooperative agreements with other organizations. The university now has a corpus of work that has been conducted on underwater sites, ranging from eighteenth-century British shipwrecks and nineteenth-century Civil War vessels to other wrecked or abandoned craft. These forgotten watercraft reflect the industrial aspects of Pensacola's history, including fishing, lumbering, and brickmaking, spanning the extensive maritime history of the region. Students are even writing their master's theses on submerged aircraft, stemming from Pensacola's role in naval aviation.

Although we have investigated all these examples of Pensacola's past, we never forgot the "Old Spaniard." The notion of searching for additional ships from Luna's doomed 1559 fleet was never far from our minds.

By the summer of 2006, UWF for years had offered a combined summer field methods course for archaeology and anthropology students, both on land and underwater. Students received hands-on experience at known sites, and they also

The research diving platform supports UWF's summer maritime archaeology field schools.

(Drone image by Patrick Reynolds. Courtesy of UWF Division of Anthropology and Archaeology)

learned how to survey for potential new finds. The maritime portion of the course involved training in scientific diving, underwater mapping and assessment of wreck sites, remote sensing surveys with magnetometers and sonar devices, and techniques in investigating the anomalies uncovered by their surveys in what were often challenging, low-visibility conditions. Earlier in 2006, UWF archaeologists had been awarded a grant from the Florida Division of Historical Resources to revisit the waters near the Emanuel Point Ship to survey with a newly purchased magnetometer. With this support, we began conducting intensive surveys during spring 2006; by summer of that year, we had a list of promising targets or anomalies for diver investigation. During the field school's scientific dive training, we instructed students in the tedious but necessary methods of conducting circle searches with reels and tapes, including how to maintain contact with their dive buddies and how to interpret a series of line pulls for underwater communication.

In August, during the last week of field school, the students investigating the seventeenth magnetic anomaly on our target list discovered a few basketball-sized stones on the bay floor, approximately 200 meters from the Emanuel Point Ship. For much of the age of sail, stones like these were used to stabilize and counteract the force of winds on ships' sails and keep vessels upright. Commonly known as *ballast*, these rocks also helped to preserve wreck sites after a ship had sunk. The general lack of natural stone in northwest Florida means any time such rocks are encountered underwater, they may be a tell-tale sign of a shipwreck.

Additional exploration and probing suggested that there was an extensive amount of rock and potentially wood under the sediment. Hand-fanning led to the discovery of lead sheathing that looked very similar to the lead strips found on the hull of the Emanuel Point Ship, which had helped seal and protect its wooden planks. After field school had finished, UWF crews continued investigating the site with induction dredges, which allowed us to carefully remove sediments and expose more stone ballast, ceramic olive jar and majolica sherds, and wooden hull timbers of a ship.

The new site, dubbed Emanuel Point II after the same point of land that reaches out into the bay near both wrecks, has been the focus of multiple field seasons since its discovery. As with excavation of the first Emanuel Point Ship (now called Emanuel Point I or EPI), key areas of the hull have been selected for study, including the port bow, the midships area where the mast step and pump structures are located, and the stern. The exposed structure suggests that EPII, like EPI, is among the larger ships in the fleet. Other similarities between the sites include the depth of water (12 feet) and their orientation (bow pointing roughly north, toward shore). The mainmast step of both ships is incorporated into an expanded keelson timber, with pumps situated aft of the mast step mortise, where the heel of the mast would have been secured into the keelson. Because this feature has been documented on several sixteenth-century Iberian wreck sites, archaeologists consider this a diagnostic component of Iberian ship construction.

A primary research question applied to submerged wrecks is how the ship sank and what degree of preservation exists, all of which is often comprised in the term "site formation processes." Both ships show extensive damage to their bow, where forces from the 1559 hurricane likely pounded the front of the ships as they were forced into shallower water near the shoreline. Both ships

An archaeologist exposes the hull timbers of the newly discovered Emanuel Point II Ship.

(Courtesy of UWF Division of Anthropology and Archaeology)

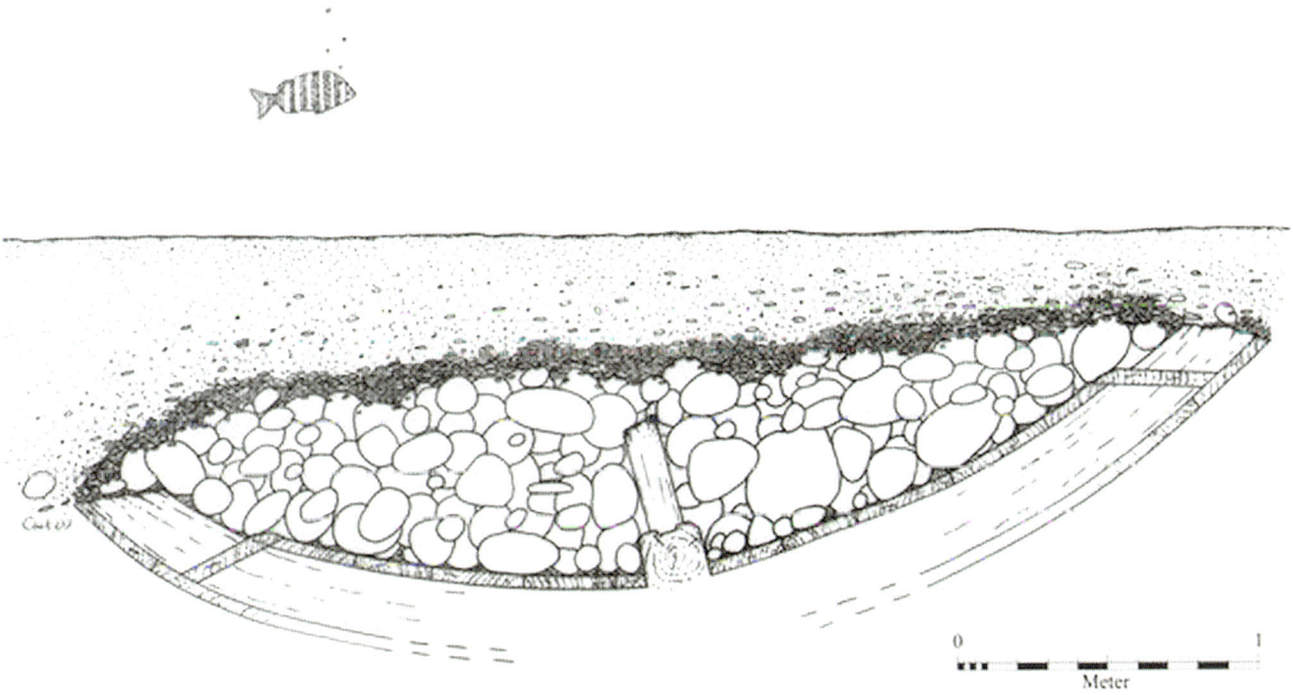

The hull profile of the Emanuel Point II shipwreck shows it listing slightly to the port side.

(Drawing by the author. Courtesy of UWF Division of Anthropology and Archaeology)

are missing their rudder, indicating the damage their stern took as they grounded. The rudder of EPI had been found off the starboard stern, but a concerted search for the rudder of EPII failed to locate this hull feature. Instead, we unexpectedly began to uncover additional frames, outer hull planking, and other features running perpendicular to the main hull section. Initially, we considered the possibility that this wreckage was from a third ship in the fleet—perhaps another vessel had slammed sideways into the stern of EPII as the hurricane raged. However, after considerable effort exposing these features, and finding such clues as deck knees and the wheel of a gun carriage, we now believe that they more likely are part of the upper side of the ship, which broke from the main hull and was wrenched into its current location by currents and wind from the storm.

As we exposed the ship's structure, we excavated methodically through the sediments and ballast that had preserved the shipwreck for more than 450 years. Although the surviving colonists likely had unloaded much of the cargo from both vessels and probably conducted additional salvage after the storm, we found the remains of things that they either did not want or could not recover. These have included a wide variety of ceramics, barrel stave fragments, and other items typically found on wreck sites from this period. Organic preservation on submerged sites typically is better than on land, and the Emanuel Point ships are no exception. Both contained bones from pigs, cows, and other species that served as food sources for the crews during the voyage, as well as rat bones and insect parts from the unwelcome stowaways on transatlantic voyages. The EPII ship's crew also apparently enjoyed the company of a cat, likely to help with the rat problem, as was evidenced by the mandible or jawbone of the animal. Weaponry of the period is indicated by the presence of stone cannonballs, painstakingly chipped out of limestone for the early naval gunnery that would revolutionize warfare at sea. Fragments of crossbow bolts and shafts of the bolts also have been found on both sites.

Occasionally, the students uncovered something truly astounding, and one such item from EPII was an ivory manicure set with rotating arms, which had been used for cleaning fingernails, ears, and teeth. Examples of these have been found on other wreck sites, sometimes made of bone or even gold, but the example from EPII is unique in that it incorporates a whistle painstakingly carved into the base of the tool. This would have been a high-status item, and its owner undoubtedly was dismayed when it became lost in the ballast of the ship.

As part of our research plan, we also continued remote sensing in the search for other vessels from the Luna fleet. In 2015, the terrestrial settlement site that had eluded our colleagues on land for so long finally was located when sixteenth-century Spanish artifacts were found during a residential construction project. The site overlooks the two shipwrecks, making it more likely that the other vessels are in the same area. During UWF's 2016 summer field school, students and staff conducted remote sensing surveys using our magnetometer and side-scan sonar, methodically covering areas of Pensacola Bay. This is done by towing sensors from our boats in narrow survey lanes to ensure adequate coverage. With the location of the land site known, we decided to cover a survey area extending from offshore of the wreck sites, all the way to the shallow waters along the shoreline. On some days, we had three operations going: dives on the EPII wreck site, a survey boat searching for new anomalies, and a target-diving boat for

Stone cannonballs like this one from the Emanuel Point II Ship were labor-intensive to make by hand, but were deadly upon impact, breaking into sharp projectiles. *(Courtesy of the UWF Division of Anthropology and Archaeology)*

~ Manicure Tool ~

Although we know that most of the cargo on the Luna ships was offloaded and that the survivors likely had access to the wrecks after they grounded in shallow water, a wide array of artifacts remained among the stone ballast inside the hulls. One of the most surprising finds was an ivory manicure or toilet set, composed of a handle with three attached implements that would have been used for personal hygiene. A hole at the base of the handle served as a whistle.

Similar hygiene sets have been found on other wreck sites, including the 1545 Tudor warship *Mary Rose* and on vessels from the 1715 Spanish treasure fleet wrecks on the east coast of Florida. Some are single instruments, and others incorporate multiple tools used for personal hygiene.

The manicure set from the Emanuel Point II wreck site after conservation.

(Courtesy of UWF Division of Anthropology and Archaeology)

The manicure set from the Emanuel Point II wreck site before conservation.

(Courtesy of the UWF Division of Anthropology and Archaeology)

Other manicure sets have included a scoop for removing ear wax, which is missing from the EPII example, but it is not uncommon for surviving samples to be broken or for parts of the set to be missing. An ornate manicure set from a 1715 wreck was made of gold, shaped like a dragon and incorporated a whistle; it was sold at auction to a private collector.

A UWF student diver goes to work in the waters of Pensacola Bay during the university's summer field school in maritime archaeology.

(Courtesy of the UWF Division of Anthropology and Archaeology)

diver investigation of anomalies located in previous surveys.

Late in the summer, we put our student divers on an interesting-looking anomaly of 59 nanoTeslas, the unit of measurement for magnetic signatures. This was the third or fourth anomaly investigated that day, and the others had turned up nothing that was culturally or historically significant. Almost immediately, they surfaced and reported that they felt "hard returns" with their probes, which could be caused by buried stones. As they extended their probe survey, we discussed conducting some exploratory hand-fanning of the bottom sediments to see whether they could determine what their probes were hitting. Soon, several round ballast stones came up, and one student said that they thought they felt wood as well. Finally, another student surfaced and shouted that she had found a ceramic sherd, which turned out to be sixteenth-century majolica, a common type of pottery for the time period.

Further investigations eventually exposed a 1×2-meter area of articulated ship timbers, including frames and outer hull planking. Nearly 50 artifacts were recovered, including iron concretions, ballast stones, ceramics, and animal bones. With sixteenth-century artifacts and intact hull structure confirmed, UWF archaeologists announced in 2016 the discovery of the third vessel from the 1559 Luna fleet. With so much work left to do on the EPII shipwreck, we decided to cover the exposed structure of the new wreck and conduct noninvasive diver magnetometer and probing surveys to get a better idea of the size and orientation of the vessel. This work is ongoing as this chapter is being written.

✳ ✳ ✳

Without doubt, additional exciting discoveries related to the Luna expedition are in the offing owing to intensive investigations of the new wreck, surveys for other vessels in the fleet, and fieldwork on the nearby terrestrial site. Having access to multiple ships of colonization from such an early expedition—as well as the settlement site itself—provides an unprecedented opportunity to increase our knowledge about early European colonizing enterprises. We already are gaining information related to the marvelous machines that allowed the Spaniards to voyage across the seas in the dawn of European expansion. Discoveries at the settlement site will provide insights into how the 1,500 colonists adapted to this new environment after the hurricane wiped out most of their food and supplies. We are fortunate to have a corpus of documents, letters, and descriptions written by the colonists themselves, but the archaeological research will allow us to analyze and explain the artifacts, structures, and tangible remains of this doomed expedition.

Dr. Roger C. Smith served as State Underwater Archaeologist for the Florida Division of Historical Resources for three decades. He is the author of three books: *Vanguard of Empire: Ships of Exploration in the Age of Columbus* (Oxford University Press, 1993), *An Atlas of Maritime Florida* (University Press of Florida, 1997), and *The Maritime Heritage of the Cayman Islands* (University Press of Florida, 2001). He also is editor of *Florida's Lost Galleon: The Emanuel Point Shipwreck* (University Press of Florida, 2018).

Dr. Gregory D. Cook is an assistant professor of anthropology at the University of West Florida. He has extensive experience working on colonial-period shipwrecks in Ghana, Jamaica, and the United States. He serves as the field director for the continuing work on the Pensacola shipwrecks and supports the students in their research and thesis work.

For Additional Information

Websites

University of West Florida, Emanuel Point Shipwreck, http://uwf.edu/cassh/departments/anthropology-and-archaeology/research/faculty-and-staff-projects/maritime/emanuel-point-shipwreck/

University of West Florida, Emanuel Point II: Second Oldest Shipwreck in the U.S., Florida Public Archaeology Network, http://www.flpublicarchaeology.org/anthro/ep2/

Publications

Dave Dunwoody, "Historical Marker Unveiled for de Luna's Emanuel Point Shipwrecks," WUWF.org, March 18, 2016, http://wuwf.org/post/historical-marker-unveiled-de-lunas-emanuel-point-shipwrecks

Thomas St. Myer, "Third Shipwreck from Luna Fleet Discovered," *Pensacola News Journal*, October 21, 2016, http://www.pnj.com/story/ncws/local/pensacola/2016/10/21/third-shipwreck-luna-fleet-uncovered/92487848/

University of Florida, George A. Smathers Libraries, The Florida Anthropologist, Vol. 62, Nos. 3–4 (September–December 2009), http://ufdc.ufl.edu/UF00027829/00207/1j

Grace Tennyson, "Shipwreck Discovered by UWF Could Be the Oldest Ship Built in America," WEARTV.com, http://weartv.com/news/local/uwf-archaeology-program-discovers-third-shipwreck-from-luna-fleet

CHAPTER 7

Florida's Sunken Treasure Galleons: Contributions of Archaeology in the Search for Treasure

R. Duncan Mathewson III

July 20, 1985. It was hard to believe that, after many years of searching, not far below me was a sunken Spanish treasure discovery that had just captured the world's imagination. Somehow I had become intimately involved with Mel Fisher's 16-year quest for the remains of *Nuestra Señora de Atocha*, sunken with more treasure than most people can imagine. Now it lay before me, pretty much the way I had envisioned it might look after I began working with Fisher's divers as an archaeological consultant 12 years earlier.

This galleon and seven other vessels in a Spanish fleet sank in a hurricane in 1622. *Atocha* took with her 260 crew and passengers and more than a million pesos in gold and silver—one of the largest single treasure cargos lost in the southern Gulf Stream.

The elusive dream of finding *Atocha* finally had become a reality. Trying not to hyperventilate as I breathed hard on my regulator, I slowly descended 50 feet to the remains of the ship, strewn more than a hundred feet along the seabed. As it gradually came into view, my mind raced over the events that brought me to this spot off the Marquesas Keys, some 40 miles west of Key West. Drifting along the undisturbed reef of silver and ballast rock that projected five feet above the sea floor, I could see tons of silver ingots, stacked in rows like blackened loaves of bread lying among intact coin chests. Swimming closer, I began to make out details among a jumbled mass of artifacts that included hundreds of copper ingots, thousands of coins, supplies and personal baggage, all lumped together just as the hurricane had left them in the ship's hold 363 years before. Next to this mound several Spanish olive jars proudly stood upright and intact—not unlike when they last held water or wine on their final voyage. Timbers of the lower hull structure clearly projected from the sides of the ballast mound. The frames or ribs of the vessel suggested that the ship had listed slightly to starboard as she settled on the seabed.

The main cultural deposit of the wrecked ship *Nuestra Señora de Atocha*. *(Photo by Don Kincaid)*

I checked my compass and quickly realized that the lower hull remains were aligned in a general northwest to southeast direction and that the stern section pointed toward the shallow, sandy shoals more than 10 miles away where the search for the galleon had begun in 1970. In fact, the hull was generally aligned on the same 130-degree bearing that had bisected nine bronze cannons we had discovered and mapped years earlier. I had used this alignment as the rough bearing of an artifact trail that we had followed from the sandy shoals into deeper water. Although it was satisfying to know that my "Deep Water Theory" for locating *Atocha*, developed in 1975, had proved to be valid, my primary thought now was on the attention and scrutiny that our handling of this unrivaled time capsule would bring.

I had to figure out how to record this cultural and historical treasure without counting on assistance from the academic or government personnel who did not support my work with a treasure-hunting company. Instead, I would have to rely on the talents and skills of the salvage community and those archaeological colleagues who accepted my invitation to help. Quite clearly, my biggest *Atocha* challenges with Mel Fisher and his staff lay ahead—well beyond the celebratory chaos and limitless exhilaration that permeated the site for several days after this thrilling discovery.

Long before I knew anything about treasure galleons, I worked as a terrestrial archaeologist surveying and excavating prehistoric and historic sites in the United Kingdom, West Africa, and

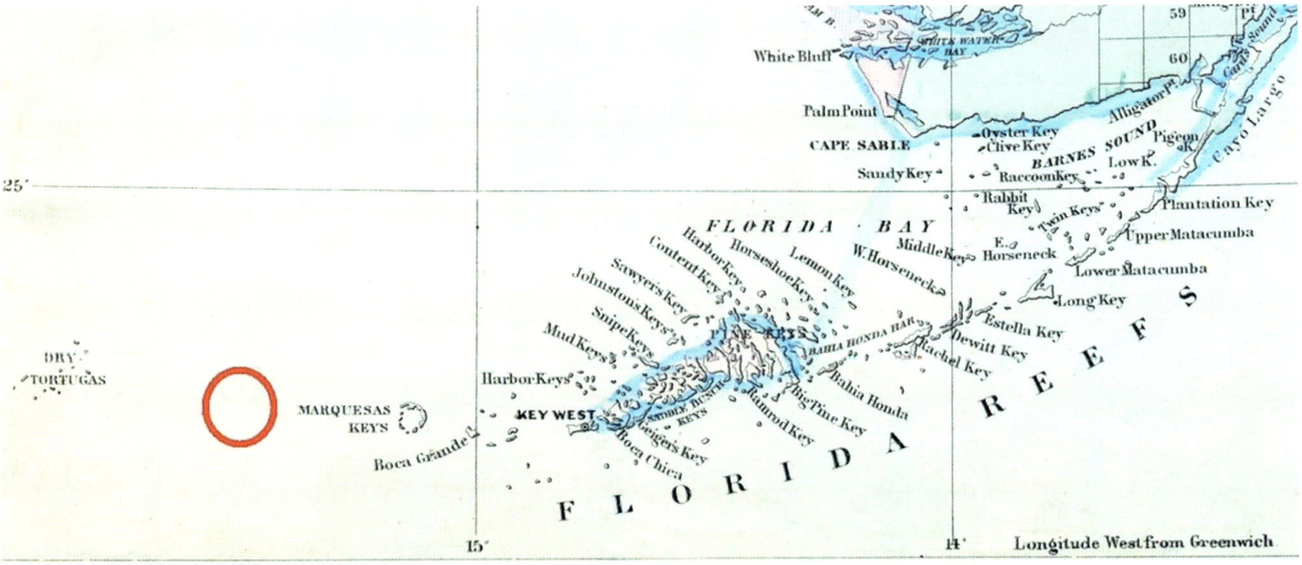

Location of the wreck sites of *Nuestra Señora de Atocha* and *Santa Margarita* to the west of the Marquesas Keys.

(Courtesy of the author)

Jamaica. The switch from land to sea was quite unexpected. I was in Port Royal, Jamaica, when I first encountered the wonderful artifacts that Edwin Link and Robert Marx had recovered during their work on the bottom of Kingston Harbor in the late 1960s. I was amazed by the variety and preservation of artifacts they had found at the pirate seaport destroyed and submerged by an earthquake in 1692. These finds humbled the meager potsherds and other bits and pieces of the past that I had recovered by slowly troweling away on land sites. Although I had heard of George Bass's pioneering research in the Mediterranean, marine archaeology was not well developed in American waters, and it was new to my graduate-level training at the University of London's Institute of Archaeology. Because I had never learned to dive, it never crossed my mind that I might become involved in one of the most heralded shipwreck projects of the time.

However, like a proverbial lightning bolt from heaven, my professional life changed direction drastically after I received a telegram from Florida treasure hunter Mel Fisher, who was hot on the trail of *Atocha* and her sister ship, *Santa Margarita*. I had never met Mel, but the little I knew about him had come from historian Eugene Lyon, researching the two treasure galleons in Spanish archives while working on his doctoral dissertation at the University of Florida. Eugene also had been assisting me with Spanish documentation of historic land sites I was excavating and had shared some of his experiences working with Mel and his Key West–based company Treasure Salvors Inc. Knowing my interest in Spanish ceramics and colonial archaeology, Eugene had persuaded Mel and his company that they needed an archaeologist to develop a scientific approach to their salvage operations and to make sense out of the increasing number of artifacts being recovered. Eugene was a serious-minded academic, so I was curious to learn more about this shipwreck project. It did not take me long to accept the invitation to visit Key West to meet Mel and his staff.

When I began consulting with Mel in 1973, American universities had little academic interest in archaeology underwater. Interest in U.S. waters had begun to develop in Florida in the

1950s through the efforts of University of Florida anthropologist John Goggin and his graduate students Stephen Gluckman and Carl Clausen. Soon after, a foundation for shipwreck archaeology was laid by commercial salvors such as Art McKee, Kip Wagner, Mel Fisher, Burt Webber, Henry Taylor, Richard MacAllister, Robert Marx, and Jack Haskins on Florida's 1715 and 1733 Spanish treasure fleets. If I was going to organize an archaeological program on the 1622 wreck sites, I would have to learn from the experiences of those who already had conducted research and recovered artifacts on historical shipwrecks. In addition, I would have to learn to dive to gain the respect of salvage divers whose assistance I would need to document wreck sites on the seabed.

The *Carrera de Indias*

Maritime trade between Spain and the Americas began in 1503 as a system of private enterprise by shipping companies and private merchants who operated under tight royal regulations governing Indies trade and navigation through the *Casa de Contratación* (House of Trade). By 1537, an armed convoy system of the *Carrera de Indias* (Route to the Indies) was established to protect Spain's merchant shipping from her powerful maritime rivals.

Two fleets usually sailed each year from Spain to the New World. Each consisted of at least two heavily armed galleons—the largest called *capitana* (flagship), and the other *almiranta* (vice-flagship). In addition, the fleets contained two *pataches* or patrol vessels, a supply or reinforcement ship, and merchant vessels or *naos* sailing under the protection of the galleons. Riding the trade winds across the Atlantic, the ships entered the Caribbean basin and headed for the major colonial ports of

Route of the Spanish treasure fleets in the New World.
(Courtesy of the author)

New Granada and New Spain (modern Colombia and Mexico).

The *Tierra Firme Armada*, or *galeones*, sailed to Cartagena and Portobelo, where it collected the trade goods and treasure of South America. The *Nuevo España Armada*, or *flota*, sailed to Veracruz not only for coins and bullion brought by mule trains from Mexico City, but also for Chinese trade goods and Southeast Asian luxury items that arrived in Acapulco from the Philippines aboard the Manila galleons. The fleets rendezvoused in Havana, Cuba, for the return voyage to Spain. After reprovisioning, the combined fleet sailed into the Straits of Florida, propelled northward by the Gulf Stream. After pilots determined that the northern Bahama islands had been cleared, the course was altered toward Bermuda, then east to catch westerly trade winds toward Spain.

Spain's economy was almost totally dependent on the treasure shipments from the New World. Because Spain manufactured little that was needed by other countries, the wealth she received from her New World colonies merely passed through her coffers into the economies of other European nations from which she purchased goods to fulfill her needs. Ironically, other countries benefited more than Spain from her New World wealth. During the seventeenth century, nearly 95 percent of the precious metals that backed Europe's monetary systems came from the Spanish treasure fleets. When treasure galleons were lost, the entire European economic structure felt the interruption.

Unfortunately, treasure fleets often failed to reach their destinations. Many galleons and merchant vessels were lost at sea during West Indian hurricanes between June and November, and dozens of Spanish treasure ships wrecked in Florida waters. Throughout the Indies, hurricanes destroyed more ships, claimed more lives, and were responsible for the loss of more Spanish treasure than all of the pirates or privateers from other nations put together.

The Spanish Galleon

Long-distance transatlantic trade required ships that could remain at sea for extended periods, were well armed to protect against pirates, and had sufficient space for passengers and cargo. After years of experimentation, the galleon best satisfied these requirements and became the workhorse of the treasure fleets by the mid-sixteenth century. The galleon design combined the best sailing qualities of the galley, the traditional warship of the Mediterranean, and the greater cargo capacity of the northern European carrack, which was better suited for rough weather on long ocean voyages.

Spanish galleons during the sixteenth and seventeenth centuries varied in size, ranging from about 300 to 700 tons of cargo capacity, and usually were between 85 and 100 feet in length and about 30 to 40 feet in beam. They had three or four masts with square and lateen sails, two or three decks above the cargo hold, and tons of ballast stones in the lower bilge to keep the vessel on an even keel. A high sterncastle provided "first-class" accommodations for officers and wealthy or high-status passengers.

Galleons were built to carry large treasure cargoes, sizable personal shipments, supplies for a voyage of several months, and 200 or more people, including crew, soldiers, government officers, and passengers. Over time, they increased in size and became more streamlined. The superstructure and shape of the hull gradually evolved into a frigate, which became the common vessel in the treasure fleets by the early eighteenth century.

The 1715 Fleet

A Spanish treasure fleet composed of 12 vessels sank in a hurricane in 1715 off the east coast of Florida, south of present-day Cape Canaveral. The loss included about 1,000 people and at least 14 million pesos worth of cargo. Spaniards salvaged much of the ships' contents, and the wrecks' locations eventually were forgotten. Centuries later, local beachcombers occasionally found bits and pieces of Spanish artifacts and coins, especially after strong storms or hurricanes. In 1928, William Beach discovered the wreck of *Urca de Lima* in shallow water off Fort Pierce. Cannons and anchors were raised and put on display outside the city hall. Charles Higgs, an amateur historian, located an old Spanish salvage camp in 1941; after surveying the site in 1946, archaeologist Hale Smith concluded that it was associated with the 1715 fleet.

Steadman Parker apparently became interested in the shipwrecks as a child after his father reportedly showed him some wreckage in 1907. In 1950, he obtained from the State of Florida an exclusive mineral mining lease for an offshore area to explore for buried treasure. Parker lacked the necessary funding to salvage materials from the ocean, but during his venture he introduced a local construction contractor, Kip Wagner, to the idea of sunken treasure. Wagner began to look for and find Spanish coins along the beach near his home and eventually convinced a local doctor, Kip Kelso, to join him in a hunt for treasure. In 1960, they obtained a 50-mile-long offshore exploration lease from the State and began to recruit local recreational divers to work on the weekends. After recovering thousands of silver coins, they incorporated the Real Eight Company in 1961 and focused on seven wreck sites, thus starting a "treasure rush" that continues today. Unfortunately, much of the commercial salvage conducted through leases and contracts with the state did not require archaeological mapping techniques beyond basic logging procedures.

Carl Clausen, Florida's first state underwater archaeologist, who was hired to oversee the 1715 salvage work, had some success at plotting artifacts in situ (in place). He persistently urged salvors to help him map the wrecks to understand how wooden vessels sink and disintegrate in a high-energy surf zone. His site plan of the Douglass Beach wreck helped me a decade later to conceptualize the distribution of shipwreck material on the 1622 wreck sites. The apparent clustering of artifacts that he mapped, particularly near the outer reef line, suggested to me a rudimentary scatter pattern of wreck material. This told me that, if a pattern could be recognized from the breakup of a wooden vessel in a turbulent coral reef environment, similar patterns within the wrecking process could be detected on the 1622 wreck sites.

Carl Clausen's 1964 site plan of the Douglass Beach wreck, which plotted the locations of artifacts relative to datum points along two chains laid on the seabed.

(Courtesy of Carl Clausen)

By the 1980s, the general lack of archaeological mapping and analysis on 1715 shipwrecks had caused considerable confusion about the individual identities and historical details of the sunken vessels between Sebastian Inlet and Jensen Beach. By this time, many cannons and anchors had been removed from the sites, rock ballast had been shifted around, and many archaeological signposts on the seabed had lost their contextual value. To evaluate what could be discovered archaeologically about the fleet, I launched the East Coast Shipwreck Project (ECSP) in 1984 as an interdisciplinary survey to investigate these wrecks. The project involved salvors working with Mel Fisher in their state contract areas and resulted in several reports that shed new light on mapping wreck sites of all periods along the east coast. Meanwhile, the state's Division of Historical Resources responded to a request by the St. Lucie County Historical Commission to declare *Urca de Lima* exempt from further salvage activities, and in 1987 the shipwreck became the first State Underwater Archaeological Preserve.

The 1733 Fleet

The largest Spanish treasure fleet disaster in Florida occurred in 1733, when 21 vessels were driven aground by a hurricane along 80 miles of the Florida Keys. A reported 20 million pesos of silver and gold were lost—the products of several years of mining and coinage minting in Mexico. Some of the ships were refloated, but those that could not be saved were salvaged successfully by the Spanish over several years. Moreover, their locations were charted, which helped modern salvors to identify more easily the sites they found.

Art McKee, known by some as the "grandfather of treasure hunters," was employed as a commercial diver on the construction of a water pipeline extending from the mainland to Key West. In 1938, local fisherman Reggie Roberts showed him a site off Plantation Key that contained iron cannons protruding from a large pile of ballast stones. After finding some silver coins and doing some research, McKee determined

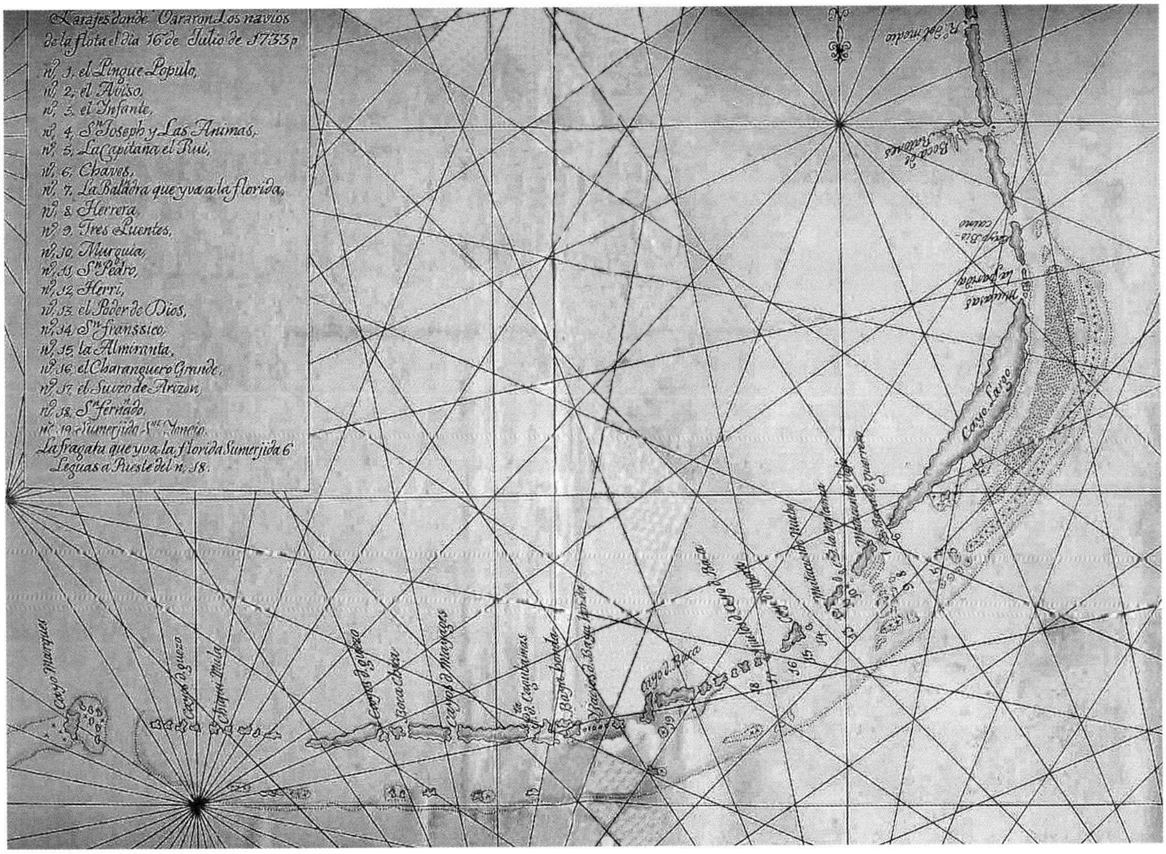

A Spanish salvors' chart of the locations of 1733 shipwrecks along the Florida Keys. *(Courtesy of the Florida Division of Historical Resources)*

Art McKee's Museum of Sunken Treasure at Tavernier in the Florida Keys.

(Photo courtesy of the Florida Memory Project, State Library and Archives of Florida)

that it was the *capitana* of the 1733 fleet. He and his friends dug through the wreckage for several years, located several associated wrecks, and in 1949 opened McKee's Museum of Sunken Treasure.

Another "treasure rush" began in the 1960s, but salvage divers recovered little shipwreck cargo apart from coins, and little archaeological mapping was done under the state contracts. An exception was the effort by Smithsonian Institution maritime historian Mendel Peterson, who worked with Edwin Link and Art McKee on the wreck of HMS *Looe* in the Lower Keys in 1951. Their underwater excavation was noteworthy because it involved the first use of an airlift together with datum mapping coordinates on the bottom, and they successfully linked documentary evidence with recovered artifacts to enable site identification.

In the mid-1960s, Peterson and National Park Service archaeologist George Fischer worked with Art McKee and Tom Gurr on the well-preserved hull remains of *San José*. This short-term project, which involved mapping the ship's articulated lower hull, demonstrated the archaeological potential of the 1733 wrecks and provided an important step toward developing method and theory in shipwreck archaeology in American waters. It also showed that professional researchers could work effectively within a commercial shipwreck project. Later work on *San José* by avocational archaeologist Ron Molinari demonstrated archaeological information was still available on the 1733 fleet after he produced careful site notes and published a book on his work.

In 1977, state field agents Roger Smith and Jim Dunbar conducted a survey of seven of the 1733 shipwrecks, creating a site plan of each and taking samples of pottery and ballast stones. Ten years later in 1987 I formed the National Center for Shipwreck Research (NCSR), a nonprofit consulting company to access 1733 wreck sites and develop educational programs with the Florida Keys Community College in Key West and the Marine Research Development Foundation in Key Largo. NCSR educational programs used field schools, workshops, and conferences relating to the 1733 wrecks to teach students and sport divers about shipwreck archaeology. My main objective was to develop an educational model for using shipwrecks as unique underwater classrooms, relying on the enthusiasm and skill of volunteers to document their wooden hull structures. Hundreds of sport divers and avocational archaeologists attended the "Dive into History" workshops that I organized for many years in the Keys and with dive shops around the country. We worked with the Atlantic Alliance for Maritime Preservation, a national sport diver group interested in shipwreck archaeology.

In 1992, NCSR and the Abyss Dive Club at Coral Shores High School mapped the hull

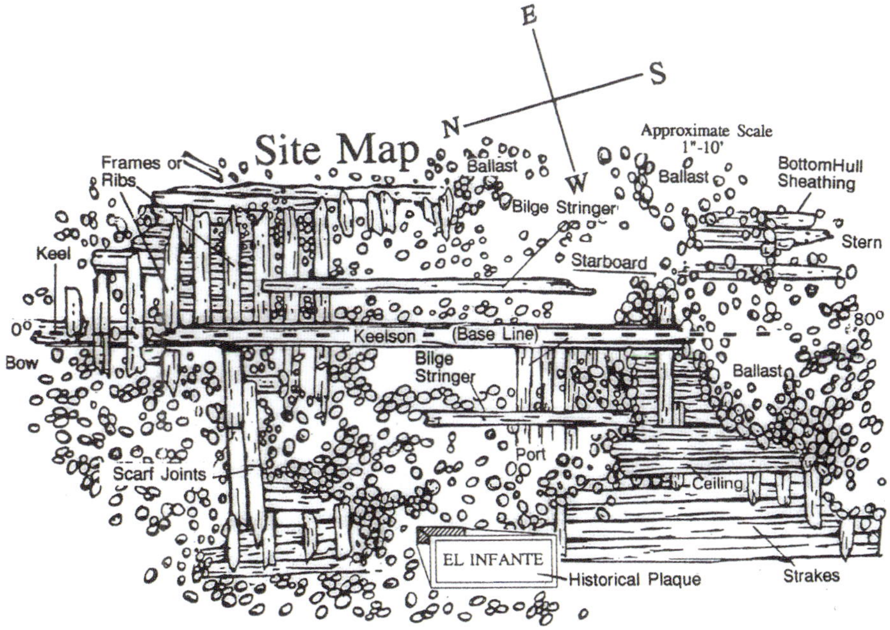

Site plan from 1992 of the 1733 shipwreck *El Infante*. *(Courtesy of the author)*

remains of *Nuestra Señora de Balvaneda*, alias *El Infante*, and placed a cement historical plaque designating the site as an integral part of Florida Keys maritime heritage.

Based on a joint Florida State University/Indiana University field school, the 1733 wreck site *San Pedro* became the state's second Underwater Archaeological Preserve in 1989. Since then, it also has been designated as a state park. In 2005, the Florida Division of Historical Resources' underwater team surveyed and recorded the 13 known 1733 shipwrecks to create a Spanish Galleon Trail in the Florida Keys National Marine Sanctuary (FKNMS) that guides visitors to what are considered the oldest artificial reefs in Florida. Each of these sites now is listed on the National Register of Historic Places.

The 1622 Fleet

On September 4, 1622, a combined fleet of 28 ships bound for Spain sailed from Havana harbor toward the lower Florida Keys, 90 miles to the north. This *Tierra Firme Flota*, commanded by the Marquis of Cadereita, was escorted by three *pataches* and eight large galleons, including *Nuestra Señora del Rosario*, *Santa Margarita*, and *Nuestra Señora de Atocha*. An enormous cargo had been loaded at Portobelo, Cartagena, and Havana, consisting primarily of gold and silver specie (coins) and bullion in ingots and bars of many shapes and sizes, tobacco, copper ore, indigo, cochineal, rosewood, and other agricultural products.

As the ships made their way into the Florida Straits, bad weather set in; by the following day, they were in the middle of a hurricane with gale-force winds coming from the northeast. The storm separated the ships and stripped them of their masts, sails, and rigging. As the wind shifted around to the south, 20 ships survived by sailing beyond the hurricane winds before heading back to Havana. However, eight ships were driven toward the lower Florida Keys, and they soon were lost.

The shipwrecks were scattered in the vicinity of the Dry Tortugas, where *Rosario*, a patache, and a small Portuguese *fragata* broke up and sank. *Atocha*

An artistic reconstruction depicting the loading of cargo on *Atocha* in Havana harbor before setting sail in 1622. The painting is by the late Cuban maritime artist, José Martinez Fernandez, based on the 1622 historical and archaeological research.

(Courtesy of the author)

reportedly sank close to *Margarita*, some "fifteen leagues," or about 48 nautical miles, east of *Rosario*. About 380 people perished aboard *Atocha* and *Margarita*, with cargo losses of almost 2 million pesos.

The Spaniards began salvage efforts immediately after news of the disaster reached Havana. The operations were directed by Gaspar de Vargas, who first located the hull of *Atocha* in 10 *brazas* (arms span) or about 55 feet of water. The ship was still intact, with her mizzen mast projecting above the water. However, the divers were unable to break into her treasure storerooms below deck because the hatches and ports were firmly battened down. The only substantial items they recovered were two bronze cannons, probably rail-guns taken off the upper deck of the sterncastle.

After buoying *Atocha*, Vargas sailed west and located and salvaged *Rosario*. In early October, another hurricane crossing the lower Keys buried *Margarita* in deep sand, and broke up *Atocha*'s hull and removed her surface buoys. Consequently, when Vargas returned to renew the salvage efforts, he was unable to relocate *Atocha*, and his African and West Indian pearl divers

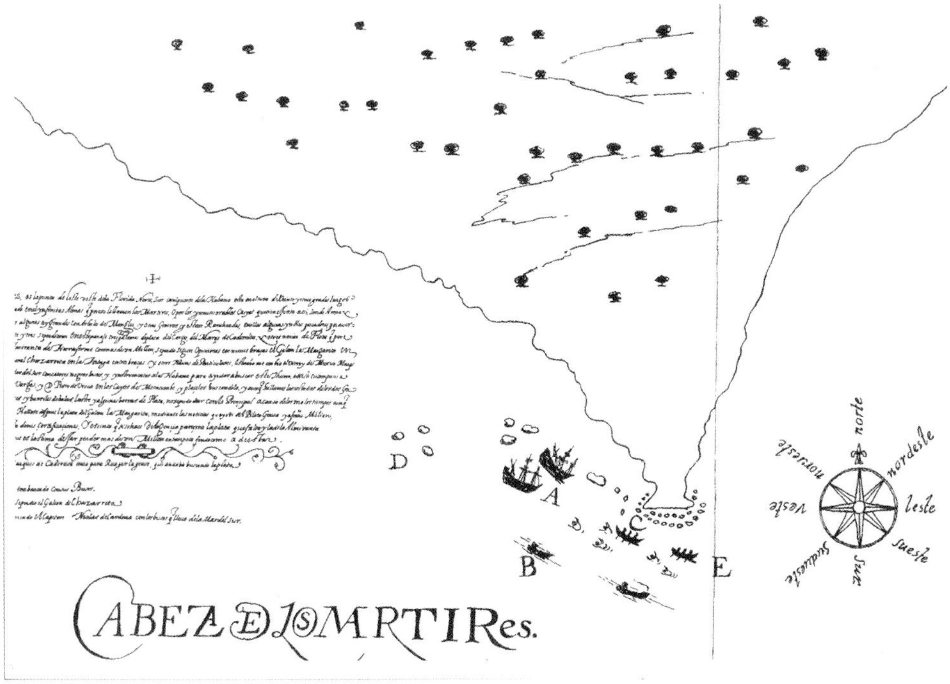

A 1623 map made by salvage engineer Nicholás de Cardona after his unsuccessful efforts to find *Atocha* and *Margarita.* The map's legend described the site stretching from the present day Marquesas Keys to the Dry Tortugas and provided a contemporary account of the salvage operation: "A. The Armada *patache* which the Marquis of Cadereita used to recover the people who went seeking silver. B. The Lost Galleons. C. The launch in which the Marquis was embarked with his divers. D. The Keys of Tortugas where Chazarreta's galleon [*Rosario*] was lost. E. The launch in which Captain Nicholás de Cardona was embarked, with the divers whom he transported from the South Sea." *(Courtesy of Eugene Lyon)*

Pedro de Ledesma described seven techniques for salvaging the 1622 treasure. This illustration notation reads: "I made this device in the year 1623 in the Keys of Matazumbi [Matecumbe] to search for the remains of the two galleons with the silver, which were *Margarita* and the galleon of Don Pedro Pasquies [*Atocha*]." *(Courtesy of Eugene Lyon)*

A sheet anchor (*ancla de salvación*) found on the *Atocha* site in 1971, one of six anchors carried on the galleon. Historical evidence indicates that it was stowed below the decks in the stern with its wooden stock removed and was used only in dire emergencies. The anchor served as an archaeological datum for mapping the artifact scatter pattern in the shallow Quicksands during the 1970s. *(Courtesy of Bill Muir)*

recovered only a small amount of material. Early in 1623, the Marquis of Cadereita came from Havana to personally direct the search from a salvage camp that had been established on nearby keys. These islands were named *Cayos del Marqués* after the Marquis and are known today as the Marquesas Keys.

After Vargas abandoned his search for *Margarita* and *Atocha* in late 1623, Cuban authorities attempted to keep the general areas of the wrecks buoyed. In early 1626, Francisco Núñez Melián began to search for the two galleons under a royal salvage contract. Equipped with a 680-pound bronze diving bell with windows to assist the operation, Melián located the hulk of *Margarita*, which his divers salvaged for more than four years. By 1630, more than 380 silver ingots, 67,000 silver coins, most of the copper ingots, and ship's ordnance were recovered.

The salvage efforts continued in the face of numerous difficulties. Operations were interrupted three times by Dutch raiding parties. Gifts of tools, beads, and comestibles were given to pacify Calusa Indians encamped on the Marquesas Keys and other nearby islands, but the Spanish salvage camp eventually was destroyed when the natives turned hostile. After Melián ended his salvage efforts on *Margarita*, the search for *Atocha* continued intermittently until 1641. A second royal contract was issued based on the belief that local Indians knew *Atocha*'s location; however, when Melián died in 1644, the wreck site still had not been found. In 1683, the Spanish House of Trade published the names of lost Spanish ships still missing in the Americas, and *Atocha* headed the list. After the deaths of the people who had been involved directly with the search and salvage of the 1622 galleons, the matter passed into history.

Melián's salvage accounts were audited, and the historical records about the lost ships eventually were transferred from Havana to the Archive of the Indies in Seville, Spain. As the centuries passed, *Atocha*'s location remained a mystery until 1970, when Mel Fisher and his commercial salvage company began to search for the last resting place of *Atocha*, *Margarita*, and their treasure cargoes 40 miles west of Key West.

Historical Secrets Revealed

Eugene Lyon's historical research on the 1622 fleet was instrumental in the search for *Atocha* and *Margarita*. Documentation about Francisco Núñez Melián's salvage efforts convinced him that the frequent use of "Cayos de Matecumbe" was a generic geographical term referring to the entire Florida Keys, rather than the Upper and Lower Matecumbe Keys where salvors had been searching for *Atocha* since the mid-1960s. When he found references that Melián had located the *Margarita* at "Cayos de Marquis," Gene made the connection to the present-day Marquesas Keys about 30 miles west of Key West. With these revelations, in 1970 Mel withdrew his Middle Keys search contract with the State and moved his search to the waters around the Marquesas Keys. This put Treasure Salvors Inc. in an area of trackless ocean more than 50 miles long and 10 miles wide.

From a starting point west of the Marquesas, a magnetometer survey recorded many "hits" from metal objects, but nothing of historical interest was encountered. However, on June 12, 1971, the monotony of dragging the mag sensor back and forth in the blazing sun finally paid off. The instrument recorded a reading that indicated a large piece of iron on the seabed. After throwing a buoy to mark the site, the crew donned scuba gear to check the anomaly. This time, it was not a fish trap or a U.S. Navy bomb fragment—it was a galleon anchor. This discovery refocused the search for shipwreck remains and became a starting point for the archaeological mapping of their locations.

Salvage Archaeology

My study of the 1622 wreck sites sought to develop direct relationships between the physical characteristics of the sites and the archaeological interpretations of cultural material recovered from them. Unlike the commercial salvage work carried out on the 1715 and 1733 treasure fleets, archaeology became an integral part of the salvage operations on *Atocha* and *Margarita*.

While consulting in Key West, I began graduate school at Florida Atlantic University (FAU) in Boca Raton to earn a master's degree in anthropology under Professor William H. Sears. I wanted to study with Sears because he had overseen the Florida commercial salvage program in the early 1960s. While assisting the Florida Antiquities Commission, he had addressed matters concerning the artifacts recovered under the state antiquities law and had maintained exclusive negotiations between salvors and state officials. Sears's mentorship helped me to see the full potential of my archaeological research design for the 1622 wreck sites—to develop successful collaborations and a pragmatic approach to preserving archaeological information. My attempt to mitigate the negative impact of commercial operations on the 1622 galleons was no different from the preservation efforts made on land sites threatened by commercial development, which was recognized in later years by academics as cultural resource management.

Based on my *Atocha* research with Treasure Salvors Inc., my master's thesis described how archaeological evidence supported my hypotheses to explain shipwreck features in artifact scatter patterns and what the patterns revealed about how the galleon sank and broke up. It contained a prediction about where the ship sank and an explanation of how its contents were scattered in the sandy shallows of the Quicksands to the west of the Marquesas Keys. In 1982, I established a publishing company to disseminate the thesis and other *Atocha* research findings to colleagues and the public.

Deep Water Theory

Although Mel Fisher and I were trying to find the same thing—the main part of the *Atocha* site—we were hunting for it for totally different reasons. Mel was looking for gold and silver and what he called "The Big Pile" or the "Mother Lode." I was looking for the "Primary Cultural Deposit" (commonly called the PCD by the divers), where maximum contextual data could reveal details about the ship, its cargo, crew, and passengers.

As an archaeologist, I knew that artifacts can explain a lot about the site if we can find the best way to interpret their message. Every item tells a different story about the cultural pattern laid out on the seabed. My challenge was to convince Mel that the primary value of each find was the information it provided about its location on the ship and how its position on the seabed explained the ship's sinking—rather than its monetary value in an investor's private collection. When trying to get this idea across, I always emphasized that the whole is greater than the sum of its parts. I told him that if he wanted to find the Big Pile,

Mel Fisher and the author inspecting photomoasics that generated archaeological data in the search for the lower hull.
(Photo courtesy of Don Kincaid)

he should direct his boat captains to stop looking for gold bars and remnants of the sterncastle in the shallows. Instead, they should search in the opposite direction, where a thin artifact trail of small ballast, potsherds, broken barrel hoops, and encrusted iron spikes led into the deeper water and where the lower hull structure and his Mother Lode most likely would be found.

Underwater Sleuths

I approached the study of the *Atocha* site just as a detective solves a homicide by reconstructing the "crime scene." in the courtroom. I used Sherlock Holmes–like inductive and deductive reasoning to work out the interrelationships between the crime scene (the site), the weapon (the hurricanes), and the location where the missing body (the lower hull structure) was lying. Each evening, the divers and I had great times on the salvage boat's fantail, discussing how the bits and pieces of "evidence" we were finding might support various hypotheses about where *Atocha* sank. Everybody had their own theory! These sessions also built camaraderie, as divers shared information and increased their own interest in piecing together the archaeological puzzle. I often mentioned Occam's Razor, the medieval axiom that in any hypothesis, the simplest explanation is always the most accurate.

I faced many research challenges and problems working with Eugene Lyon and Mel Fisher, but the central issue was always whether enough credible archaeological information could be recovered to reconstruct the process in which *Atocha* sank and broke up. How could details from Gene's historical documents fill gaps in our evidence from the seabed and provide insights about the recovered artifacts? I first needed to understand why finds were scattered as they were throughout the Quicksands, the deep sandy shoals where our mapping of *Atocha* began. To do this, I had to convince the divers to help me gather information to address questions that could only be answered by knowing the location of artifacts on the seabed. This meant persuading them that archaeological evidence was as important to recover as the treasure. Despite academic colleagues' doubts about combining archaeology with commercial salvage, I knew from experience that if I could gain the divers' respect and pique their curiosity about the ship's sinking, I could convince some to think archaeologically and realize that holding a measuring tape or laying a mapping grid was not such a strange thing to do.

Fingerprinting History

The Spanish Archive of the Indies in Seville played a major role in finding and understanding the 1622 sites. The archive contains millions of records that chronicle the activities of the *Carrera de Indias* through time. Thousands of documents tied into bundles called *legajos* were written in a flowing script called *procesal*, which is a barely legible, unbroken scroll of Arabic-like letters with little or no punctuation. Gene's ability to decipher and translate more than 20,000 pages of worm-eaten documents about the 1622 fleet led to his discovery of key evidence for solving the mystery about where *Atocha* and *Margarita* sank and the material goods and people on board when they went down.

The Bank of Spain

A main part of the Quicksands was situated on the edge of a shoal that the divers called the "Bank of Spain" because several thousand Spanish silver coins had been found there in 1973. These eight-*reales* coins commonly are referred to as "pieces of eight" in pirate literature. Clusters of all kinds of artifacts found in the deep sand indicated that it was the prime area to begin mapping archaeological finds as they were recovered. Understanding how the ship sank and broke up depended on the degree to which spatial relationships between different artifacts could be established.

As on any land site, it was important to determine the position of each artifact before it was removed from its original context, if it was going to explain the archaeology of the wreck. But how could this be accomplished where constantly shifting sand dunes had moved items around for more than 350 years? Additional disturbance came from the use of "blowers." These elbow-shaped metal ducts (also known as "mailboxes") were invented by Mel Fisher on the 1715 fleet to fit over a boat's propellers to dig through sand with the downward thrust of the engines while the boat is anchored. Although the forceful propwash thrust can be controlled by the engine throttle, in shallow water it has a negative impact on delicate artifacts. The action also dislodges artifacts, making it impossible to map them in situ.

Never having had this problem on land sites, I had to find a solution if the shipwreck artifacts were going to tell *Atocha*'s story properly. Because it was impossible to map individual artifacts in the sand, we compromised by recording all finds that appeared together in each blow hole of about 20 to 30 feet in diameter. By mapping separate clusters of finds as individual groups across the site, it was possible to get an overall impression about how the artifacts were distributed. Blower holes were plotted by triangulating compass bearings from spar buoys attached to a surface grid about 100 yards long and 50 yards wide in the "Galleon Anchor Corridor."

After two summers of work, it was possible to create a mosaic map of finds that suggested how the artifact distributions might reveal how the vessel broke up. The absence of cannons, hull remnants, and a well-defined ballast mound indicated that this particular wreck material was a secondary scatter derived from a primary hull deposit located where the vessel originally sank somewhere to the southeast.

Determining the stratigraphic position of the finds in sometimes up to 15 feet of sand was another problem. It was impossible to maintain

Precious Clues

Gold bars usually were marked with stamps and seals noting the purity of the gold, the mint where they were cast, and a royal stamp indicating that the king's 20 percent tax had been paid. Unlike the silver ingots on *Atocha*'s cargo manifest, the gold bars were never identified individually and were only listed by karat.

Silver ingots were identified individually. For instance, one of the ingots has the same inscribed weight and fineness that was listed for ingot 569 (in Roman numerals) on the cargo manifest. The IZ shipper's monogram is the same mark Eugene Lyon found in the left-hand margin of the manifest. Linking historical documentation with archaeological evidence from the seabed was an important step toward establishing the wreck site.

One of three silver ingots weighing about 70 pounds each found at the Bank of Spain in the Quicksands.

(Photo courtesy of Treasure Salvors Inc.)

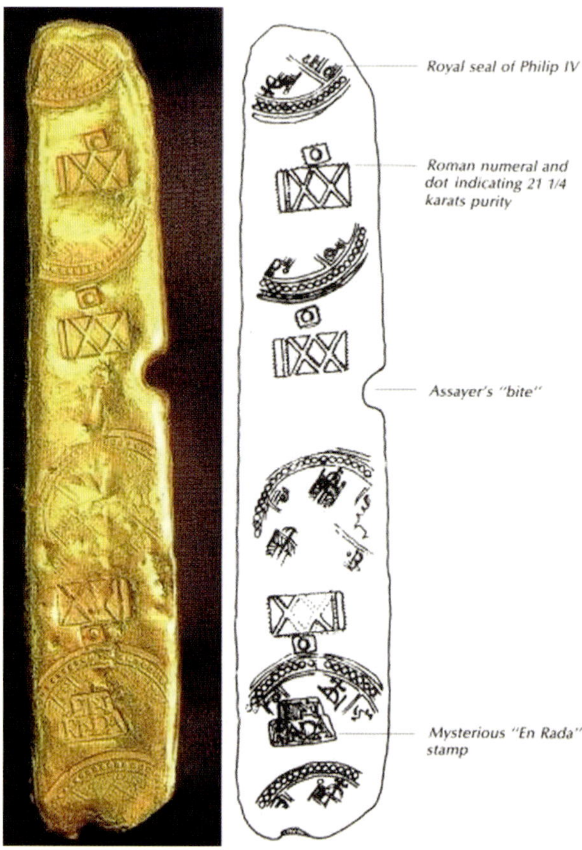

A one-pound, five-ounce gold bar found in September 1974 within the Quicksands that characterizes other gold bullion being shipped from the New World.

(Photo courtesy of Treasure Salvors Inc.)

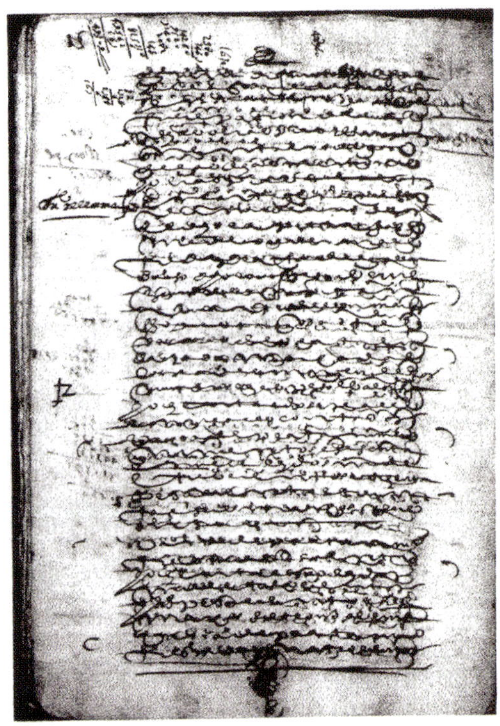

Fingerprinting the 1622 sites involved matching documentary information from the archives with archaeological evidence from the seabed. Matching marks on silver ingots recovered underwater with identical markings in the cargo manifest provided incontrovertible details for identifying the 1622 sites.

(Courtesy of Eugene Lyon)

a good stratigraphic section through the sand to determine how finds were deposited vertically in the sediments. However, we attempted to roughly gauge the relative depth of certain artifacts and ballast by the length of the throttle time and power of each thrust of the boat's engines. Although this recording procedure involved too many variables to make the resulting data very precise, it provided a fair idea of how artifacts were distributed vertically and enabled us to identify upper and lower depositional zones based on the size and weight of the ballast and individual objects.

Vertical measurements down the sides of blower holes also helped to determine the origin of major artifacts and the scatter of ballast deposits. This rough mapping procedure indicated that the larger rock ballast, encrusted objects, coin clumps, and heavier artifacts had accumulated in a lower stratum near the bedrock. Potsherds, barrel hoops, and lighter artifacts more commonly were found "floating" in the upper zone, where they were more affected by the movement of sand, prevailing currents, and sea state. The lower strata had less displacement through time than the lighter artifacts in the upper zone. This stratigraphic evidence provided a key piece in the archaeological puzzle because the finds in the lower zone pointed in a southeasterly direction, from which the secondary deposits most likely came.

Galleon Archaeology

The concentration of rock ballast, silver coins, pottery sherds, gold and silver bullion, navigational instruments, encrusted objects, and other artifacts found in the "Bank of Spain" defined a definite pattern that appeared to trail off toward the northwest. Using the size of the stones and a rough estimate of how much had been uncovered, I calculated the weight and volume of the Quicksands ballast at no more than about 60 tons. Knowing that a galleon the size of *Atocha* probably carried about 180 to 200 tons of ballast, if this was the main wreck site, where was the rest of the ballast? The lack of a well-defined mound indicated that the vessel did not sink at this part of the site.

A careful sweep of overlapping blow holes across our survey corridor, using a grid of datum points, baselines on the sea bed, and a surface grid system to control the mapping of the excavation holes, had failed to reveal any of the 20 bronze cannons we knew *Atocha* had on board when she sank. In addition, the lack of wooden hull remains and a sizable quantity of Spanish olive jar fragments was conspicuous. The absence of these important archaeological markers clearly indicated that the artifacts recovered in the Quicksands were from secondary deposits, away from where the vessel originally had sunk.

Although spectacular treasure finds of great intrinsic value, including silver bars and coins, gold bars, and personal jewelry, were found in the northwest quadrant of the site, the archaeology was telling me that they represented the final disintegration of the sterncastle, where affluent passengers of high social rank, the captain, and senior officers were accommodated. The other artifact trail consisting of potsherds, broken barrel hoops, corroded iron spikes, and ballast led in the opposite direction toward the southeast.

Historical documentation told us that *Atocha* sank in 55 feet of water, so why were we finding vessel remains in depths of no more than 25 feet? How could the historical information be reconciled with archaeological evidence from the seabed? Could the Quicksands artifacts be from one of the three smaller, unaccounted for ships in the 1622 fleet that also sank in the hurricane? Or was this the site of *Margarita*, known to have sunk in shallow water in sight of *Atocha*?

Although historical evidence provided by markings on three silver ingots recovered in the Bank of Spain indicated they were part of *Atocha*'s cargo, the archaeological evidence suggested that we had recovered only a small part of what would be expected from a 500-ton galleon. Because this part of the site did not represent the lower hull deposits, evidence supported the likely scenario that *Atocha*'s primary remains were in deeper water somewhere in the middle of Hawk Channel to the southeast.

To confirm the theory that the main part of *Atocha* lay in the deeper water, an artifact trail had to be identified leading from the Bank of Spain southeast across the "Coral Plateau," an expansive limestone hardpan in about 25 feet of water with soft coral and sponges and a thin layer of sandy silt overburden. I urged the boats' captains to anchor where divers could search the bottom and crevices methodologically with metal detectors in an effort to locate coins, iron spikes, barrel hoops, and other pieces of discarded metal from the wreckage.

Not all captains wanted to leave the Quicksands where gold coins, bars, and chains were being recovered, but Dirk Fisher, Mel's eldest

Dirk Fisher finding the first five cannons fully exposed on the bare bedrock. Four other cannons were discovered nearby by Pat Clyne and divers as they excavated the area.

(Photo courtesy of Don Kincaid)

son, believed in the Deep Water Theory and began to search for the artifact trail on the Coral Plateau. While Dirk was checking one of his boat anchors on the bottom, he suddenly came face to face with five bronze cannons sitting in full view on the hardpan. Four other cannons were found nearby in a separate cluster, buried in silt and mud.

Bronze Cannons

Aboard the salvage boat, I drew a field map of the nine bronze cannons from drawings and measurements recorded on underwater slates. Because the Coral Plateau cannons were beyond the Galleon Anchor Corridor, they linked the shallow, sandy area with secondary shipwreck material and the deeper water in which my predictive model projected the primary lower hull deposits would lie. Careful in situ mapping of the cannon features, including a photomosaic, provided critical information toward confirming the Deep Water Theory.

The four buried cannons had inscribed weight markings that confirmed they were from *Atocha*. Their relative positions on the seabed supported the working hypothesis that the main part of the wreck would be found to the southeast along a 130-degree compass bearing. As the salvage boat swung across the cannon site and cleared the overburden in successive digging positions, divers searched the area for shipwreck debris with metal detectors and by hand-fanning in bedrock crevices.

The position of the cannons suggested that they likely tumbled off both sides of the gundeck as it and timbers of the upper superstructure wallowed toward the Quicksands, driven by wind and waves of the second hurricane. The distance between two gun clusters was a little more than 30 feet, approximately the beam of *Atocha*. The 130-degree bearing bisecting the two cannon features was construed to be a wreckage path coming from the direction in which we needed to search.

As we followed a trail along the 130-degree bearing from the cannons into the deeper water, hundreds of anomalies detected by side-scan sonar and magnetometer had to be checked. When anomalies were recorded, two divers with a handheld metal detector conducted a circle search within a predetermined radius around a marker

The author, Eugene Lyon, and Mel Fisher (in the background) inspecting one of nine bronze cannons that confirmed the *Atocha* wreck site. *(Photo courtesy of Don Kincaid)*

After the encrustation was removed from one of the bronze cannons, weight markings, with the Hapsburg Coat of Arms, and the date 1616 became visible. *(Photo courtesy of Don Kincaid)*

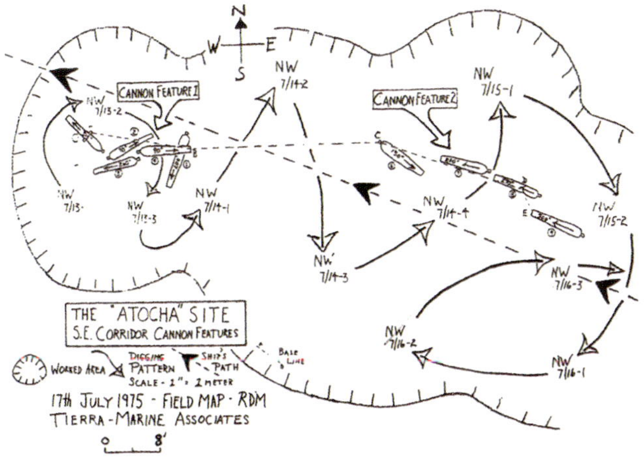

Field map of the cannons uncovered on the Coral Plateau.

(Drawing by the author)

laid on the seabed. Often the targets turned out to be shell-encrusted bomb fragments from a nearby World War II practice bombing range.

Following a trail as narrow as 50 feet was never easy—a ballast rock here, a potsherd or iron spike there. The path traversed terrains ranging from turtle grass on sandy overburden to bare limestone, hardpan, and soft corals, and finally the hard-packed mud bottom in the deepest parts of Hawk Channel. The salvage boats defined the edges of the trail with each successive find as they continued farther to the southeast.

In 1980, while searching for *Atocha* in Hawk Channel, divers picked up an artifact trail that eventually led to the *Margarita* site. Distinguishing two different galleon artifact trails was not easy, but a line of wreckage consisting of a large copper cauldron, crumpled lead sheathing, standing rigging, iron spikes, and a thin scatter of rock ballast connected with three galleon anchors near the outer reef and *Margarita*'s impact site. This was directly to the north of where she went aground in the first hurricane in only 15 feet of water. A widely dispersed artifact scatter of gold bars and chains, coins, and silver ingots suggested that the second hurricane tore apart *Margarita*'s hull and distributed the contents northward more than two miles.

Margarita Timbers

The *Margarita* timbers represented a 23-foot-long, top-timber section of the starboard side of the sterncastle. Designed by the company's videographer Pat Clyne, a sliding camera track attached to a PVC grid allowed us to use video and overlapping photomosaic to record architectural details not easily seen by visual inspection. Unfortunately, the grid and photo track were not easy to

Pat Clyne and Mel Fisher using the camera track to create the photomosaic of *Margarita*'s wooden hull structure.

(Photo courtesy of Don Kincaid)

use in the brisk ocean current (often two knots), and Pat spent several weeks ensuring that his photographic coverage of the feature with 130 overlapping photographs was precise and complete.

Margarita's timbers harbored a large concentration of finds, including personal effects from the passengers accommodated in the sterncastle. While hand-fanning in the area one day, Don Kincaid and I found tell-tale signs of daily life at sea. An experienced National Geographic photographer, Don always was thrilled when artifacts said something about the lives of the people on board. Pig bones, chili peppers, and a shoe sole told a different story than gold bars and other prized finds. The most spectacular artifact Don and I recovered from *Margarita* was an encrusted fragment of a book that had somehow been preserved under the timber structure. Later, as it carefully was cleaned in the company's Key West conservation laboratory, we were excited to see traces of writing and color decoration in a page margin. We had great expectations about what further conservation treatment in the state laboratory might reveal, but unfortunately, this artistic treasure was lost in cleaning before more could be recorded from it.

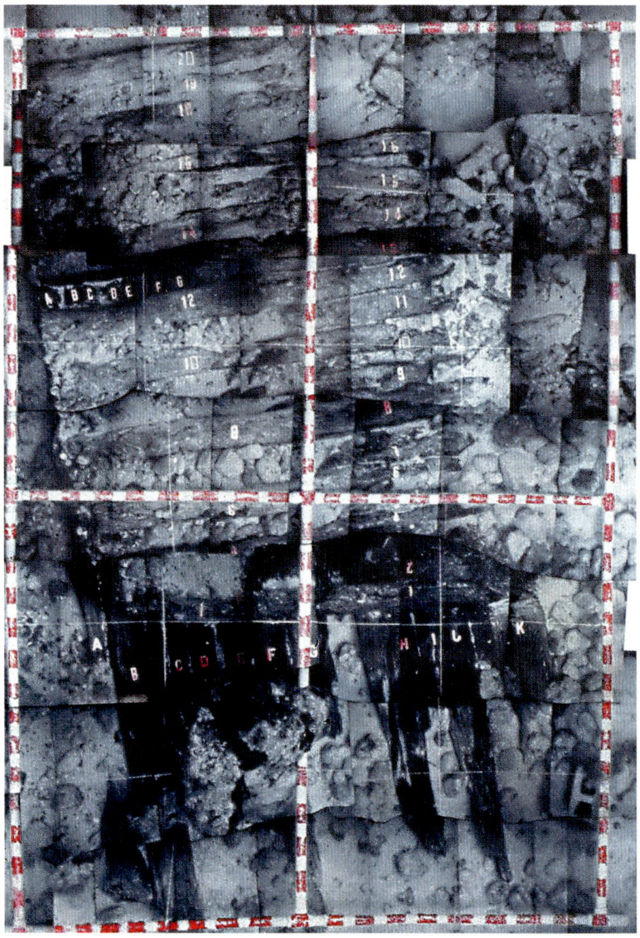

A photomosaic of *Margarita* timbers revealed scarf joints holding the framing timbers together. *(Photo courtesy of Pat Clyne)*

It also was exciting to find *Margarita* artifacts that had come from different areas of the world. One example was the lid of a small ivory box with silver hinges still in place that was intricately carved with figures of lions, eagles, and other mythical creatures. We later learned that this priceless artwork represented the legend of the first royal family of Ceylon (present-day Sri Lanka). Its figurines were similar to those on a box dating to the sixteenth century in the Victoria and Albert Museum in London. The box likely had come across the Pacific from the Philippines on the Manila galleon

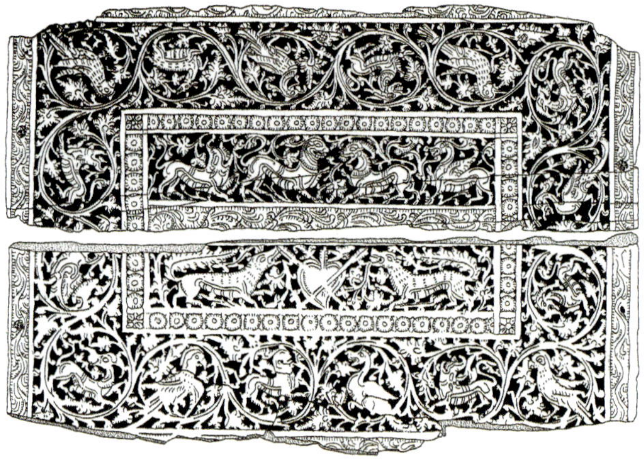

This ivory box lid (ca. 10 × 3.5 cm) represents the flow of luxury goods into the Caribbean Basin from halfway around the world. *(Drawing by D. Larissa Dillin)*

trade as part of Spain's global imperial commerce, which the 1622 wreck sites represented.

Mapping Hull Structures

Careful study of lower hull timbers and structure of wooden vessels can provide information about the design of ships from an era in which little was recorded about their construction. Archaeological materials associated with historic wooden-hulled shipwrecks provide invaluable evidence about how the vessels sank and disintegrated on the seabed under the influence of currents and weather. *Teredo* worms (warm-water mollusks) undermined the integrity of a ship's hull by boring into the wood and destroying its structural fabric. However, the lower hull timbers of a wrecked ship often were preserved under ballast stones—and, in the case of *Atocha*, under heavy silver and copper cargo—as well as being covered by a thin layer of sediment.

Excavating, mapping, and studying *Margarita*'s wooden structure in 1980 prepared us for recording *Atocha*'s lower hull when it was discovered in 1985. All timbers were marked with a letter or number to prepare them for the photomosaic and to facilitate their later study after being moved to a safe saltwater storage in the lagoon at the Florida Keys Community College.

Mapping both 1622 galleon sites revealed the difference between the artifact scatter patterns of *Atocha*, which sank quickly in deep water, and *Margarita*, which sank slowly in shallow water. *Margarita*'s structure evidently had been buried for some time, which protected the timbers from *teredo* worms and prevented ballast rocks from accumulating barnacles and other growth.

In 1616, *Atocha* was contracted to be constructed by Alonso de Ferrera in the royal shipyard in Havana and was completed in 1620. The ship was built as a three-masted, 500-ton guard galleon, 110 feet in length, 33 feet in beam, and drawing 14 feet of water. The hull was designed with a towering sterncastle and space for 20 bronze cannons on the main gundeck below the weather deck. Early structural problems on her maiden voyage in 1620 led officials to charge Ferrera with using inferior materials and not following the construction contract. Our underwater study of the timbers and fasteners revealed

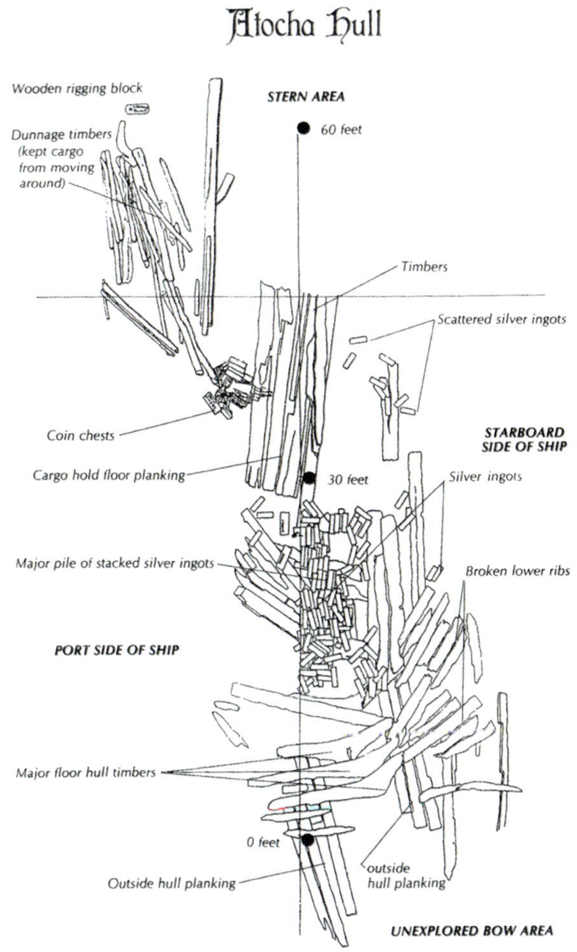

Site plan of *Atocha*'s primary deposit including the lower hull floor timbers, planking, and the main pile of stacked silver bars and coin chests. Note the jumbled condition of the frames and the conspicuous absence of a keel and keelson, reflecting traumatic impact and disintegration of the hull on the bottom.

(Courtesy of Treasure Salvors Inc.)

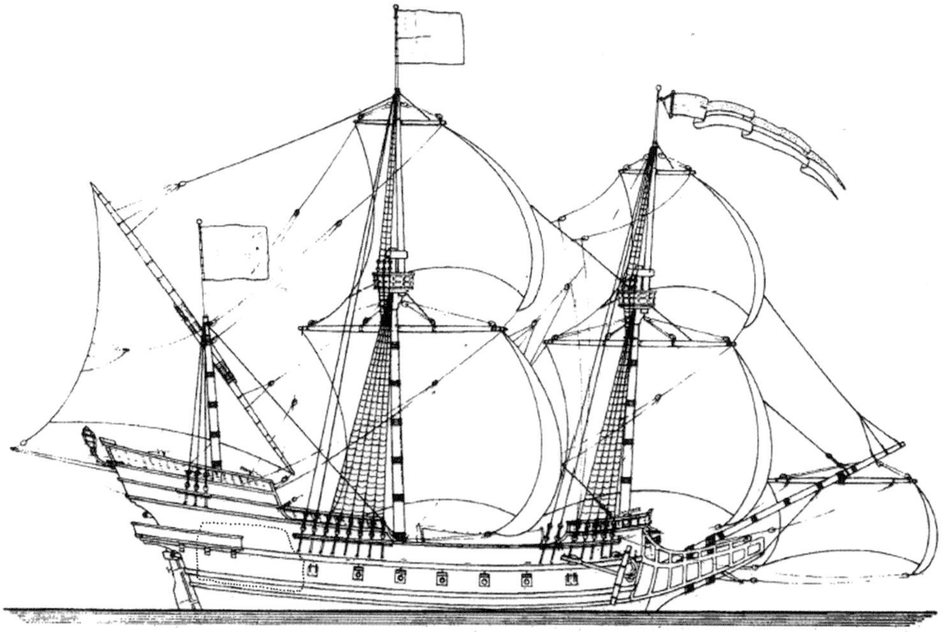

An architectural reconstruction of *Atocha* compiled by ship historian Bill Muir was based on documentary evidence from the construction contract and archaeological measurements and descriptions of the ship's timbers recorded on the seabed. The dotted section on the stern castle represents the location of the timber structure found on the *Margarita* site.

(Courtesy of Bill Muir)

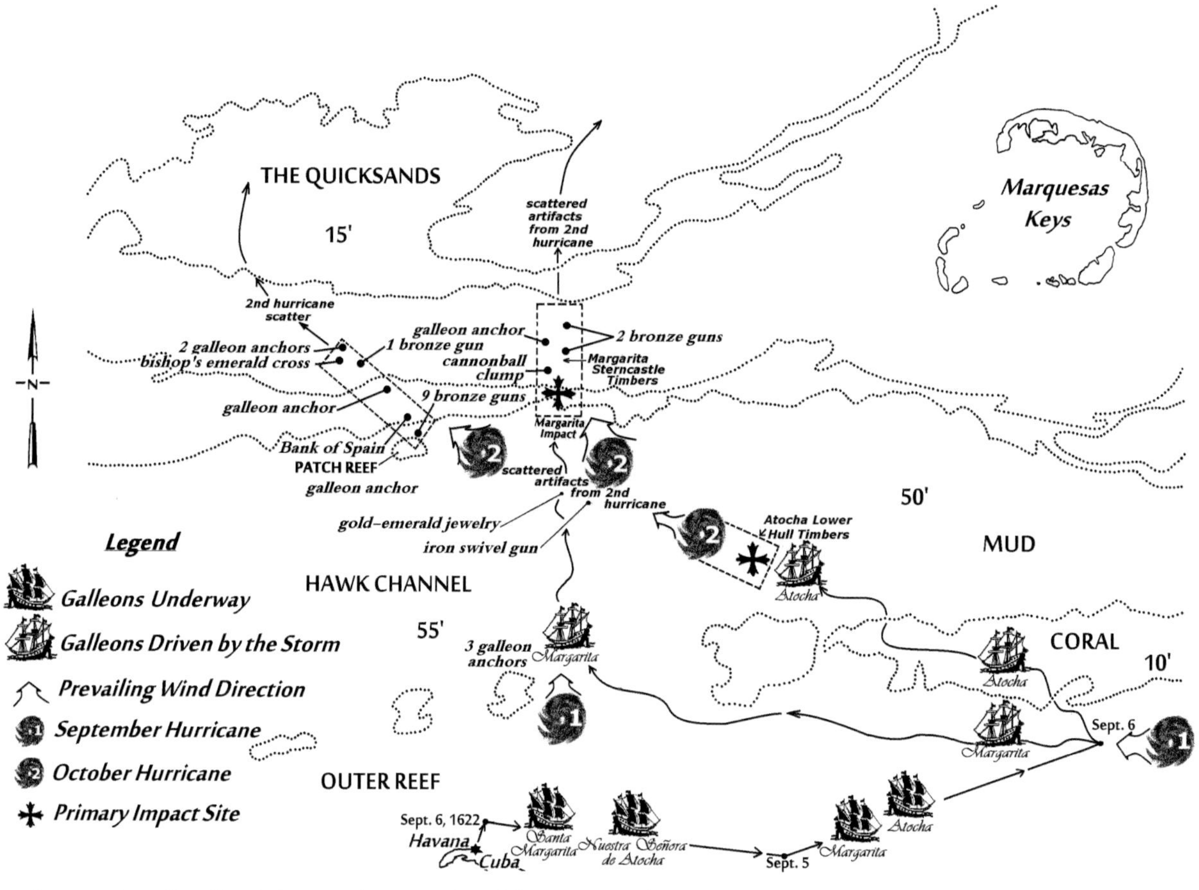

Schematic map depicting the sinking and progressive disintegration of *Atocha* and *Margarita* on the Florida reef tract. Note how *Atocha*'s upper hull structure was carried by storm action in the second hurricane toward the northwest, crossing the artifact scatter pattern associated with *Margarita*'s gradual demise during the first hurricane.

(Drawing by D. Larissa Dillin and the author)

that the shipwrights had made shortcuts in framing the lower hull, which probably contributed to the way *Atocha* sank and disintegrated on the seabed.

As soon as we found the lower hull deposit, I realized we needed a full professional effort to record the remains. I assembled an eight-member team of consultants who worked with the salvage divers and our own archaeological assistants to map and record the hull and all types of associated artifacts. As with any mapping effort, we encountered and overcame a variety of challenges, from creating a suitable grid frame in the prevailing current to keeping track of each diver's bottom time to avoid decompression problems.

Mapping the lower hull deposits presented a number of difficulties. The first mapping frame we laid over the site was a 30 feet by 20 feet PVC grid which did not work well at all. It was too cumbersome to assemble on the bottom and too difficult to secure on the seabed to provide a steady frame for mapping the deposits in the prevailing current. Eventually, we established a baseline extending 150 feet along the middle of the site with datums and buoys every 10 feet. We used measuring tapes along the baseline to triangulate artifact locations and the sizes and orientation of each timber.

We used airlifts and water dredges to uncover artifacts, and we excavated stratigraphic units to expose the lower orlop deck deposits and rock ballast in the bilge. We learned that *Atocha* was framed with mahogany timbers rather than oak as were used on *Margarita*.

The cultural legacy of *Atocha* and *Margarita* was always far more important to me than the monetary value of the treasure. I was pleased that part of the artifact assemblage was kept intact

The 1622 ceramic assemblage displayed in the MFMHS Museum is one of the largest collections of early Spanish colonial pottery in the Americas. Many pots provide specific archaeological dates for ceramic design and decoration often not available elsewhere from land sites.

(Photo courtesy of Corey Malcom and the MFMHS Museum)

and exhibited at the Mel Fisher Maritime Heritage Society (MFMHS) in Key West, a nonprofit museum and conservation laboratory created in 1982 to preserve and exhibit the 1622 collection. In addition to dissemination of our research findings, the museum encouraged owners of 1622 artifacts to donate unique objects to museums, thus transferring items from this assemblage from private collections into the public domain.

Research on the 1622 fleet went a long way toward developing method and theory in historic shipwreck archaeology. My archaeological study of the 1622 fleet was based on knowledge acquired from artifact scatter patterns on 1715 wreck sites and the successful linking of historical and archaeological evidence that enabled identification of the 1733 wreck sites. Tracking *Atocha*'s trail of wreckage along the seabed for more than 10 miles was based on the tenet that the contextual positions of artifacts on the site were as important as the objects themselves for the wreck's interpretation. Archaeological mapping was crucial to understand the wrecking process and to formulate working hypotheses and predictive models for locating *Atocha*'s lower hull deposits. By focusing on the integration of onboard activity areas as reflected by different artifact assemblages, I was able to determine the types of artifacts that would be associated with different parts of the ship. Priceless cultural assemblages from the 1622 shipwrecks have provided new insights into the *Carrera de Indias* and early seventeenth-century Spanish maritime culture, as described in numerous publications, professional papers, and websites.

Dr. R. Duncan Mathewson III is a renowned marine archaeologist who was instrumental in identifying and mapping Spanish shipwrecks from the 1622, 1715, and 1733 fleets. He is the author of *Treasure of the* Atocha: *A Four Hundred Million Dollar Archaeological Adventure* (Pisces Books, 1986), and a marine science and archaeology middle school module titled *If Shipwrecks Could Talk* (Delta Education, 1995), a publication based on his Ph.D. dissertation at the Union Institute and University. He would like to acknowledge the assistance of his wife, Arlene, for helping with the manuscript, Larissa Dillin for her expert illustrative skills, and all those who helped to locate, map, and record the 1622 archaeological treasure.

For Additional Information

Publications

Joshua Goodman, "Shipwreck of the *Atocha*," *Florida Memory Blog* (Florida State Archives), September 26, 2014, http://www.floridamemory.com/blog/2014/09/26/shipwreck-of-the-atocha/

Michael Imig, "The Spanish Galleons," Isle of Standauffish Renaissance Guild, 1995, http://www.landoflegendslv.com/01library/05research/02top/20ship/SpanishGalleons/Galleons01.html

"The Spanish Treasure Fleets of 1715 and 1733: Disasters Strike at Sea," National Park Service, Teaching with Historic Places Lesson Plans, https://www.nps.gov/nr/twhp/wwwlps/lessons/129shipwrecks/

Kyle Teal, "Duncan Mathewson: Archaeologist Has Spent Career with Shipwrecks, Salvors," *Florida Keys News,* July 11, 2008, http://www.flkeysnews.com/living/article79608527.html

Websites

The 1733 Spanish Galleon Trail, Florida Department of State, Division of Historical Resources, http://info.flheritage.com/galleon-trail/

McLarty Treasure Museum at Sebastian Inlet State Park, http://atochatreasures.com/mclarty.htm

Mel Fisher Maritime Museum, 1622 Fleet, http://www.melfisher.org/1622.htm

The *San Pedro*, Florida Keys National Marine Sanctuary Shipwreck Trail, http://floridakeys.noaa.gov/shipwrecktrail/sanpedro.html

San Pedro (shipwreck), U.S. National Park Service, https://www.nps.gov/nr/travel/flshipwrecks/ped.htm

San Pedro Underwater Archaeological Preserve, Florida's "Museums in the Sea," http://www.museumsinthesea.com/sanpedro/index.htm

Urca de Lima (shipwreck), U.S. National Park Service, https://www.nps.gov//nr/travel/flshipwrecks/urc.htm

Urca de Lima Underwater Archaeological Preserve, Florida's "Museums in the Sea," http://museumsinthesea.com/urcadelima/index.htm. Multimedia site.

Videos

"The Search for the Atocha," A&E Television, 1998, https://www.youtube.com/watch?v=RRwVHTuED2E

"The Sinking of the Galleon Atocha, 1622, The Model," Mel Fisher Maritime Museum, 2010, https://www.youtube.com/watch?v=UarOFggLqMg

CHAPTER 8

Anatomy of a Slave Ship: *Henrietta Marie*

David D. Moore and Corey Malcom

During the summer of 1972, a shipwreck was discovered on New Ground Reef, approximately 14 miles west-northwest of the Marquesas Keys. Melvin Fisher's company, Treasure Salvors Inc., had been searching for the legendary Spanish galleon *Nuestra Señora de Atocha*, which wrecked during a hurricane in 1622. But the recovery of an assortment of artifacts seemingly associated with the transatlantic slave trade—including shackles, trade beads, and ivory elephant tusks—made it likely that the wreck represented the remains of a slave ship. Additionally, the recovery of numerous examples of English-marked pewterware strongly suggested an origin somewhere in England.

The site was only investigated for a few days due to the lack of a proper permit from the State of Florida, but the company came back in 1973 with an appropriate permit and continued its investigation for another 14 days. During this time, cannons, anchors, hull structure, and numerous associated artifacts were located and examined, and many items were recovered. However, after this initial investigation, the site remained undisturbed for a decade while the company focused its continuing efforts on locating the final resting place of the treasure galleon *Atocha*.

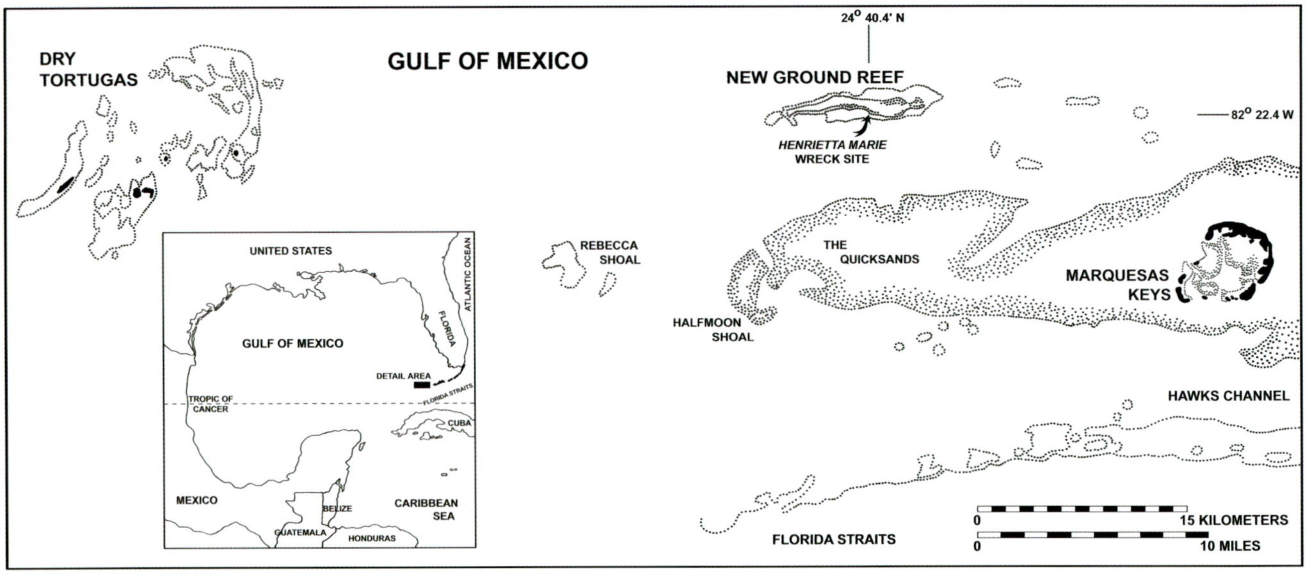

Location of *Henrietta Marie* wreck site on New Ground Reef, Florida. *(Drawing by David D. Moore)*

Henrietta Marie: In the Beginning (David Moore)

In 1983, private researcher Henry Taylor, who had an interest in the pewterware found at the site, subcontracted with Fisher to reopen the investigation of the slave ship's remains. I was hired in June 1983 to work with Taylor and provide archaeological oversight on the effort. After working in the often-murky coastal waters of North Carolina the previous few years, I welcomed the opportunity to dive among coral reefs and tropical fish as a change in scenery.

Initially, the site proved difficult to relocate. After we spent two fruitless days of visual searching at the long-range navigation (LORAN) coordinates recorded 10 years before, Don Kincaid was asked to come out with us to help find the wreck. Kincaid, who had worked with the Fisher organization for years as a diver, photographer, and board member, had been one of the captains on the site when it was first located in 1972–1973, and he knew the area well. Not surprisingly, he was able to locate and buoy the coral-encrusted iron box and nearby iron cannons in about 15 minutes. This would not be the last time that Kincaid's experience and memory of the slave shipwreck would prove extremely useful to archaeologists.

Our 1983 dive team operated from Henry Taylor's 28-foot boat, *Trident*, set up with a small compressor for filling tanks and operating air lifts and a pump for dredging. Although designed primarily for day trips, taking the boat 35 miles out to New Ground Reef from Key West and staying for three to five days at a time strained the small vessel's capability at times. This was particularly true if any type of adverse weather appeared, which happened on several occasions, making for rather uncomfortable and wet living conditions.

We spent the next 25 days examining the site and studying its features. Using surface-supplied air greatly increased our time on the bottom. The northern-most cannon was established as a permanent datum, and the areas to the south, east, and west then were surveyed both visually and using handheld metal detectors. Although we mapped and recovered a substantial number

Bronze ship's watch bell bearing the embossed inscription THE HENRIETTA MARIE 1699.

(Photo by Dylan Kibler, courtesy of the Mel Fisher Maritime Heritage Society [MFMHS])

of artifacts, most were surface-scattered material that had escaped detection during the 1972–1973 operations. However, during this period the wreck's most significant artifact was discovered. The ship's bronze watch bell was recovered on July 7, which had both the name and the date embossed around its waist: "THE HENRIETTA MARIE 1699." This one discovery allowed us to focus immediately on a specific ship in the historical shipping records.

Locating and recovering the ship's bell indeed was fortuitous, but the way in which it was removed allowed me to make a strong point with our divers. We previously had established a north-south baseline on the site to enable us to record artifact locations; however, the bell was brought aboard the boat quite rapidly, without any attention to these formalities. I quickly made it clear that the bell would be the last artifact to be recovered in that fashion. Fortunately, the impression that the bell had left in the bottom sediments remained, and its provenience was easily and quickly recorded. The fact that the bell location rested less than 20 feet from the baseline and was clearly within its sight in visibility that usually exceeded 50 feet made my point much easier to make.

As the 1983 field season came to a close, we found numerous disarticulated structural components, primarily planking and frames. However, one wooden artifact stood out among the rest: an intact upper section of one of the ship's bilge pump tubes.

Taylor elected not to return to the site in 1984, so on-site investigations were continued by another subcontractor, Anton Kopp. We began operations in October in the south sector of the site where loose structural components and the bilge pump fragment previously had been located. The position of the south cannon was established as an additional datum, and the coherent hull structure, last examined in 1972–1973, was relocated. We surveyed and excavated the area around the south cannon using air lifts and induction dredges. In addition to mapping and recovering artifacts, the intact hull structure was re-excavated, examined, photographed, and recorded.

We spent 37 days on the site with dive operations that continued into March 1985. As in 1983, surface-supplied air helped to maximize our bottom time, with most divers spending from six to eight hours a day underwater. After the cramped conditions on Taylor's boat the year before, Kopp's vessel, a 90-foot, two-masted topsail schooner named *Illusion*, was the lap of luxury. The year before, we had dreaded the all-too-common midnight rain squall blowing across New Ground, when all we could do was to hunker down under

Author David Moore signaling his arrival on the surface to the ship's mascots. *(Photo by Kimberly Monk)*

whatever foul-weather gear we had. On *Illusion*, we had our own personal cabin and a comfortable bunk. In addition to Kopp's four-year-old daughter, who had the run of the vessel, we always were met at the top of the dive ladder by one or both of his overly friendly Dobermans, who always seemed quite interested in what we brought up from the depths or what we had recorded on our slate.

Historical Research on *Henrietta Marie*

Discovery of the ship's bell with the name *Henrietta Marie* and the 1699 date indicated that the shipwreck was an English slave ship. Archival research provided substantial information about the ship and her operators, and revealed that she was an independent English slaver, or "separate trader," operating against the long-held monopoly reserved by the Royal African Company. After the company lost its monopoly by Act of Parliament in 1698, the ship's trading operations became legal when her owners paid a 10 percent duty to the company on the goods used to acquire enslaved Africans on the West African coast.

Henrietta Marie appeared in numerous documents, all of which told us a more complete story of the ship's operations. The vessel was listed in the Barbados and Jamaica Shipping Returns, revealing at least two voyages through both Caribbean islands, respectively, in 1698 and 1700. Treasury records provided names of men placing trade goods aboard the ship destined for Africa in 1699, and these undoubtedly represent at least some of the vessel's owners. Probate records containing the last will and testaments of at least eight people associated with ship operations (owners, captains, and seamen) offer interesting insights into the social connections associated with a typical slave ship. Moreover, almost every document located during our research gave us dates that further reflected the vessel's operational profile.

Unfortunately, despite continued historical research over the past few decades, one of the only things that has yet to be identified is the ship's origin. We suspect that *Henrietta Marie* originally was French because the various shipping records in which she is listed mention that the vessel was "foreign-built." The English captured approximately 1,300 prizes during King William's War (known in Europe as the War of the League of Augsburg, 1689–1697), which ended the same year that *Henrietta Marie* first appeared to be sailing as an English slave ship. The ship possibly was named for the French queen of the English king Charles I and would have been an appropriate name for either a French or an English vessel. However, she also could have been christened after a similarly named wife or daughter of one of the ship's owners. Research continues on the origin of *Henrietta Marie*.

Material Culture Recovered from *Henrietta Marie*

Although the recovered artifact assemblage is not very large—less than 3,000 objects, not counting thousands of trade beads—many of the artifacts are unique, and they provide a detailed glimpse of the cargo and functions of a typical, small West Indian merchant ship transporting enslaved Africans to the Caribbean from the west coast of Africa. The assemblage essentially can be divided into two categories. The first are cargo items transported to Africa to trade for enslaved Africans and sometimes pepper, ivory, and gold dust. The second category includes the ship-related artifacts such as gear and equipment, and objects related to the actual fabric of the ship itself.

Ship's Cargo

Elephant Tusks

The trade in ivory elephant "teeth" or tusks was closely related to the trade in enslaved Africans due to their local availability. On her first triangular voyage, *Henrietta Marie* brought ivory back to London that was sold to merchant Christopher Astley in 1699. The master of the slave ship *Dispatch*, Captain William Barry, received instructions from the vessel's owners in 1725 to purchase "240 Choice slaves, besides a Quan'y of teeth the latter of which are always to embrace provided they are large, seeing in that Commodity there's no Mortality to be feard." More contemporary with *Henrietta Marie*, the owners of the slave ship *Blessing* of Liverpool directed her captain

Author Malcom recovering one the six elephant tusks found on the slave ship. (Photo by Dylan Kibler)

in August 1700 to "dispose of all y^r^ cargo [at Whydah] slave y^r^ ship to her full Reach if you can and if any remainder be left lay it out in Teeth and [gold] Dust as ye have opportunity."

We recovered six intact elephant tusks from *Henrietta Marie*. Most were found in the central portion of the site, along the southern face of New Ground Reef, with some still resting exposed on the seabed after 300 years. The tusks have maintained their general shape and are quite recognizable, but their surfaces are pitted and discolored from long underwater immersion.

Glass Trade Beads

Historical documents indicate that merchants Thomas Starke and Daniel Jamineau placed 2,074 pounds of beads aboard *Henrietta Marie* prior to her last voyage in 1699. Although more than 13,000 beads have been recovered and processed to date, this amounts to far less than a single pound. The vast majority of those recovered are

Selection of glass trade beads: (lower) including both "seed" beads and gooseberry types. Middle: Several seeds still strung on original iron wire. Upper: A typical mass of bead-laden concretion. *(Photo by David D. Moore)*

nondiagnostic "seed" types, although a few larger striped varieties known as "gooseberries" also were found in addition to a few tube types.

The "seeds" appear in at least 10 colors, two of which appear to have significant historical implications. The journal of James Barbot, supercargo aboard *Albion Frigate* in 1699, stated, "The Blacks objected much against our . . . green beads, . . . yellow beads, and some other merchandize, as of little or no demand there at the time." Among the beads recovered from *Henrietta Marie* more than 85 percent comprised these two colors, suggesting that she encountered the same discriminating tastes and consequent trading difficulties as did *Albion Frigate* several months earlier.

We do not know exactly where *Henrietta Marie* traded on the African coast, but the fact that both of these ships were separate traders from London suggests that *Henrietta Marie* visited the same location as *Albion*—the Calabar area in present-day Nigeria, a common destination for many of the non-Royal African Company slave ships. It probably was not a coincidence that both Daniel Jamineau and James Barbot were involved with placing cargo aboard both ships.

Pewter

Pewterware was one of the many commodities popular on the West African coast for the trade in slaves. Numerous manifests, accounts, and logs of slave ships mention pewter "basons," tankards, spoons, and plates. Examples of all these were found on *Henrietta Marie*. More than 300 examples of pewter have been identified, most bearing touchmarks (maker's marks) of artisans manufacturing their wares in London between 1660 and 1710. Six types of pewterware are represented in

Examples from the *Henrietta Marie* pewter assemblage (left to right): large flagon with threaded lid, bottle, four-pound bowl (back), two "portrait" spoons (front), two-quart tankard, and plate (note the knife cuts on surface). *(Photo by David D. Moore)*

our recovered assemblage, including large bowls or "Guinea basons," tankards, spoons, plates, bottles, and a large flagon or jug.

Large bowls possibly were the most popular pewter objects traded in Africa. Thomas Phillips, captain of the slave ship *Hannibal* in 1693, stated that "the goods they most covet are pewter basons, the larger the better." The bowls were manufactured in sizes of one, two, three, and four pounds although only three- and four-pound versions have been recovered from the wreck site. Many of these bowls remain in excellent condition, and the marks of three London pewterers have been identified—Joseph Hodges, Thomas Winchcombe, and George Hammond—all stamped on the bottom of the rims.

The recovered tankards represent typical styles of the period, with squat tapering bodies and flat type lids. The cargo manifests indicate that sizes of one, two, three, and four pints were traded as well, although only two-pint (one quart) and four-pint (two quart) sizes were recovered. Only one maker's mark has been revealed among the tankards, that of London artisan William Eddon.

Numerous pewter spoons have been recovered, including 72 found inside a crushed pewter flagon. Known as "Royal Portrait" spoons for the bust of King William III positioned at the top of the tri-lobed handles, the well-decorated spoons also bear the initials "SB" within a small, spoked wheel, which was the stamp of London craftsman Stephen Bridges.

One of the more interesting and significant artifact types is the approximately 20 pewter bottles with a little more than a one-quart capacity. Their significance lies in their rarity, and the number recovered strongly suggests the bottles were cargo items. Several examples are marked with the touch of John Emes Jr. Although apparently rare in the world of pewter research, they in fact may be the "Guinea Juggs w'th Corks" mentioned in the manifest of the slave ship *King Solomon* in 1720.

As noted previously, 72 of the recovered portrait spoons were found inside a large crushed jug or flagon that was configured to receive a threaded lid. Unfortunately, the two-gallon jug bore no discernible maker's mark, but it did have decorative design features similar to the pewter bottles. Although they were not specifically listed on cargo lists examined to date, Thomas Phillips, captain of the slave ship *Hannibal*, noted in his journal that the "goods [the Africans] most covet are . . . large screw'd pewter jugs, which they did much affect." This reference suggests a container very similar to that recovered from *Henrietta Marie*.

Only two pewter plates have been recovered, and both 9¼-inch-diameter units are in excellent condition and bear several maker's marks. The primary touchmark belonged to Joseph Hodges, whose same mark is seen on some of the bowls. The secondary marks are similar in configuration and reveal the place of origin was London. However, perhaps the most interesting marks are the initials "HM" stamped on both plates, suggesting the name of the ship, *Henrietta Marie*. Although pewter plates were traded in bulk on the West African coast, these two items undoubtedly served the crew, and the numerous knife scars indicate a substantial usage.

Voyage Iron

Iron bar stock, sometimes known as "voyage iron," was another popular trade good on the African coast. Twenty-eight examples, averaging 2.2 pounds in weight, 13.5 inches long, almost two inches wide, and 0.5 inches thick, were recovered from the site. Similar bars were traded by the thousands and even by the ton on the West African coast. On her last known voyage, *Henrietta Marie* shipped at least 33 tons of iron for merchant Anthony Tourney, an iron monger and probable part-owner of the ship.

Ship-Related Furniture and Equipment

In addition to many cargo items, numerous artifacts associated with ship-related furniture and equipment were recovered. Many of these artifacts have provided additional insight into the day-to-day operations of the ship and in some cases revealed the actual structural dimensions of particular areas of the vessel.

Copper Cauldrons

The remains of two copper cauldrons were recovered from the site in 1973. Although the smaller of the two was in poor condition when found, enough remained to enable a graphic reconstruction illustrating its original size and shape. The container is constructed of punch-riveted sheets of copper and features two separate chambers, one of seven gallons, the other holding 9½ gallons. Both chamber openings have coamings to allow fitted lids to cover each, although no such lids have been identified at the site to date. The larger of the two cauldrons is single-chambered, has an 85-gallon capacity, and undoubtedly was designed to cook meals for a much larger enslaved African cargo. A large mass of concreted chain found within the interior was probably meant to suspend the cauldron over a heat source.

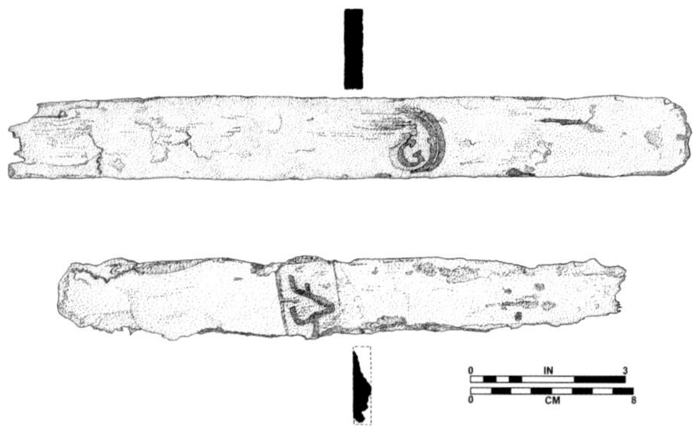

Bars of "voyage iron" bearing unidentified manufacturer's or shipping marks. *(Drawing by David D. Moore)*

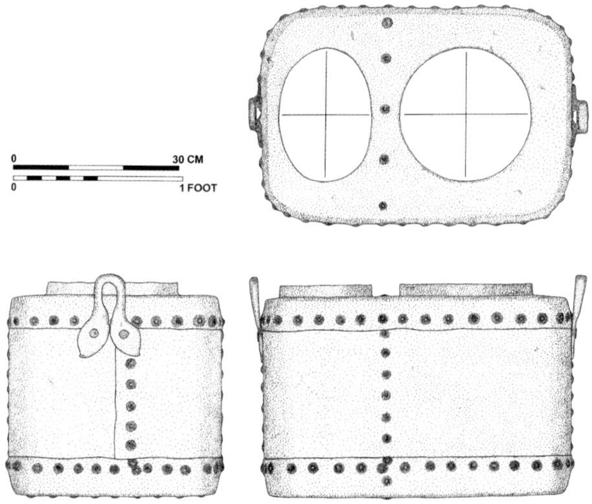

Reconstructed view of a two-chambered copper cauldron used to prepare meals for a limited number of crew. *(Drawing by David D. Moore)*

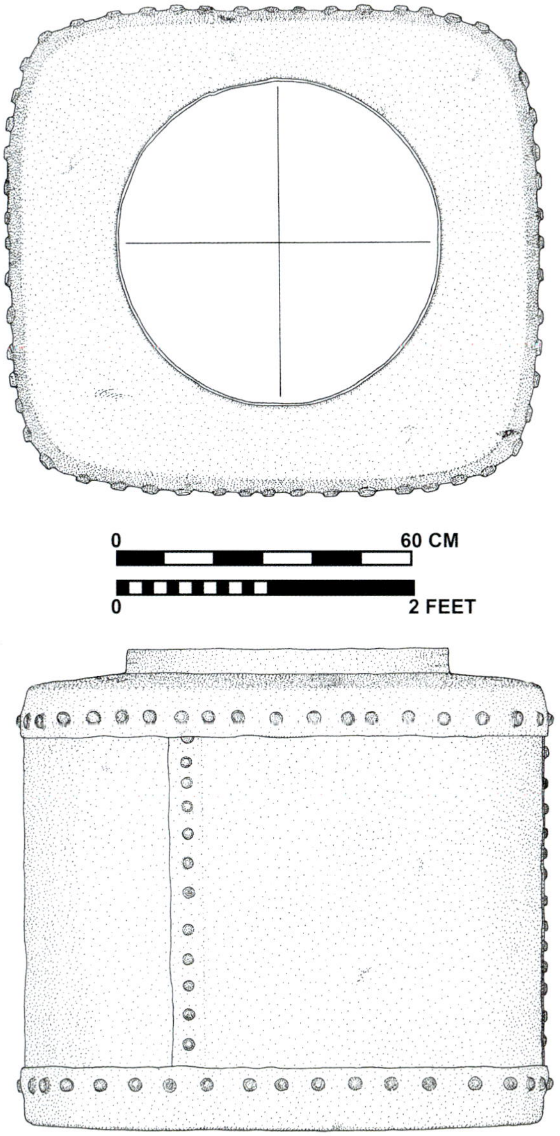

Large copper cauldron designed to prepare and hold a large volume of food for a substantial number of people, probably an enslaved African cargo. *(Drawing by David D. Moore)*

Cannons

Historical records reveal that *Henrietta Marie* was armed with eight cannons. We found only two on the site, both of which were recovered for research and exhibit purposes. They were found to be minions, or four-pounders, weighing 780 and 776 pounds, respectively, according to the typically English weight marks incised into the top of each gun tube. The cannon balls recovered from the wreck site came in both three- and four-pound sizes, suggesting the size of the original guns carried aboard the ship.

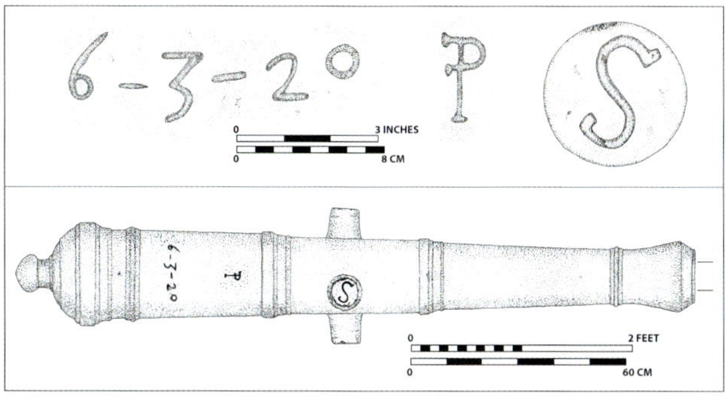

One of two four-pounder cannons (minion) recovered from the *Henrietta Marie* site bearing typical English weight marks. *(Drawing by David D. Moore)*

Bilge Pump

One of the more significant artifacts we recovered was the bilge pump, arguably the single most important piece of equipment aboard any ship. When I first noticed it on the bottom in 1983, lying among a number of disarticulated planks and frames, it appeared to be just another of the ship's structural components. However, on closer inspection it became apparent that the five-foot section of timber had been bored out and had a three-inch diameter hole drilled in one side about two feet below the iron bracket around the intact end of the tube. After a few minutes studying this component, it finally dawned on me that the small hole was a discharge port where the water from the pump tube emptied out onto the vessel's deck during pumping operations. There also was an encrusted bracket mounted around the upper end that still held remnants of the pump brake (handle) support. Additionally, there was a block-style "M" carved into one side of the tube near the broken end. Also visible at this end is the lower terminus of a metal sleeve fitted within the bore,

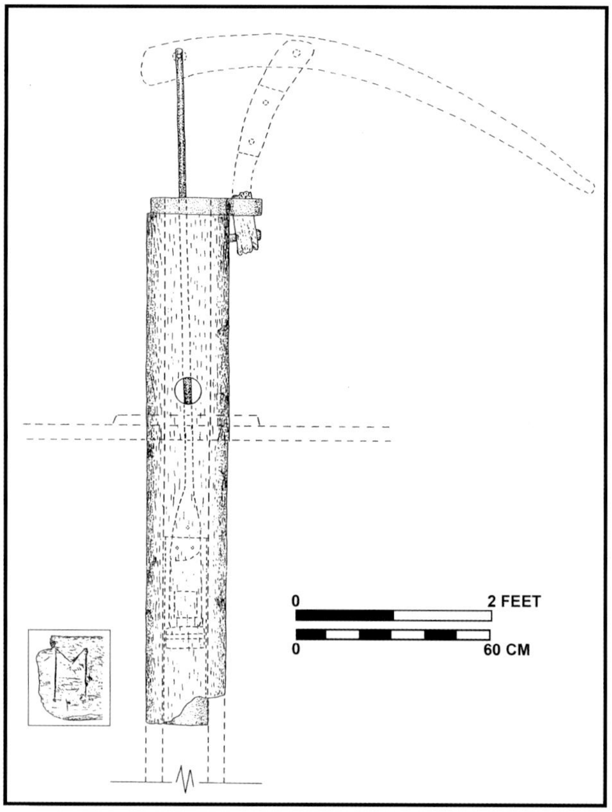

Reconstructed schematic of an upper bilge pump tube recovered from *Henrietta Marie*. Note the block "M" carved into one side and the metal friction sleeve; also the pump spear connecting the pump break (handle) and bucket valve that was recovered from another part of the site.

(Drawing by David D. Moore)

undoubtedly designed to prevent friction wear from the pump bucket valve.

"Pissdale" Tube

Known from examples from several other late-seventeenth-century and early-eighteenth-century shipwrecks, a large, conical lead tube almost three feet long was recovered from *Henrietta Marie* and identified as a "pissdale" or toilet tube, which allowed human waste to empty from an inboard location directly outboard into the sea. The identification of the ship's intact lower stern section in this area of the site suggests that the artifact was associated with the captain's cabin.

Lead Scupper Liners

More than a half-dozen heavy, lead tubes have been recovered and identified as scupper liners. The shorter examples had larger diameters and probably were located along the main deck to allow breaking waves or water brought up from the hold by the bilge pumps or to drain overboard. The length between the outer and inner flanges provides evidence for the thickness of the side of the ship near the main deck. The longer examples had smaller diameters and probably were designed to pierce locations through an upper wale. The difference in the diameter of the respective tubes indicates a position or location at different deck levels; the larger diameter was designed to drain more water accumulated on a lower deck. The smaller diameter scuppers would have been positioned at a higher forecastle deck, quarter deck, or half deck location, where there would have been a smaller volume of water to drain.

Rigging

Numerous examples of different types of rigging components have been recovered from the site, both running and standing rigging. These include deadeyes and chain assemblies, a shroud truck, deck cleats, forelocked ringbolts, hooks and hook thimbles, blocks and sheaves, and several different sizes of cordage, including shroud and lanyard fragments.

Ship's Hull Structure

The most significant artifact that we observed and recorded on *Henrietta Marie* unfortunately continues to lie some 34 miles west of Key West on New Ground Reef. The large and relatively intact

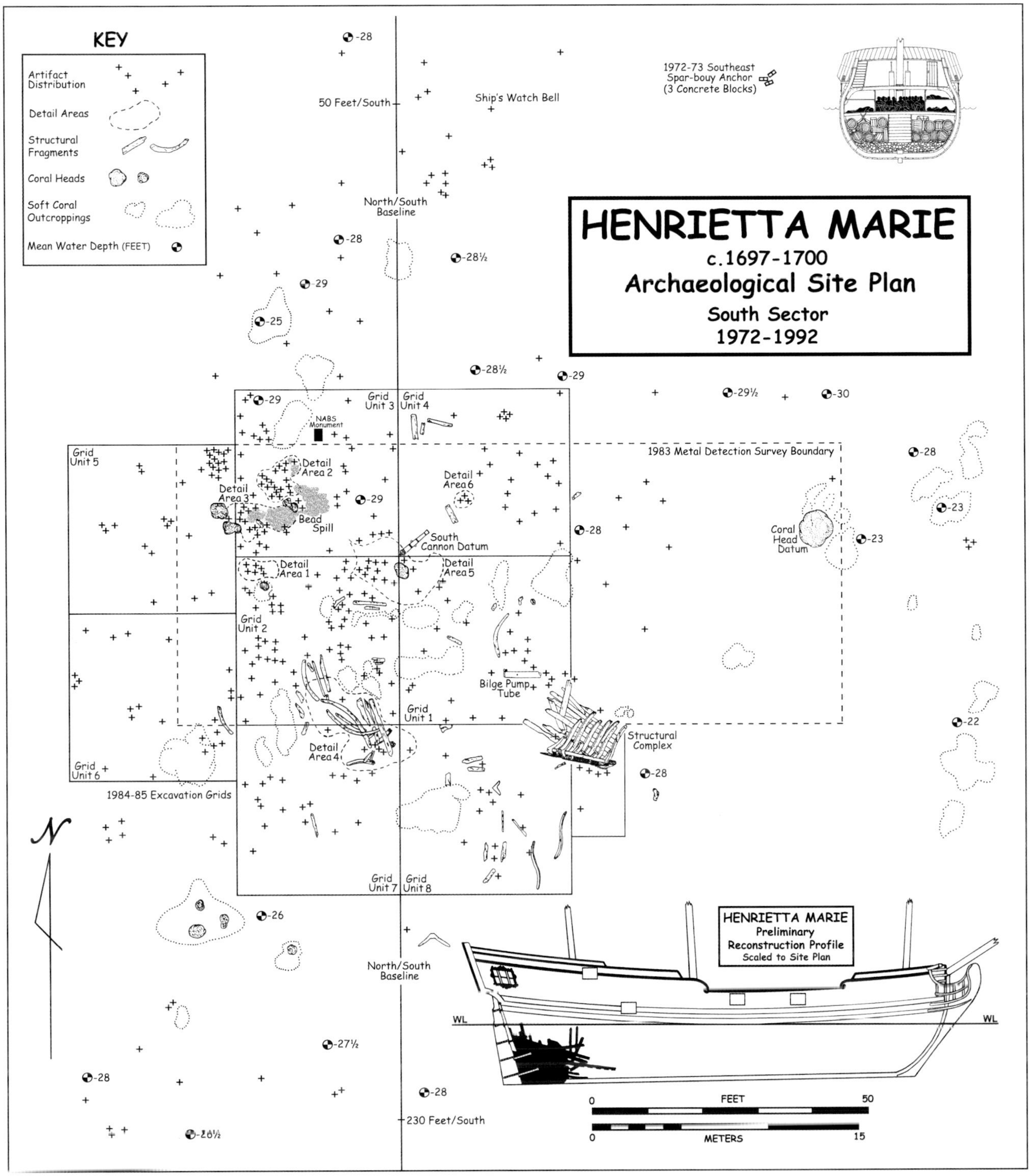

Henrietta Marie site plan, south sector. Hypothetical reconstruction profile (lower right) and cross section (upper right) of the ship are rendered at the same scale as the site plan for perspective. The darkened area illustrated on the stern of the profile illustrates the limited amount of hull structure from the original ship identified and recorded to date. *(Drawing by David D. Moore)*

Slave Shackles

The artifacts most indicative of *Henrietta Marie*'s function as a slave ship are the many sets of shackles recovered from the site. Loop and bolt components representing about 80 sets of manacles of varying sizes have been recovered.

Instructions to the captains of slave-trading vessels verify the importance of using such restraints, as attested by a 1725 letter to Captain William Barry from the owners of the slaver *Dispatch:*

> So soon as you begin to slave let your knetting [netting] be fix'd breast high fore and aft and so keep 'em shackled and hand Bolted fearing their rising or leaping Overboard, to prevent which let always a Constant and Carefull watch be appointed to which must give the strictest Charge for the preservation of their Own Lives, so well as yours and on which the Voyage depends, which per sleeping in their Watch has often been fatall and many a good Voyage (which otherwise might been made) entirely ruind.

In a historical account more contemporary with *Henrietta Marie*, Captain Thomas Phillips of the Royal African Company slave ship *Hannibal* wrote during a voyage in 1693–1694 that, once the enslaved Africans had been transferred from land to shipboard, "the men were all put in irons, two and two shackled together, to prevent their mutiny, or swimming ashore." Captain Phillips's great concern over the potential trouble certainly was conveyed in the following statement:

> When our slaves are aboard we shackle the men two and two, while we lie in port, and in sight of their own country, for 'tis then they attempt to make their escape, and mutiny; to prevent which we always keep centinels upon the hatchways, and have a chest full of small arms, ready loaden and prim'd, constantly lying at hand upon the quarter-deck guns.

The shackles were located throughout the wreck site, singular components as well as in several large conglomerates, suggesting a common storage arrangement aboard the ship. During preparation for electrolytic treatment, a shackle loop was found to be wrapped with small cord, possibly to prevent the chafing of ankles or wrists.

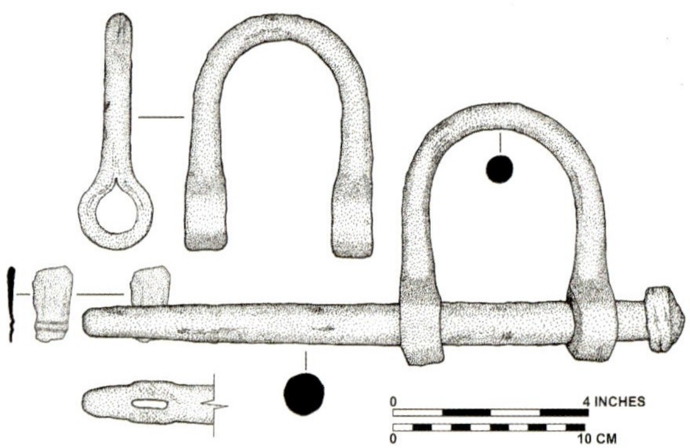

One of the better examples of a full set of shackles recovered from *Henrietta Marie*. *(Drawing by David D. Moore)*

Wrapped shackle loop recovered from *Henrietta Marie*. *(Photo by Dylan Kibler)*

lower stern of the ship has been measured, photographed, and documented with video, but it is simply too large and problematic to recover at this time. However, study of the structure continues to provide us with insight into ship construction and naval architectural practices during the late seventeenth century.

Henrietta Marie: The Next Chapter (Corey Malcom)

In 1987, Mel Fisher and the directors of Treasure Salvors Inc. decided to dissolve the corporation and sell the rights to the *Atocha* and *Santa Margarita* shipwreck sites to another group. As part of this transaction, all the artifacts in the Treasure Salvors' collection, including those from *Henrietta Marie*, were transferred to the permanent collection of the not-for-profit Mel Fisher Maritime Heritage Society (MFMHS). Ultimately, the purchasers of the shipwrecks defaulted, and the galleon sites reverted back to Treasure Salvors Inc. However, the artifacts remained with the MFMHS.

With this transfer of materials, a multi-year campaign of conservation of many of the uncleaned *Henrietta Marie* pieces began. This treatment was needed because artifacts that have been underwater for prolonged periods of time have undergone profound physical and chemical changes. It takes time and energy to undo the effects and to stabilize the materials, but conservation is essential so the objects can be exposed to the air again. In the case of *Henrietta Marie*, this meant stabilizing iron, pewter, glass, lead, and bronze pieces, with each type of material requiring its own treatment.

Iron artifacts can be especially challenging to clean because they are encased in a thick marine concretion of calcium carbonate and sand mixed with rust from the artifact. This concretion masks the artifact underneath, and details such as markings or even the condition of the piece are hidden until it is removed. Small chisels are used to carefully chip away at the concretion, slowly exposing the remains of the artifact. A number of surprises were uncovered in the laboratory—for example, the shockingly small size of some of the shackles and the cryptic markings of ironmongers on iron bars sold to the ship's trading partners. One shackle loop was bound with twine, perhaps as an anti-chafing measure to help protect the valuable human cargo against damage, and this required much patience and a steady hand to separate the hard concretion from the delicate organic wrapping.

Once the artifacts were freed from their centuries-old covering, they still required more treatment. Metals are especially unstable and highly susceptible to further corrosion because they have become permeated with salts during their time in the sea. For iron objects, this required an electrochemical process called "electrolytic reduction" or "reverse electrolysis" to force the

Conservator Monica Brook carefully deconcretes the iron components of a lifting jack from *Henrietta Marie* in the MFMHS laboratory. *(Photo by Corey Malcom/MFMHS)*

salts out of the metal. This process is quite slow, and iron objects can require as much as a year of treatment. Other metals such as pewter, bronze, and lead are more resistant to the effects of salt and corrosion and can be treated more quickly. Ceramics and glass also need to be treated by soaking in baths of fresh water to leach out the salts. If the salts are not removed, they will crystalize when they dry and damage the pieces by cracking them or spalling their surfaces. All in all, the conservation laboratory work for a shipwreck project requires much patience and many years of effort to stabilize the recovered materials.

In 1991, a new executive director of the Mel Fisher Maritime Heritage Society came on board, and she saw immediately that there was a tremendous and powerful story with *Henrietta Marie*. Artifacts coming out of the laboratory would make a terrific exhibit and would help people understand an aspect of history that had not really been put before the public in such a tangible way. We all agreed, so while the conservation moved forward, planning began for a large-scale *Henrietta Marie* exhibit.

Although years of fieldwork had yielded a sizable and varied collection of artifacts, two cannons had never been recovered, and areas of New Ground Reef around the shipwreck had not been explored. In addition, despite diligent efforts, the project really had not generated the number of quality underwater photographs that would be needed to convey the nature of the *Henrietta Marie* site. In summer 1991, one of Mel Fisher's boats visited *Henrietta Marie* and reported that the cannons were still there and accessible. Based on the needs of the planned exhibit, we decided to organize an expedition to recover the cannons and expand the understanding of the shipwreck.

In September, MFMHS began its first underwater field project at the site. A photographer came along to document the day-to-day activities. A 42-foot Keys lobster fishing boat named *Tropical Magic* was chartered to serve as a work platform for a week. She was a tough work boat with virtually no creature comforts, but she provided a stable home away from home for five people on New Ground Reef.

With calm weather and clear water, we had an uneventful four-hour, 35-mile trip to the reef. *Tropical Magic* was equipped only with a relatively crude LORAN navigation system (satellite Global Positioning System was not yet publicly available), so as we approached the site, all eyes were on the water to look for telltale signs. Luckily, as we came up on the reef from the south, we passed directly over the large iron box that sat in about 10 feet of water at the northern end of the site. In the clear water, it was easy to see. Now all we needed to do was to anchor in a good spot and begin the project.

As the equipment was unpacked and organized, it quickly became apparent that we had made a big mistake—the earpieces for the metal detectors had been left at the museum. These pieces emitted a squealing buzz whenever the detector passed near metal, and they were the only way for a diver to know whether an artifact was hidden or buried nearby. Without them, searching would be ineffective. We radioed the office to try to arrange for a fast boat to bring the earpieces to us, and fortunately, this could be done.

We began the project by laying a baseline from the iron box to a point 100 feet due south. The current at New Ground can be quite strong, and this day was no exception. Laying a straight baseline was quite a challenge as the line shimmied and bowed in the ocean's flow. After much pulling, tightening, and checking of compasses, the line was set. Our initial task was to conduct visual

The iron cannon found in the northern part of the *Henrietta Marie* site. (Photo by Dylan Kibler/MFMHS)

search surveys along the line to see what wreckage was visible to the naked eye. The northern cannon was located on coral pedestals on the reef in about 12 feet of water. The position of the second cannon, in about 25 feet of water south of the reef, was mapped and marked. To spice up the underwater work a bit, late summer is high season for moon jellyfish in the Florida Keys, and hundreds of these pulsating creatures drifted with the currents throughout our workspace. It was a constant and ultimately futile challenge to dodge them, so we learned to accept mild stings.

The next day, the northern cannon was chipped free from the reef, the southern gun was uncovered from the sand, and the earpieces arrived from Key West. In addition, an abundance of glass beads was found buried just below the surface of the sand near the south cannon. These tiny "seed" beads are barely one millimeter in diameter; to collect them, we had to lie belly-down on the bottom, pinch them individually between the fingers, and collect them in plastic bags. Each diver staked out a territory, and worked intently at the task until the beads stopped appearing—some 7,000 beads later. As if that was not enough, right next to where the beads had been, a concentration of small lead scattershot appeared, so we applied the same tedious process to collect them. It was a bit like picking raisins out of a cake.

The next morning, we decided to make a small airlift, a suction device made from a PVC tube and a scuba tank, to vacuum away some of the remaining sand to see if we had missed any of the beads. While we were testing the device, one of the other divers swam over with a set of iron shackles that he had discovered nearby. Everyone felt a rush of excitement and a chill of reality. These iron devices were used to hold Africans two-by-two during the Atlantic crossing, and although finding artifacts such as this was exactly why we were there, the cruel core of *Henrietta Marie*'s mission was right in front of us. This spurred us on to continue westward, toward the location of the shackles, to look for other wreckage. We discovered two lead musket balls about 100 feet west of the central baseline, but they were the westernmost artifacts that we found.

Our next goal was to explore northward in the high reef, pushing beyond where wreck remains previously had been seen. This meant laying a series of 250-foot-long baselines that created six 25-foot-wide lanes. The high reef at New Ground is a remote and beautiful place, with many corals, sea fans, and fish. Our work was limited to metal detecting and hand fanning any "hits" that were not readily visible. The metal detector is a useful tool in a survey like this, especially when a wreck is widely scattered, because in this type of environment metal objects are the likeliest to have survived. In addition, because the reef generally has hard bottom with sand only in pockets, artifacts were not buried deeply and readily could be found within the two-foot penetration range of the detector. Within the clearly defined lanes, it was easy to search across the entire area thoroughly with little chance of anything being missed.

Author Corey Malcom (left) and Wayne Lusardi (right) with artifacts from *Henrietta Marie*, 1991.

(Photo by Dylan Kibler/MFMHS)

A *Henrietta Marie* cannon being hoisted on board *Tropical Magic*, 1991. From top to bottom: Wayne Lusardi, Jim Stowell, Corey Malcom, and Gunther Fojuth. *(Photo by Dylan Kibler/MFMHS)*

We found many interesting artifacts buried in sand pockets or wedged in crevices. Among these were pewter basins, still stacked as they had been stowed on board, and a small, circular lead weight, stamped with an English crown and official marks from the City of London. Scratched into the back side were the letters "WD," almost certainly the initials of William Deacon, captain of the ship's first voyage and an investor in its second and final venture. The geared cranking mechanism and lifting bar for a jack, a device to lift heavy loads onto the ship, was recovered. Many smaller items such as cargo hooks and iron spikes from the ship's hull also were found. A small elephant's tusk was buried near the iron box, and many hundreds of glass beads, especially a larger variety called "gooseberries," were scattered across one section of the reef, buried in pockets of sand. Our reef survey certainly pushed the boundaries of the *Henrietta Marie* site farther northward and westward, but it also defined its limits; we found no wreckage beyond our search areas.

After our explorations ended, it was time to recover the cannons. These guns were quite heavy, and were made even more so by the concretion around them. Nonetheless, the lifting process was straightforward. A diver rigged them with rope barrel-sling rigs, then surfaced to notify the onboard crew, who lifted them with a davit and winch system. The guns were heavier than *Tropical Magic*'s davit would have liked, and the system seemed as though it would buckle, but with plenty of straining and heaving, both guns were recovered safely. Now that they were exposed to the air, we wrapped them in towels and plastic sheets to keep them wet and retard any corrosive effects during transit back to shore.

Back in Key West, the museum staff were waiting at the dock to hear about what we had accomplished at the site. Even Mel Fisher was there to see what had come in from the wreck, a site he had not seen in nearly 20 years. Reporters from Key West and Miami newspapers also were there, and their stories spread the news about the latest work at this remarkable shipwreck site.

Among those who read the accounts were members of the National Association of Black Scuba Divers (NABS), a relatively new organization to promote diving and the underwater world within the African American community. The existence of a wrecked slave ship near the Florida Keys was a compelling idea for them, and they wanted to know more. The president of NABS called to invite us to make a presentation about *Henrietta Marie* at their premier annual meeting in Fort Lauderdale.

Their response was remarkable. Members of NABS were deeply moved by what they saw and heard about *Henrietta Marie*. A small exhibit with the bell, shackles, and other objects, and our words about the ship's history and what was happening with its remains were like an epiphany for the group. They knew that they wanted to be involved with the shipwreck in some way. That desire evolved into the idea of honoring the Africans forced to sail on *Henrietta Marie*, as well as the 12 million other captive people constrained to cross the Atlantic Ocean during the 350-year history of the transatlantic slave trade. The members of NABS decided to create an underwater memorial as the best way to remember these ancestors. After much planning and design work to develop a monument that would survive in the sometimes-rough environment at New Ground, a one-ton concrete pyramid with a brass plaque was built. The plaque read:

HENRIETTA MARIE

IN MEMORY AND

RECOGNITION OF THE COURAGE,

PAIN AND SUFFERING OF

ENSLAVED AFRICAN PEOPLE,

"SPEAK HER NAME AND GENTLY TOUCH

THE SOULS OF OUR ANCESTORS."

An initial plan to install the monument in November 1992 was squelched by bad weather, so the group gathered again in Key West in May 1993. The one-ton memorial was attached to an inflatable lift-bag and towed in the water during the 35-mile journey to New Ground Reef. The weather was perfect, with a nearly flat, calm sea. A small flotilla including the tow-boat with the monument, a dive boat chartered by NABS, and boats from the newly formed Florida Keys National Marine Sanctuary gathered at the wreck

The *Henrietta Marie* Monument created by the National Association of Black Scuba Divers before its deployment to New Ground Reef. *(Photo by Dylan Kibler/MFMHS)*

site. Words were read to honor the Africans and to dedicate the monument to them. Then a small group of divers got in the water, slowly let out the air from the lift bag, and escorted the monument to the seabed. Everything proceeded without a hitch, and the monument was set in 25 feet of water on the south side of the reef, with the plaque facing eastward toward Africa. There was only one problem. The water was pretty murky that day, and no one could tell exactly where on the *Henrietta Marie* site the monument had been placed.

The following year MFMHS organized an expedition to revisit the *Henrietta Marie* site to check on the status of the monument. NABS members joined the team because they wanted to make sure the memorial's materials were holding up as designed. The summer of 1994 was notable in the Florida Keys because migrants from Cuba, desperate to flee the difficulties of life in their country, were crossing the Florida Straits to the Keys in just about anything that would float. Many of their watercraft were made of inner tubes and blocks of foam—nothing that would be considered safe or seaworthy. As we made the trip to the site, we saw many of these rafts scattered along the mangrove shores of some of the western Keys and the sandy shallows between them. There was no one with any of these vessels, and there was no way of knowing whether their users had been rescued or had perished. It was another sad and eerie reminder of the ocean's often painful and tragic role in the human journey. The monument was located again with relative ease, and everyone was pleased and relieved to find it in good condition.

At the museum, the *Henrietta Marie* exhibit was moving forward with a flurry of planning, continued conservation work, and new historical and archaeological research. Telling the story of this important shipwreck became the focus of a team of MFMHS staff and outside experts. Historical records from England helped to fill in the story of the ship, the people who had owned and outfitted it, and those who sailed on board. Among the most telling data were tax records from London that listed the cargoes put aboard *Henrietta Marie* just before she sailed for Africa. These lists compared favorably to what had been found on the site. The exhibit still had to be designed, and this meant deciding which artifacts would be presented, writing the related texts, outlining a floor plan, developing an itinerary, and figuring out how to pay for it all. The working mantra was to stay focused on the ship and her stories without getting sidetracked or succumbing to the temptation to editorialize. *Henrietta Marie* told a powerful story that had never been examined in such a tangible way. This was an opportunity to share those truths with the public, no matter how unpalatable they might be.

The exhibit "A Slave Ship Speaks: The Wreck of the *Henrietta Marie*" opened in a large, newly built second-floor gallery at the Mel Fisher Maritime Museum in May 1995. Much of the Key West community and hundreds of tourists came to see it during its six-month exhibition. This was a good sign, but how would it play on the outside, away from a friendly hometown audience? As it turned out, the exhibit was very well received. It toured throughout the United States and the Bahamas for 18 years and was seen by nearly 3 million people. Everywhere it went, people lined up to learn about *Henrietta Marie* and her authentic, honest story from the often poorly understood slave trade. Long-lost artifacts had a way of making everything about the ship tangible, real, and undeniable, and this resonated with people curious about her story.

The *Henrietta Marie* exhibit at Daytona Museum of Arts and Sciences, 2003. *(Photo by Corey Malcom/MFMHS)*

Getting *Henrietta Marie* on the road was not the end for the ship's underwater site. We still had unanswered questions about the shipwreck that we wanted to resolve. For example, the known site and its artifacts represented perhaps half of the ship, so where did the rest of it go? Could it be found? How was the known portion of the ship's hull faring? It was buried in the sand, but was it being preserved there? These and other questions would be answered over the next few years.

Among the easiest questions to address was the nagging issue about the NABS monument—where was it on the site, if it was even there at all? In October 1996, a combined team from MFMHS and NABS set out to plot its location. High winds and rough seas kept us in port longer than we anticipated. Once at New Ground, the monument was fairly easy to find, but *Henrietta Marie* was not. We knew we were in the right area, but it took quite a bit of swimming to get our bearings. Eventually, with five people in the water and two days of searching for clues in the high reef, the large iron box was located. From this point, the monument quickly could be tied into the site plan. A baseline was run 250 feet due south from the box, with markers placed at 25-foot-intervals. The monument's position was triangulated by measuring its distance from the nearest two points. When scaled-down versions of these distances were plotted on a chart on the boat, we realized that the monument was in a nearly perfect spot—roughly 225 feet south of the box and 75 feet northwest of the ship's buried hull remains. It was a very central location, and it indeed was facing east toward Africa. The concrete portion of the monument was already being colonized by corals and other marine growth, turning it into a miniature reef.

To determine whether missing portions of *Henrietta Marie* still might be located, MFMHS partnered with the fledgling RPM Nautical Foundation to begin additional survey work at New Ground. RPM recently had acquired a magnetometer, a device that measures the earth's magnetic field. This is a useful search tool because iron from shipwrecks—cannons, cannonballs, or a hull full of spikes—will cause a disturbance in the natural magnetic field, which the magnetometer detects. The magnetic data can be linked with location data from the GPS system, providing an excellent way to find scattered and buried sites that are not readily visible to the naked eye. With so much of the ship missing, including six of the eight iron cannons she had carried, a survey seemed well worth the effort.

Initial magnetometry proved quite promising. Many anomalies were detected in the area immediately around the *Henrietta Marie* site, some of them quite large, and there were plenty of others within two miles of the site. We also found other shipwrecks, including a 1950s-era shrimp boat. However, because we were learning about "magging" as we did it, our techniques were not always up to snuff, and some of our data were not reliable. Nonetheless, we prepared a report for the marine sanctuary outlining our initial findings. In short, we discovered that anomalies of interest existed around *Henrietta Marie*; we just needed to organize a more formal search for them.

By 2001, another question began to loom concerning the wooden hull remains of *Henrietta Marie*. The section of the ship's lower stern had never been fully uncovered and recorded, and although it had been buried and presumably was safe in its sand bed, it not been in seen in many years, leaving us wondering how it was faring. We decided that it would be wise to uncover the hull to check its condition and to document it more fully. An application to do this work was permitted by the FKNMS, and *National Geographic* magazine wanted to cover the project as part of a broader story of *Henrietta Marie*. The hull excavation was planned in partnership with RPM Nautical Foundation and was based from their boats *Lakota* and *Robo*. We left Key West at the end of May to begin a week-long study of the wooden remains of *Henrietta Marie*.

The site was easily relocated; the area where the hull was thought to be buried was outlined and buoyed, and equipment—dredges, hoses, lines, markers—were placed on the bottom in preparation for digging. Two four-inch diameter venturi dredges, fed by water pumped from the boat, were used to suck the sand off the wreck. The goal was to locate and uncover the intact portion of the hull and a deposit of disarticulated timbers that had been collected during earlier explorations and buried near the hull. By the afternoon of the first day of digging, we found some of the wooden remains and soon uncovered a small, intact portion of the hull. Disarticulated planks and frames were gathered and moved to an open area where each piece was measured and photographed to help us determine its original position in the hull. The structure that had survived intact was a small part of the entire ship—a section of the lower stern, where the keel and the sternpost came together, with some of the framing and planking attached to the starboard side. An iron strap that had helped to hold the rudder was attached to the after end of this section. The wooden section was about 8 feet by 7 feet by 10 feet, representing some 5 to 10 percent of the original ship. During our excavation, we completely uncovered the structure on its upper and port faces, exposing the keel for the first time. The other side was left cradled in the sand for support because the waterlogged wood had softened and the fasteners largely had corroded. In addition to the overall dimensions, we recorded details such as the width of planks, distances between fasteners, and curvature of the frames. This information can be used to re-create these particular remains and draw larger conclusions about the size and design of *Henrietta Marie*.

The long days, cool water, and heavy work load took their toll on the crew. After the fifth day, a cold started to make its way around to everyone, and with this many ear infections developed. People were miserable, but the job had to be done, so diving continued. The *National Geographic* photographer had such badly infected ears that he could not get up and down in the water very easily; he found it easier and less painful to just stay down and have fresh scuba tanks brought to him, which he changed underwater.

By the last day, all the measurements had been taken, and the dredges were turned around to pump the sand back onto the hull structure so it would be preserved for future research. Despite the illness, our project was a success. The hull

Author Corey Malcom using a venturi dredge to uncover the hull of *Henrietta Marie*, 2001. *(Photo by Dylan Kibler/MFMHS)*

remains were documented thoroughly, many new photographs and videos were acquired, and a few new artifacts were discovered.

Six weeks later, another chapter of the *Henrietta Marie* project began. Our objective this time was to locate missing portions of *Henrietta Marie* by continuing magnetometry surveys along New Ground Reef and to document other shipwrecks in the area. Another partnership with RPM Nautical Foundation allowed use of their boats as the survey and dive vessels. This survey was more structured. Three magnetometers were towed behind *Lakota*, with travel lanes that ensured that each unit passed east to west along every 10 meters of the survey zone. All magnetic data was tied to the GPS system and collected and stored in onboard computers to be processed later. Divers used the data-generated plots to investigate and identify the magnetic anomalies. With this systematic coverage, there was little likelihood of missing anything.

This tedious method of surveying required steering the boat along parallel lines across the area of interest, like a farmer plowing a field. The

Author David Moore documenting futtocks, or "ribs," of *Henrietta Marie*, 2001. *(Photo by Dylan Kibler/MFMHS)*

RPM Nautical Foundation's magnetic survey vessel *Lakota* at New Ground Reef, 2001. *(Photo by Corey Malcom/MFMHS)*

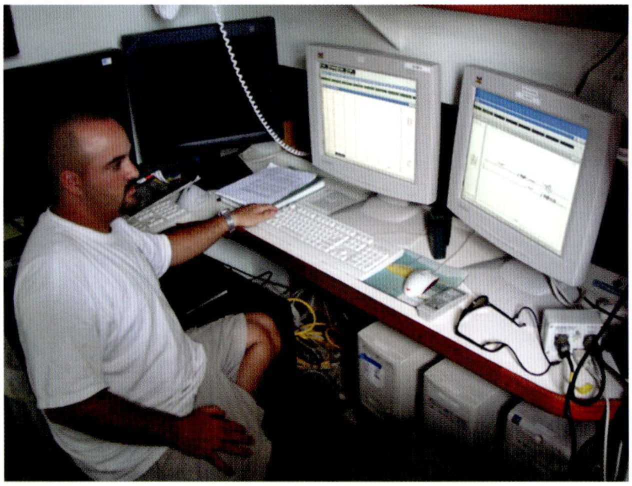

Archaeological technician Brian Blanco monitoring the New Ground magnetic data as it is collected.

(Photo by Corey Malcom/MFMHS)

Student intern Aubrey Kozak and Craig Jones of the RPM Nautical Foundation review a printed chart of magnetic anomalies to formulate a diving plan. *(Photo by Corey Malcom/MFMHS)*

captain used software that laid out lanes over an electronic chart, and he steered between the lines. A crew member on the aft deck to kept an eye on the magnetometers so they did not snag on obstructions or get tangled in the turns. Below deck, another crew member watched two computers to endure that the mag data streamed in as it should. These days were long and uneventful, punctuated by the seismographic squiggling lines that indicated a magnetic anomaly. This surveying took place during a two-year period.

When plotted, the results revealed many well-defined magnetic anomalies around the site and across the entire New Ground area. Some were even organized in long, straight lines that looked like "spill trails," a type of debris field created when a stricken ship is blown or drifts while breaking up and dropping its contents. We found very large hits approximately one mile south of *Henrietta Marie* that were especially intriguing in light of the six missing iron cannons. Other anomalies were scattered just to the west of the wreck. Once the entire area had been covered, the survey revealed hundreds of magnetic anomalies.

A list of particularly interesting hits was compiled, chosen for their relationship to *Henrietta Marie*, their size, or because they might be from other shipwrecks. As dive teams began to "ground-truth," or visually inspect the anomalies, some were very easy to identify; large anchors, pieces of shrimping gear, and long runs of heavy chain were spotted before the divers hit the water. Items camouflaged by the reef had to be located with metal detectors. Iron plates from a shipwreck dating to the late 1800s or early 1900s were so overgrown with marine life that they looked like any other part of the reef and were unrecognizable to the naked eye. About a half-mile to the south-

southwest of *Henrietta Marie*'s hull structure, we found a scupper liner, a lead tube that poked through the hull at the deck level to allow seawater and rain to flow overboard. It was found on the surface by a diver looking for a mag hit that had never been located.

Most anomalies were buried, some so deeply that even the metal detectors could not locate them, so we used a more powerful handheld magnetometer to pinpoint these items. Six compelling and promising anomalies were selected for study because of their size or relationship to *Henrietta Marie* and because they seemed likely to be missing portions of the wreck.

The first anomaly was east of the wreck site and had a strong, intriguing magnetic profile. Dredging quickly revealed that it was a foot or so beneath the sand and encrusted, but its odd and complex shape was not readily identifiable. After a couple of hours of dredging, the piece proved to be a two-wheeled hand truck that still had rubber on the wheels; it was obviously no more than 30 or 40 years old, and probably had been lost by a commercial fishing vessel.

The second anomaly, initially detected during the 1998 surveys, had always been high on our list for scrutiny because it had a very large reading. Over the years, more than one conversation had focused on it being the shipwreck's missing cannons. Located 45 feet deep, the anomaly was a mile south of the slave ship site in an area far from the actual reef, with a flat bottom of silty sand. The target was pinpointed with the handheld magnetometer and marked with fiberglass stakes that we strung with line to delineate the area. As we excavated, we could only dive an hour per shift because the greater water depth created a risk for decompression sickness. Digging through

Left: Author Corey Malcom dredging on a magnetic anomaly. *Right:* A blue glass seed bead found during the excavation.

(Photo by Howard Phoenix/RPM Nautical Foundation)

the silty, compacted sand, each team made the hole deeper and wider. Visibility often was quite poor, especially between tides, and only shells and oddly blackened chunks of limestone broke the monotony of the white sand matrix. But then, a tiny speck of unnatural blue was spotted, and the dredge head was moved back to avoid sucking it up. The speck was a small glass bead of a type carried in *Henrietta Marie*'s cargo. To avoid losing it, the tiny bead was brought to the surface, photographed, and safely stowed on the boat. Everyone was more than excited; this surely was evidence we were about to uncover a significant, new portion of *Henrietta Marie*. Although the next group did not find anything, a diver who had gathered a few shells as souvenirs was in for a big surprise. While cleaning them, another blue bead popped out! This truly confirmed that we were in the right place.

Team after team of divers dug more deeply, but the now four-foot-deep hole still showed only sand, silt, shells, and rocks. Finally, one of the divers surfaced early and said, "There's a whole bunch of wood down there." He had a small piece in his hand, and it had a distinct pine smell to it. This was really it—the rest of *Henrietta Marie* surely had been found! Most of the crew raced to the bottom to see, but on closer inspection the wood

A deposit of organic debris uncovered as a magnetic anomaly in 50 feet of water near New Ground Reef. (Photo by Dylan Kibler/MFMHS)

did not look like anything from a shipwreck. Rather, it appeared more like branches and small trunks from trees, mixed with a layer of organic material. A one-square-meter area was cleared that revealed other oddities, including shells from oysters and shallow-water snails attached to some of the wood; a piece of wood that had been burned on both ends; a waterlogged pinecone; and more black rocks. Nothing seemed related to *Henrietta Marie*, but the feature was measured, mapped, and photographed, and samples were collected for identification and analysis.

Back on shore, the wood samples were sent to laboratories for species identification and carbon-14 dating analysis, and conservation began on some of the other pieces. After a short wait, the results began to arrive. We learned that two types of wood had been recovered, mangrove and yellow pine, neither of which were associated with *Henrietta Marie*. When the carbon-14 dates arrived, they were beyond belief—the samples dated to 8600–8350 BP. What we had found was 8,500 years old! We had discovered an area that was once the coastal zone of prehistoric, ice-age Florida. Thousands of years ago, water was locked up in glaciers and sea levels were much lower. What was now about 50 feet underwater had once been land, and plants and trees that once had foliated that land were nicely preserved in the mud off New Ground Reef.

There was still more exploring to do to find the rest of *Henrietta Marie*. The last anomalies to be excavated were west-southwest of the site and were within a long line of such hits suspected to be a trail of artifacts from the wreck. Again, these areas were in an expanse of silty sand, this time in 30 feet of water. When the first hit was pinpointed, excavation yielded blackened rocks and bits of wood charcoal until a layer of peat-like organic material appeared about 4 feet deep. We knew from our earlier experience what was happening and took some photographs, but halted the work. At the next magnetic anomaly, a hole that eventually penetrated 11 feet into the sea-

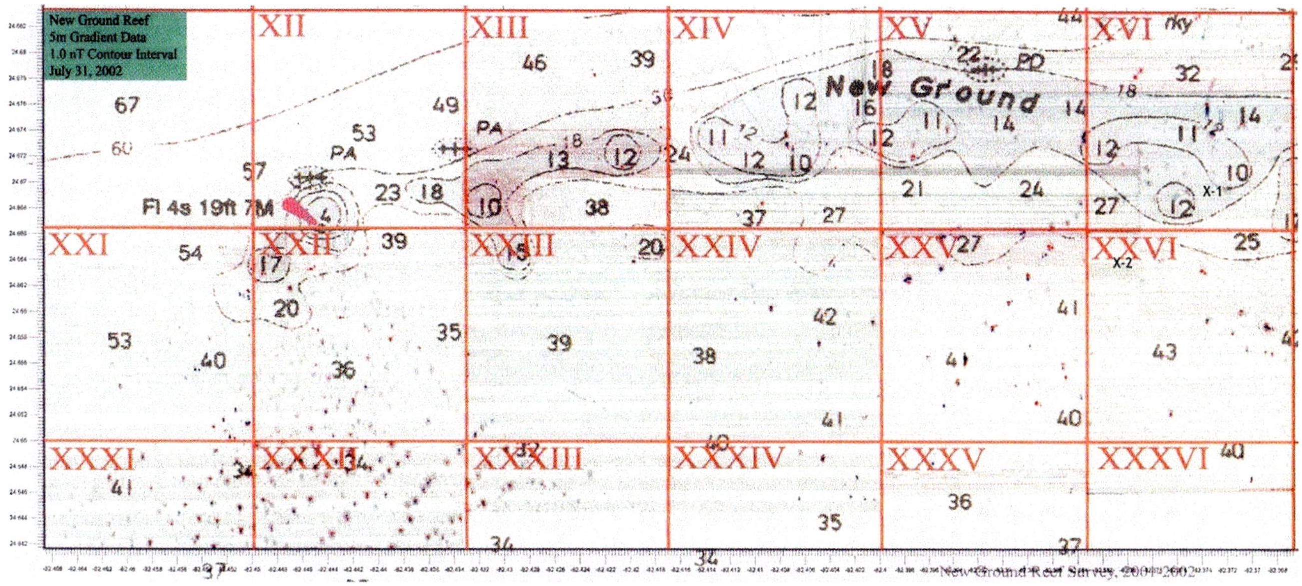

Magnetic data collected across New Ground Reef, 2001–2003. The red and blue spots are anomalies. *(Image by RPM Nautical Foundation)*

bed also revealed only sand, shells, black rocks, and charcoal. We ended this excavation because the hole was unstable and dangerous for divers, and it was unlikely that wreck material was this deep.

We clearly had not found more of *Henrietta Marie*, but what had we detected in the mud south of New Ground? The common features of these mysterious excavations were ancient, deeply buried organics, blackened rocks, and evidence of fire in the form of burned wood and charcoal. Why would these things be linked with such strong magnetic anomalies? It took much research, but eventually it appeared that we had encountered a phenomenon called "thermo-remnant magnetism," a heat-induced magnetic realignment of materials. When anything is heated above about 600 degrees Celsius, its magnetic particles are realigned to the prevailing magnetic field of the place and time. This essentially creates a magnet that becomes stuck in time. While the rest of the earth's magnetic field constantly shifts and changes, the once-heated feature retains its realigned field and stands out as an anomaly in the modern magnetic situation. These thermo-remnant magnetic fields stand out like sore thumbs to a magnetometer. When we looked at data from the mag charts, we saw hundreds of hits in long lines, all looking much like those we had just excavated. We realized that these most likely were the same ancient magnetic fields. We probably had discovered an age-old landscape where low land and shallow water came together. The water created long, thin strands of land in alignment with its flow. These skinny islands were fringed by mangroves and had pines in the interior that were susceptible to fires from lightning strikes or perhaps human activity, creating hotspots that became magnetically realigned. Over time, and with enough fires, these narrow strands were scarred with lines of anomalies that we can find today. This discovery was a clear example of never knowing what to expect when we begin an investigation, and while very interesting, it was a hard-won piece of knowledge that we had not been seeking.

This new understanding of the magnetic features of New Ground Reef made our original goals more daunting. We had found some evidence of *Henrietta Marie*—two beads and a lead scupper liner—but the likeliest magnetic anomalies had proved to be something else entirely. Our survey found no evidence that the missing parts of the slaver were anywhere nearby. With time, money, and patience evaporating quickly, we called off our search with the hope of a future effort using search methods better suited to the setting. The rest of *Henrietta Marie*, wherever it might be, would have to wait. Although much of the site first discovered in 1972 has been explored and the vast majority of artifacts associated with the wreck have been recovered, the present assemblage is numerically far short of what we might expect if the entire ship had been lost in this one area. Somewhere, there must be a small mound of ballast, the lower hull, and six additional cannons waiting to be found.

Henrietta Marie probably sank without survivors, but we still do not know what circumstances put the ship on the bottom. The timing of her return voyage and documentation related to other European ships in the area during the summer of 1700 strongly suggest that she met her end during a hurricane. Although portions of *Henrietta Marie* still are missing, our study of what has been found has changed the way we see the past. Historical research and archaeological efforts have combined over the past several decades to paint an exciting, albeit sobering, picture of a very typical slave ship operating at the end of the seventeenth century. Both the research and the shipwreck provide a rare glimpse of the nuts and bolts of the African slave trade. *Henrietta Marie* offers tangible relics of the infamous Middle Passage, exposing the economics of the brutal business and providing an authentic example of what a "slave ship" was.

Henrietta Marie was one of thousands of such ships that crossed the Atlantic Ocean and delivered nearly 12 million people into lives of bondage in the Americas. Although we do not know the names of the Africans who were forced to sail on *Henrietta Marie*, we do have a much greater understanding of their experience, and we can appreciate the ship's role in shaping lives and cultures on both sides of the Atlantic. *Henrietta Marie* might have been found largely by accident, but the many decades of careful archaeological research that followed this discovery have made all of this possible.

David D. Moore, the nautical archaeology curator at the North Carolina Maritime Museum, is well known for his archival research and archaeological fieldwork on the pirate Blackbeard's ship *Queen Anne's Revenge* and the slave ship *Henrietta Marie*.

Corey Malcom, director of archaeology at the Mel Fisher Maritime Heritage Society Museum, has worked extensively on shipwrecks in Florida and the Bahamas, including the remains of three slave ships. He has extensive experience with artifact conservation and analysis, and museum interpretation and display.

For Additional Information

Publications

Teresa Coppens, "History of the Henrietta Marie Slave Ship," HubPages, June 4, 2013, https://hubpages.com/travel/History-of-the-Henrietta-Marie-Slave-Ship

"A Slave Ship Speaks, The Wreck of the *Henrietta Marie*. A Prospectus for the Exhibition Tour," Mel Fisher Maritime Heritage Society, 1994, 2007, http://melfisher.org/pdf/HMPropectus.pdf

Websites

The *Henrietta* Marie, Mel Fisher Maritime Museum, http://melfisher.org/henriettamarie.htm

A Slave Ship Speaks: The Wreck of the *Henrietta Marie*, Historical Museum of Southern Florida, http://historical-museum.org/exhibits/hm/henmarie.htm

Videos

"Deep Sea Detectives: Slave Ship Uncovered," History Channel, September 23, 2003, https://www.youtube.com/watch?v=Htwb4lWB4HU

Mel Fisher Maritime Museum, "Documenting the Slave Ship *Henrietta Marie*, December 28, 2012, https://www.youtube.com/watch?v=ucLIH3-4qLY

CHAPTER 9

Maritime Archaeology in the Nation's Oldest Port: A Regional Template

~ Chuck Meide ~

LAMP 1.0

I remember the exact moment when I knew I was going to be an underwater archaeologist. It was a chilly March afternoon in 1992, and I was chest-deep in the Wakulla River, in the rural Gulf coast county of that name, near the sleepy fishing village of St. Marks, Florida. At the time, I was an undergraduate student at Florida State University (FSU), where my double major in English and anthropology reflected my long-standing goal of becoming a professional writer and my rapidly increasing interest in archaeology. FSU had a number of underwater archaeology classes on the schedule, so while I joyfully toiled by day at a dig on a Spanish mission site, at night and on weekends I took a scuba course at the local dive shop. The dive instructor looked at me like I was crazy when I told him I wanted to do underwater archaeology.

The next semester, I enrolled in the FSU class "Techniques of Underwater Site Research," which brought me and another student to the cold Wakulla River. For many unsuccessful days and hours we had been searching for a lost ship. We had been told about the alleged shipwreck by state archaeologist Jim Dunbar; it seemed to be the perfect option for the required student field project, so we had set out to find it with nothing more than snorkeling gear. We did not even bring a dive flag, which had gotten us kicked out of the water by the Marine Patrol on an earlier day. But this was the final day. My partner, Terei Tarter, was frustrated to the point of anger, after countless hours of swimming (probably in circles) and searching fruitlessly through the thick sea grass on the river bed. She cursed Dunbar, questioned his knowledge of these waters and this supposed wreck, and clearly was ready to quit. Not wanting to give in so easily but with the sinking feeling that the cause was lost, I suggested that we swim one more time, from where we were standing toward an observation deck far upriver. "One more try," I promised, "and if we find nothing we can go home and forget about this wreck."

So we swam together in one long line. Below my questing eyes in the dim water, I noticed parallel strips of mud without sea grass, one after another. Suddenly the strips of sand became timbers. Rows of timbers, bristling with spikes and bolts. We had found our shipwreck. After a brief exploration, we stood on the timbers with our heads and shoulders out of the water, no longer noticing the cold and chattering excitedly. This could be a Spanish merchant ship or a pirate ship, we said, knowing that a nearby seventeenth-century Spanish fort had suffered both shipwreck and pirate attack. It could be a Civil War gunboat or a steamboat hauling cotton. It could be anything, and the only way to solve the mystery was through an archaeological investigation. Then it suddenly clicked in my head, and I said to myself, "This is what I want to do." I knew, right then and there, that I had found myself.

Over the next 13 years, there were many more discoveries and mysteries. I worked on Spanish shipwrecks in the Dry Tortugas and in Pensacola Bay, and Norwegian lumber barks in the Gulf of Mexico and off the rocky coast of Ireland. I discovered a bronze cannon from the 1686 ship of the French explorer La Salle in Texas, and an anchor from the Spanish Armada of 1588 in Ireland. It was in Ireland in the summer of 2005 while I was working on my dissertation research that I received three emails that would change my life.

Two were from colleagues, and one was from the executive director of the St. Augustine Lighthouse and Museum (now the St. Augustine Lighthouse & Maritime Museum), who, unknown to me at the time, would by my future employer. All three emails were calling my attention to a job opening coming up in St. Augustine, Florida, that might be of interest. Of course, I was familiar with the job. The director of the Lighthouse Archaeological Maritime Program Inc. (LAMP) had left his position and was moving on. LAMP, now known as the St. Augustine Lighthouse Archaeological Maritime Program, had been founded by the museum in 1999 as an archaeological research institution. It serves as the research arm of the museum, and to me it had always seemed like a dream job.

I had always wanted to live in St. Augustine, in part because I had grown up in Atlantic Beach, just a short drive from there. Founded in 1565, St. Augustine is the nation's oldest city, with streets that were laid out in the 1570s. It has a charm and feel that is unique and more akin to old European cities than their American counterparts. I had been visiting St. Augustine since I was a kid and had always loved the palpable feel of its history, evident everywhere from its seventeenth-century fortress Castillo de San Marcos to its eighteenth-century colonial cityscape to its magnificent Gilded Age hotels and churches.

Aerial view of the St. Augustine Lighthouse & Maritime Museum. In the background can be seen the confluence of the Matanzas River, Tolomato River, and Salt Run, and (at top right) the mouth of the St. Augustine Inlet.

(Courtesy of St. Augustine Lighthouse & Maritime Museum)

But for an underwater archaeologist, St. Augustine has an even more compelling appeal. It is the oldest port in the country, and as such it has seen ships coming and going for more than 450 years. Furthermore, it really was a lousy port. It was widely known for its notoriously dangerous inlet, which was shallow and plagued by an ever-shifting sandbar. This means shipwrecks, and lots of them. Spanish shipwrecks, English shipwrecks, American shipwrecks, and even some early French shipwrecks. There was plenty of job security for a shipwreck archaeologist in St. Augustine, and plenty of exciting finds awaiting discovery!

So I found myself traveling home to prepare for a job interview at the museum. Perhaps I had the home team advantage or I was just a perfect fit for the job, but I accepted their offer and became the new LAMP director in March 2006.

450 Years of Maritime History in the Nation's Oldest Port

St. Augustine was a city born in storm and shipwreck. It was founded in 1565 by Pedro Menéndez de Avilés, who had been sent by the Spanish king to drive out by "fire and blood" the French who had established the settlement of Fort Caroline just to the north, in present-day Jacksonville. After a brief naval skirmish with the French off the mouth of the River of May (today's St. Johns River), Menéndez retreated to the next inlet to the south, landed his men, and founded the settlement he named *San Agustín*. He hastily began digging trenches and piling earth to fortify it, and his expectations of French aggression were prescient: his French rival, Jean Ribault, attacked only three days later with his four largest ships.

Menéndez, who had been offshore lightering supplies in a smaller vessel, was almost captured, but he took the great risk of hurtling across the shallow sandbar at the mouth of the St. Augustine Inlet. The French galleons were simply too large to follow without waiting for a higher tide. Instead, they were swept up in a sudden and violent hurricane that raked the coast, which drove the French ships south to their destruction in the vicinity of Cape Canaveral. The wrecking of these vessels—and the subsequent slaughter of the shipwreck survivors—sealed the fate of the French in Florida and cemented the Spanish foothold in North America at St. Augustine.

Menéndez was a keen mariner and naval tactician, and the lessons of this event were not lost on him. He did not move his base of operations to a different port with a deepwater inlet. The sandbar guarding the entrance to St. Augustine undoubtedly was dangerous, but it nonetheless provided the best defense for his fledgling colony. St. Augustine from the outset was not intended as a commercial port but as a military outpost responsible for guarding Spanish shipping routes farther out to sea. As such, Menéndez chose to maintain his provincial capital behind a treacherous inlet. For the next 200 years, St. Augustine was supplied primarily by small vessels from Cuba. The large armed galleons and fat merchant *naos* that silently traversed the horizon, following the Gulf Stream home to distant Spain, never made harbor at the town that was charged with their protection.

The role of the St. Augustine bar changed as the city and its function within the Spanish empire evolved, but its presence was always first and foremost in the minds of its residents and visitors. As St. Augustine shifted over the centuries from a peripheral military town to a more cosmopolitan (if still somewhat backwater) city, its infamous sandbar went from being a source of security to a liability for shipping and a hindrance to economic health. Its constantly shifting sands meant no published sailing directions or pilot books were of use for long, and with such shallow channels only small vessels could safely enter or exit the port. By the eighteenth century, shipwrecks were so common that the lookout would sound an alarm whenever even friendly ships approached the inlet to alert the locals to launch boats in case a rescue was required.

In other respects, St. Augustine's physical maritime landscape was conducive for trade. The Matanzas, Tolomato, and San Sebastian Rivers (along with countless estuarine creeks) provided conduits for moving goods between the hinterland and the port, while the bay fronting the town proved a safe and capacious anchorage for the ships that did make it safely over the bar. A series of wooden forts, culminating in 1695 with the coquina masonry fortification Castillo de San Marcos, were erected on the city's waterfront to protect residents from seaborne attacks, which became increasingly common as English colonies encroached upon Spanish territory in the 1600s and 1700s. In 1738, Fort Mose, the nation's first legally sanctioned, free African-American settlement, was built along the estuary two miles from St. Augustine to protect it from attacks from the north. Fort Matanzas was built 14 miles to the south at Matanzas Inlet to guard the rear entrance to St. Augustine from enemy ships.

When the British took control of Florida in 1763, they were determined to stimulate trade in their newest colonial capital. The ambitious authorities brought in mooring anchors for the harbor, heightened the existing watchtower and converted it to a lighthouse, and funded hydrographic surveys of the inlet. Nonetheless, the inlet was always St. Augustine's Achilles' heel. Johann Schoepf, a British army surgeon and visitor to

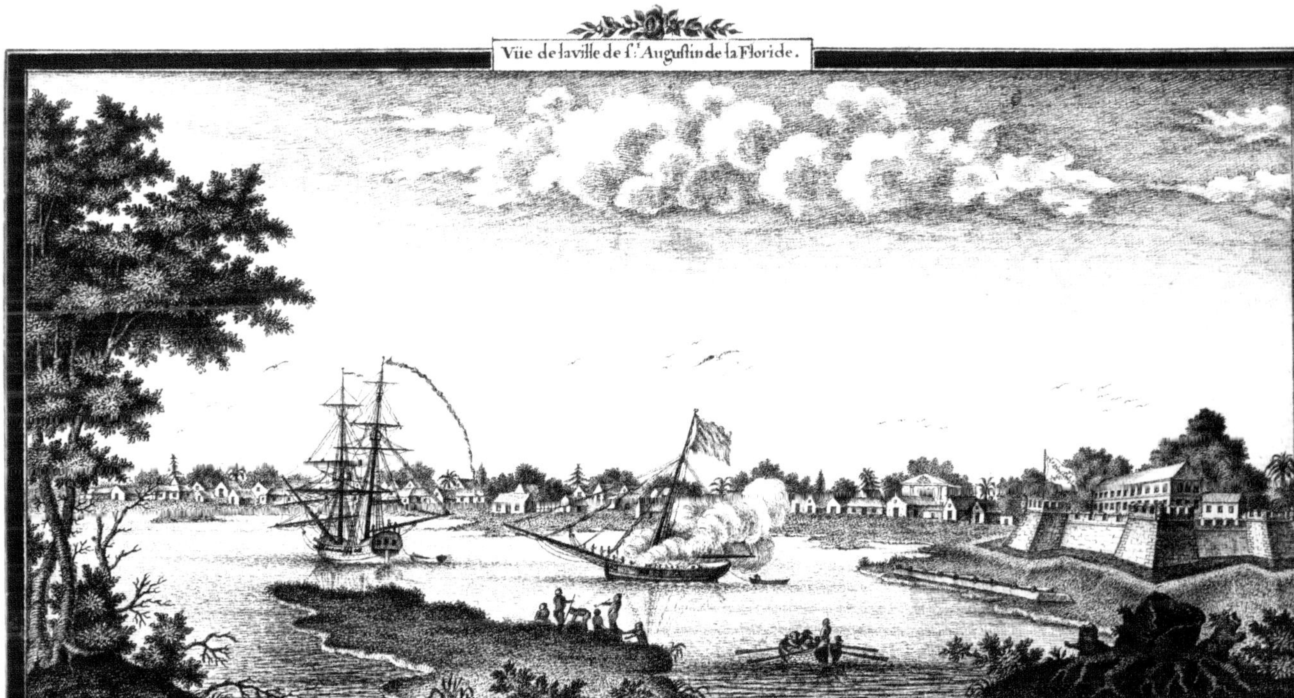

View of St. Augustine's waterfront during the First Spanish Period, circa 1750. *(Courtesy of the St. Augustine Historical Society)*

St. Augustine in 1784, wrote that St. Augustine's bar was "unquestionably the most dangerous" of all the colonies because it was the shallowest and "at the same time exposed to the total force of the ocean playing upon it." He went on to paint a vivid picture of what it was like to sail into the port:

> It is indeed a fearful thing to hear the wild tumult of these breaking seas and to behold them on all sides foaming and tossing . . . In coming in and going out the 'seas' are put to use, 3–4 waves commonly lifting the vessel over the shallowest spots otherwise impassable. But for this, keen attention, great skill, and good fortune must all be united. The wave which is to raise the ship must strike it full, and no other must come against it, athwart for instance, at the same time, else the ship is driven from the narrow channel on to a bank, and soon knocked to pieces or laid over. A great quantity of dismal remains of vessels protrudes on all sides from the sand and the water.

Schoepf estimated that a ship was wrecked on this coast every two weeks to a month and that one could not walk 100 paces on the beach without encountering the skeleton of a lost ship. Vessels regularly had to wait one to two weeks, and sometimes five or more, for a favorable tide and winds in order to cross the bar.

Despite the danger and inconvenience of the inlet, trade did prosper at St. Augustine. Given the shallow passage, it is not surprising that commerce was carried out primarily in small, coastal vessels, usually between 20 and 25 tons and rarely more than 50 tons. Larger vessels visiting the port typically anchored offshore and ferried cargo or passengers ashore on lighters. Havana was the primary trading partner during the First Spanish Period (1565–1763), although Charleston, South Carolina, and Savannah, Georgia, increasingly became important (even when English trade was outlawed by the Spanish king) and eclipsed the Cuban port by the British Period (1763–1783). Although most British commerce was limited to neighboring coastal colonies, ships from as far away as Philadelphia, New York, Bermuda, the Caribbean, the Canary Islands, and Cork in Ireland engaged in the St. Augustine trade. Imports primarily were manufactured goods (furniture, soap, tools, and hardware) and foodstuffs (pork, poultry, cheese, oil, wine, and rum). Florida is still known for its oranges, and St. Augustine's most important export was both sweet and sour oranges and their juice. Other exports included cattle hides, deer skins, oysters, hogs, lumber, and live oak timber for shipbuilding. Privateering was established during times of war in the First Spanish Period; it peaked in the British Period during the American Revolution, when the war-starved city depended on this piratical activity as the most reliable source of food and commodities.

During the Second Spanish Period (1784–1821), St. Augustine's farmers, laborers, merchants, and mariners formed a truly multicultural community. The St. Augustinians who identified as ship owners or sea captains before 1800 included Spanish Americans, Anglo-Americans, Minorcans, Greeks, Italians, Canary Islanders, and at least one free African American. After 1800, this maritime community was augmented by French, Irish, Scottish, and American immigrants. Trade remained brisk for the most part, but in the nineteenth century St. Augustine was eclipsed as a commercial port first by Fernandina and then by Jacksonville. Both of their inlets were

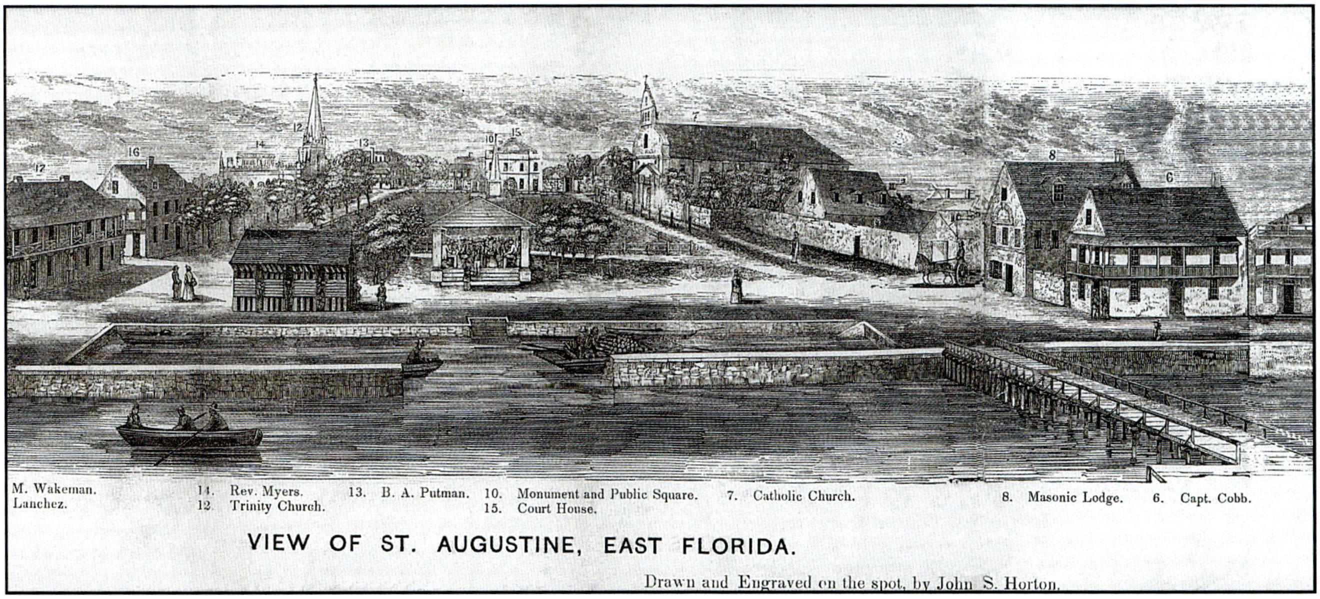

Detail of an 1855 engraving depicting St. Augustine's waterfront as seen from Matanzas Bay, facing the old boat basin and the central plaza. The wharf in the foreground on the right is in the approximate location of today's Bridge of Lions.

(Courtesy of the St. Augustine Lighthouse & Maritime Museum)

deeper and safer for shipping. By the advent of river steamboat transportation, it was more common and safer to travel to St. Augustine along an inland maritime route from Jacksonville. Ships arriving there would transfer goods or passengers to steamboat, travel up the St. Johns River to the landings at Picolata or Tocoi, and then travel overland to St. Augustine by coach or, after 1858, horse-drawn rail.

After the Civil War, St. Augustine suffered economic hardship from years of blockade and wartime devastation, the abolition of slavery, and the forced hiatus of Northern tourists. Florida's tourist industry dates back to as early as the 1820s, when land speculators attempting to attract visitors to St. Augustine and northeastern Florida touted its warm and salubrious climate. The region became popular with seasonal visitors, initially wealthy Northerners with respiratory ailments seeking refuge from harsh winters. This tourist market reemerged shortly after the war, as evidenced by a local who when asked how St. Augustinians made their living, replied "sweet taters and sick Yankees."

During the Gilded Age, industry expanded rapidly when developers such as industrialist Henry Flagler transformed St. Augustine with railroads and grand hotels. Maritime recreational opportunities were popular, including sail and steam cruising, rowing, fishing, sailboat racing for cash prizes, and oyster roasts. Recreational fishing, sailing, boat charters and rentals, and tour boats remain an important part of St. Augustine's maritime economy today. One Minorcan family, the Usinas, for three generations has operated tour boats in St. Augustine waters and currently offers daily excursions on the bay aboard the *Victory III*, the third boat of that name to do so since around 1900.

Even though oceanic trade in the late 1800s had diminished compared to previous centuries, St. Augustine's waterfront continued to see sail and steam traffic. Consequently, maintaining the harbor and its aids to navigation was still a priority for the federal government. In 1871, when it became clear that the old coquina lighthouse was endangered by erosion, plans were drawn for a new, modern lighthouse. On October 15, 1874, the new tower with its first-order Fresnel lens was operational, and the light forever was extinguished at the former Spanish watchtower. Six years later, the old coquina tower succumbed to encroaching tides and collapsed into ruins during a heavy storm; its foundation still can be seen today at low tide and has been documented by LAMP.

America's modern shrimping industry began at the turn of the century in Fernandina, where the highly effective "otter trawl" nets were first drawn by powered boats, an innovation credited to a Sicilian immigrant named Sallecito Salvador. Around 1920, the better school system in St. Augustine enticed Mediterranean immigrant families to make the move from Fernandina, and the center of this booming industry shifted to St. Augustine with them. Soon the First Coast region, with trawler fleets based in St. Augustine, Mayport, and Fernandina, was supplying shrimp by the ton via iced railcar to the New York market. The expansion and growth of this fishery created a new maritime infrastructure of shipbuilders, ship chandlers, canneries, shippers, ice factories, and boat maintenance yards. By World War II, the fleet measured in the hundreds. The largest shrimp boat builder was DESCO (Diesel Engine Sales Company), which had built 500 shrimp boats by 1954, 1,700 by 1971, and a trawler every four days by 1981. These vessels were destined for fisheries as far away as South America, Africa, the Middle East, and Asia. Although this booming industry subsequently collapsed in the 1980s and 1990s, a few shrimp trawlers still are ported in St. Augustine, and the San Sebastian River remains a working waterfront to this day.

Underwater Archaeology in St. Augustine Waters: The Early Years

If the rate of shipwrecks described by Johann Schoepf in 1784 held true for St. Augustine's entire history, there would be somewhere between 335 and 670 lost ships dating to before the twentieth century. The rate of wreckings actually is related to the frequency of shipping, which varied over time and this likely yielded a smaller number than the estimate, but it still is clear that multitudes of historic shipwrecks are hidden beneath St. Augustine's seas, surf, and sand.

The potential for underwater archaeology in St. Augustine was recognized early. The first underwater investigations were diver surveys lead by FSU professor and National Park Service archaeologist George R. Fischer at the Castillo de San Marcos and Fort Matanzas in 1978 and 1979. However, these initial projects were limited in scope; the first extensive, research-oriented archaeological effort to discover and study St. Augustine shipwrecks took place almost 20 years later. In 1995, a survey conducted by the nonprofit research institution Southern Oceans Archaeological Research (SOAR) led to the discovery of a number of shipwrecks, including the oldest yet found in northeast Florida—the 1764 British supply ship *Industry* (see Chapter 5). Funded by a state historic preservation grant, the survey used a marine magnetometer deployed from a research vessel to search the estimated area of the historic inlet. Researchers used the magnetic signatures discerned by this device to pinpoint the location of several historic shipwrecks.

The year before, the St. Augustine Lighthouse had opened to the public as a maritime museum after an extended restoration that had begun in 1980. By 1997, realizing archaeology's potential contribution to public interpretation of St. Augustine's maritime heritage, the museum's administrators began to provide additional funding for SOAR's ongoing research excavations at the *Industry* wreck site. In 1999, the lighthouse went a step farther and established its own research organization, LAMP. In the summers of 1999 and 2000, LAMP archaeologists conducted further excavations at *Industry* and investigated an unidentified nineteenth-century steamship wreck. We have continued to conduct maritime archaeological research in St. Augustine waters to this day.

Artifacts from *Industry*—including a cannon, a box of axe heads, shovels, handsaws, a copper teapot, an iron cauldron, and small personal items—were conserved and displayed at the lighthouse, notably in a long-term exhibit titled *Beans and Bullets* that extended from 2004 to 2016. LAMP archaeologists have been interested in not only shipwrecks but also other types of maritime archaeological sites. LAMP has searched along inland waterways for wharfs, landings, anchorage sites, and groins (jetty-like structures designed to divert current flow to maintain navigational channels). One of the more interesting non-shipwreck sites discovered and investigated was the Tolomato Bar Anchorage site, an anchorage with associated wharf remains and an abandoned boat. It was situated on the Tolomato River at the site of a sugar cane and indigo plantation owned by the first British governor, James Grant (1764–1771). The docks and wharves were associated with the British plantation and also with Minorcan farmsteaders who settled there in the Second Spanish Period.

LAMP 2.0

In 2005, the original founder and director of LAMP, Billy Ray Morris, left his position for other adventures, and LAMP underwent a complete staff turnover. This made the job even more appealing for me when I took the helm the following year because I could hire my own people and reshape the program to my own vision. I wanted to build a first-class maritime archaeology program that incorporated more participation from students and community members of all ages. I also wanted a program that conducted meaningful archaeology that could be translated into unique and exciting educational experiences for our museum's visitors and community. My team and I have been doing this ever since, in what we have affectionately nicknamed "LAMP 2.0."

I have built quite a team, and in all honesty the successes LAMP has achieved have been due to our talented and dedicated staff and the support of the greater museum team. My first hire was Sam Turner. A long-time friend, Sam and I had worked together on a number of shipwrecks, including the 1837 Mississippi River steamboat *Ben Sherrod* and an unidentified 1700s French shipwreck in the Caribbean. Sam is always enthusiastic and has the glowing personality of the eternal optimist. He is full of wild but wonderful ideas and has been diving for decades, since he was a child growing up in Puerto Rico. Sam is a paleographer, which means he can read and translate Spanish from as early as the sixteenth century, and his knowledge of and passion for the history of Spanish exploration and colonialism makes him a perfect scholar for St. Augustine.

Next, I brought in Brendan Burke. A native Virginian and proud of his state's history, Brendan is another perfect fit for LAMP. I met him when we were students at the College of William & Mary, and I immediately was impressed with his intellect and skills. Brendan is an academic who grew up on a farm. He can discuss anthropological theory with the best of them and fix a broken boat motor or explain in detail the components of a historic steam engine. He is another experienced diver and a very skilled boat captain. He has excelled at the technologies of finding shipwrecks and has become a largely self-taught specialist in the use of side-scan sonar and magnetometers.

In 2010, I hired Starr Cox, an archaeological conservator who was trained at Texas A&M University. Her specialized skills in stabilizing and preserving artifacts were absolutely critical if we were going to excavate shipwrecks and recover waterlogged artifacts. The museum currently is building a new Maritime Archaeology and Education Center, which will greatly expand our conservation laboratory and give Starr and her team of conservators more space to preserve the artifacts we recover from the sea.

The most recent addition to the team is Olivia McDaniel. Olivia was a hard-working young archaeologist when she took our field school in 2012, and she joined us as a staff member in 2014. She is dedicated, dependable, and highly organized, and has become an indispensable member of the team. Above the water, she helps with grant management, writing archaeological reports, and organizing the field school; underwater, she can be relied on to complete any task no matter how challenging.

It was the support of the museum and the State of Florida's historic preservation program that allowed me to build this team and to meet our goals for growing LAMP. Shortly after my

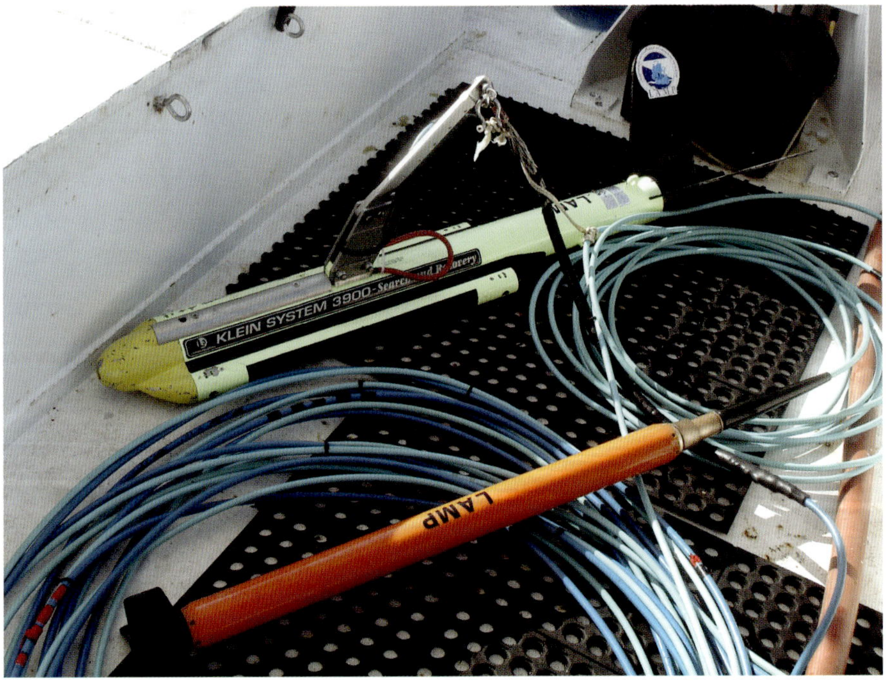

Compact and portable, side-scan sonar (top) and marine magnetometer (bottom) sensors towed from the boat can detect targets that might be historic shipwrecks.

(Courtesy of the Search for the Lost French Fleet of 1565 Expedition, NOAA-OER/St. Augustine Lighthouse & Museum)

arrival at LAMP, we secured a state grant for more than $280,000 to fund the 2007–2009 First Coast Maritime Archaeology Project. This allowed us to purchase 12 new sets of diving gear, thus enabling the cultivation of a large team of volunteer divers and an annual field school for graduate and undergraduate students. The funding also paid for new remote sensing equipment and software, including a marine magnetometer and side-scan sonar, as well as two of our staff positions. This grant was to prove critical for LAMP because state and federal funding became scarce in the recovery years after the Great Recession of 2008. The equipment and volunteer support gained through this grant, and the new LAMP staff positions for which the lighthouse would later assume funding, allowed LAMP to continue fieldwork and conservation treatment each season for the ensuing years when state funding largely was unavailable. In recent years, grant funding has become more reliable, and we recently secured a state grant for almost $500,000 for the 2017–2018 First Coast Maritime Archaeology Project.

Field School and Lessons Learned

One of the programs we started with the original First Coast Maritime Archaeology Project was our Maritime Archaeology Field School. A field school is an essential part of any archaeologist's training. It allows for hands-on training by working side by side with professional archaeologists. Given the inherit risks of diving, often in less than ideal conditions, a field school in underwater archaeology is critical for those seeking a career in this discipline.

Our first field school was run in partnership with Flinders University in Australia. Mark Staniforth and Jen McKinnon brought their students to St. Augustine to learn how to do underwater archaeology on the Steamship and Ballast Pile Wreck. This is an apparent double-shipwreck site, where a steamship and a sailing ship came to rest right next to each other. We think that the steamship might be *Cricket*, which was lost in 1860, but we have yet to solve this mystery.

Some of the lessons the students learn have nothing to do with archaeology. An important one is how fast a storm can strike in St. Augustine. I remember working with the Flinders students on the wreck site one beautiful, sunny day. It was in the early days of LAMP 2.0, when our two research vessels were the 28-foot, fiberglass-hulled *Island Fever* and a smaller boat, *Nickerin*, which had been donated to us. The clear, sunny skies suddenly went dark, and those of us on the surface realized the storm clouds were headed right for us. The safety diver splashed into the water to recall our working divers, and we hastily prepared to pull in anchors and go. I was driving *Nickerin*, and Sam was driving *Island Fever*.

The storm hit just as we were entering the inlet, about the worst place to have problems in a boat as the currents rip through it at incredible speeds. Fortunately, we motored forward through the inlet as the seas began to heave and lightning crashed all about us. The pelting rain and dark clouds reduced visibility, but we had safely traversed the inlet. We were entering the bay when the real trouble began. Just as we were passing the Castillo, what appeared to be smoke began pouring out of *Island Fever*'s engine compartment. *Island Fever* yawed to one side as her momentum stalled, and they deployed her anchor to keep her from being blown ashore or into another boat. In *Nickerin* we raced around to lend assistance, approaching the larger boat from astern. But just as we got close, our engine died!

Aboard *Island Fever*, Mark was screaming at us to come get the students off his boat, which we all feared might have a fire in the engine compartment. I was screaming back that our own engine was dead. The students on *Island Fever* were all donning life jackets. I turned my head around to look back at Brendan, who had removed the cowl on *Nickerin*'s outboard. "I could use that engine, Brendan!" I hollered into the wind. Afterward, one of our passengers, Kurt Knowles of the Museum of Underwater Archaeology, noted that it was "just like a *Star Trek* episode." And as though we were indeed in a TV drama, at that moment Brendan pulled it off, and the motor roared to life. We sped to *Island Fever* and begin shuttling students to nearby docks and safety.

Every field school has adventures and stories, and this certainly has been true in our case over the years. We now have completed 11 field schools, and we have gotten better at it each year. We prepare our students for working in poor visibility waters through a blacked-out mask obstacle course in the pool, and we prepare them for emergencies with rescue and accident manage-

The students and staff of LAMP's 2014 Field School, on board the research vessel *Roper*, on loan from the Institute of Maritime History. *(Courtesy of St. Augustine Lighthouse & Maritime Museum)*

ment training. Our students have learned real-life lessons about overcoming adversity through teamwork and tenacity. They have gone on to graduate schools and positions as professional archaeologists across the country and abroad. Now we use the research vessel *Roper*, a 36-foot steel-hulled former trawler, which is a solid, seaworthy, and capable diving vessel, on loan to us from David Howe and the Institute of Maritime History. We have made some of our greatest discoveries in this boat.

Finding and Diving on Shipwrecks in St. Augustine

In 2009, the first year we used *Roper*, we conducted a new magnetometer and sonar survey. Countless hours were spent towing the high-tech equipment back and forth at numerous search areas in the vicinity of the historic inlet. Some of these search areas included known sites—the 1764 *Industry* wreck, the Steamship and Ballast Pile site, and the Centerboard Schooner wreck—to better understand the magnetic and sonar signatures of shipwrecks of various types and from different time periods. Most of the other search areas were positioned to include previously determined traces of magnetism that had never been located by divers.

The survey was highly successful, and by testing the magnetic data, we discovered four historic shipwrecks between 2009 and 2016. All were completely buried beneath the sand, which is the hardest kind of shipwreck to find! The first discovery was made in August 2009 in the search area code-named "Storm." I happened to be the diver to find this one, and I was working alone, tethered by my air hose to the boat where Sam was tending my line. As is often the case in St. Augustine, the water was utterly black on the bottom, and I was working blind. I was using a hydraulic probe, which is simply a 10-foot-long pipe connected by a fire hose to a water pump on the boat. The pipe jets out water, and when man-handled into an upright position and thrust downward it sinks into the sediment like a hot knife through butter. The first probe, disappointingly, hit nothing under the sand, but the second struck a hard object, which I eagerly exposed by jetting away the sand. After a period of digging blindly but determinedly, I groped in the blackness and felt a wooden plank, ballast stones, and several encrusted iron objects. This was a good sign! One of the corroded iron objects was round and large, the size and shape of a gigantic beach ball. Carefully feeling it in the dark, my questing fingers came to a flared rim and a large opening at one end. It was hollow. Trembling with excitement, I realized what it was: a large cauldron or cooking pot. With wood, stone, iron, and a recognizable historic artifact, there was nothing else this could be but a shipwreck site! We named it the Storm Wreck, after the survey area code name.

The following year the cauldron was raised to the surface in the summer of 2010, seeing sunlight for the first time in 228 years. However, an even bigger discovery on this wreck would occur on December 17, 2010. This time Sam was in the water. It was a cold December day, but the seas were uncharacteristically calm for winter, and we wanted to look at the Storm Wreck a few months after the close of our first excavation season there. Once on the dive site, no one really wanted to be the first into that frigid water, but Sam volunteered along with Mike Chapman, a member of the local sheriff's dive team. I remember actually apologizing to Mike in advance for the dive, which I assumed would be cold and dark. I even promised that if he joined us next summer, he would have a better dive experience and see some real archaeology on the wreck site. Boy, was I wrong!

Sam was utterly surprised when they descended into the cold, green waters and discovered they could still see the bottom! For the first time, he could see 10 feet or more on this shipwreck, and almost immediately he noticed a cluster of large objects. At some point the sand had shifted, so everything that had been buried by a few feet of sand just a few months ago was now exposed, including five cannons and the ship's bell!

With hearts pounding, Sam and Mike raced to the surface to share the news, which I did not even believe until Sam insisted, and I saw on his face that he was not joking. We recorded and brought up the bell that day, worried about the safety of such an important and delicate object exposed on the sea floor. During a unique event at the museum, Starr Cox cleaned the bell in front of a crowd of more than 200 people, all holding their breath in anticipation. Alas, there was no name inscribed on the bell, nor a date. Although we were disappointed at this, we were still eager to get back to the Storm Wreck; during the 2011 excavation season, we and our field school students raised two cannons from the wreck. The smaller of these, a type known as a carronade, had been invented during the American Revolution and had a date inscribed on its trunnion: 1780. Not only was this the oldest known carronade at that time, but it helped us date the Storm Wreck.

Six years were spent digging on the wreck, between 2010 and 2015. A total of 1,371 dives were completed on the wreck, comprising 1,094 hours and 12 minutes of bottom time, without any significant diving accidents. Ninety-two divers have participated in the excavation, including 55 students and dozens of volunteers. The Storm Wreck has never been identified by its original name, but it has been confirmed as one of 16 refugee ships lost in December 1782 while attempting to cross the sandbar and enter the port. Carrying British soldiers and Loyalist civilians, these vessels were members of the last fleet to evacuate Charleston, South Carolina, at the end of the Revolutionary War. Thousands of individual artifacts—including personal items, household objects, tools, ship fittings and rigging, cookware, tableware, artillery, and firearms—have been recovered by LAMP archaeologists during the excavation. Collectively, these artifacts have given us unique insights about not only daily colonial life but also what it might have been like to be uprooted hastily from home and hearth and forced to flee to an unfamiliar land in the face of wartime atrocities.

Some of the unearthed objects are simply amazing. Three British military muskets were found, two of which are still loaded (as seen in X-ray imagery). Three gold guinea coins were found, dated 1774, 1775, and 1776, that probably belonged to a gentleman. A small, delicate boxlock pistol was found, manufactured by Thomas Ketland in Birmingham, England. A refugee of less means, who likely could not afford a fashionable pocket watch, probably owned the false watch we found, whose hands were cast in pewter and could have never moved. Shoe buckles, spoons, plates, kettles, buttons, pins, locks and keys, clothing irons, tools, and even a tombstone fragment all provide a perspective on the lives of the variety of craftsmen, farmers, gentry, soldiers, slaves, and sailors from all different social classes who were literally in the same boat.

One of the small cauldrons we recovered contained, remarkably, the remnant of the last meal its owners had eaten: a single green pea. Even smaller

The ship's bell from the Storm Wreck, recovered on December 17, 2010. The bronze bell along with its wooden headstock and iron clapper were all preserved. Despite a long-standing maritime tradition, the name of the ship or its year of launching was not inscribed on the bell, so the identity of the Storm Wreck remains a mystery.

(Courtesy of the St. Augustine Lighthouse & Maritime Museum)

Author Chuck Meide (at right in wetsuit) and Brendan Burke (at center behind cannon) carefully guiding the 4-pounder cannon raised from the Storm Wreck onto the research vessel *Roper* on June 28, 2011. *(Courtesy of the St. Augustine Lighthouse & Maritime Museum)*

Director of Archaeological Conservation Starr Cox uses an airscribe to clean the carronade recovered from the Storm Wreck. This gun was originally cast in 1780 at the Carron Iron Company in Falkirk, Scotland.

(Courtesy of the St. Augustine Lighthouse & Maritime Museum)

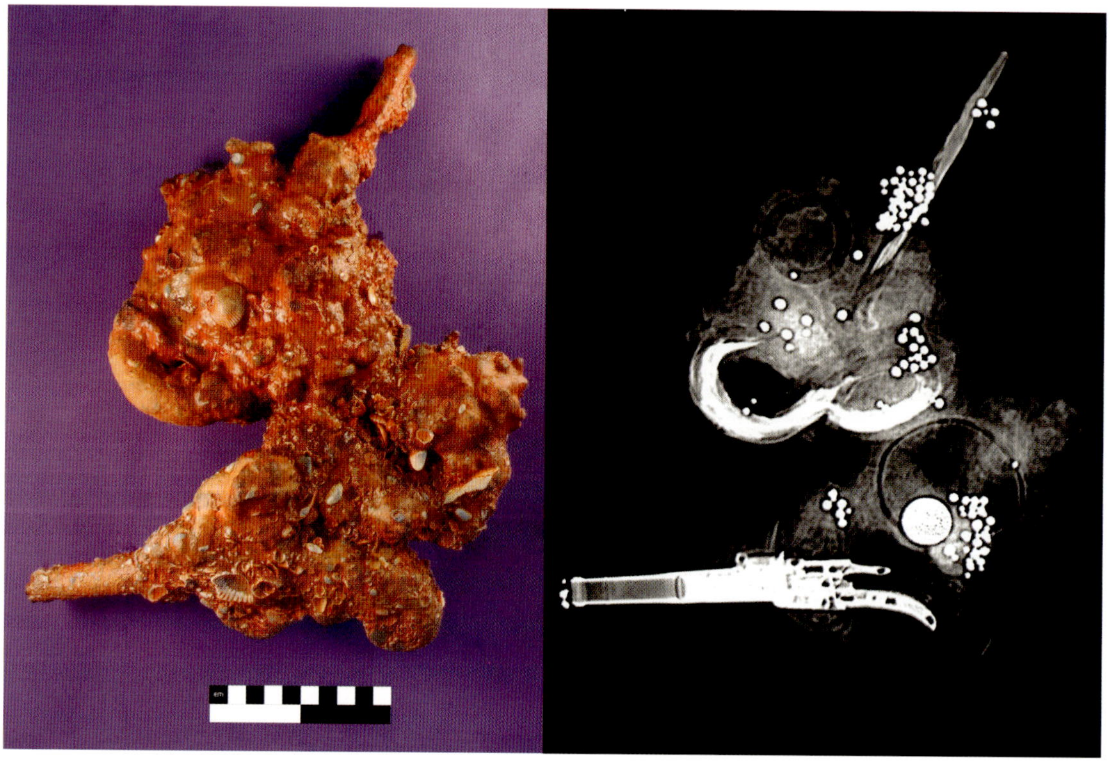

A concretion recovered from the Storm Wreck, with an X-ray image of its interior showing a large spike, numerous lead pellets (birdshot), an iron rigging hook, a rigging hank, an iron ring of unknown function, a gold coin dated 1774, and a small and very rare Queen Anne's flintlock pistol. The scale is 10 cm in length.

(Courtesy of the St. Augustine Lighthouse & Maritime Museum)

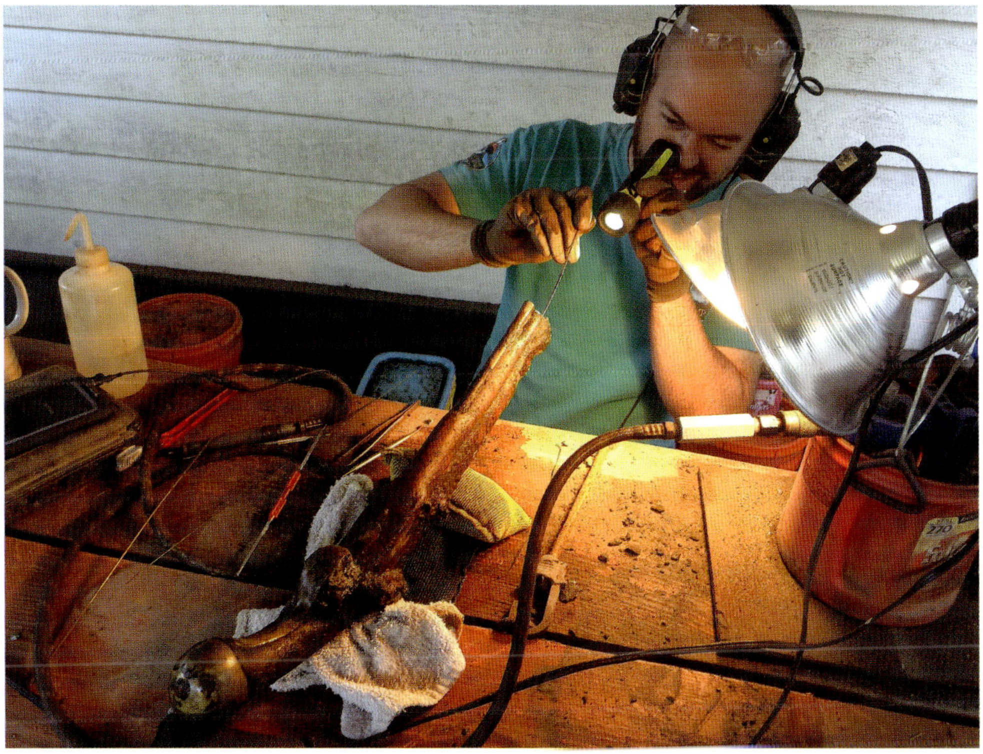

Archaeological conservator Andrew Thomson inspecting a British Navy sea service pistol he has cleaned. The pistol was recovered from the 1782 Storm Wreck.

(Courtesy of the St. Augustine Lighthouse & Maritime Museum)

LAMP Field School Supervisor Annie Carter and East Carolina University graduate student Julie Powell air scribing the largest and smallest cauldrons recovered from the Storm Wreck.

(Courtesy of the St. Augustine Lighthouse & Maritime Museum)

things survived in the sand, to be collected and forensically analyzed by archaeologists, such as the heads of the wood-boring ants that infested the wooden crates and barrels, and the body and wings of a tiny beetle that would have lived off fungus growing in a sack of grain. Many of these finds have been stabilized in the conservation laboratory and are now on display at the St. Augustine Lighthouse & Maritime Museum as part of the major new exhibit *Wrecked!*, which opened in May 2016.

Our current excavation project is known as the Anniversary Wreck, so called because we discovered it during St. Augustine's 450th anniversary in the summer of 2015. Like the Storm Wreck, this buried shipwreck scatter was found from magnetic data generated by LAMP's 2009 survey. The 2016 and 2017 field schools focused on the excavation of this shipwreck, which has proved to be another exciting find. The artifact scatter at this site is even denser than that at the Storm Wreck site. It features at least 28 iron cauldrons or cooking pots, similar in shape to those observed on the Storm Wreck but packed more closely within what appears to be the ship's cargo hold. In addition to the cauldrons there are a number of

LAMP Field School student Silvana Kreines excavates stacks of cast-iron cauldrons exposed on the Anniversary Wreck, believed to be a merchant ship lost while trying to enter St. Augustine sometime between 1750 and 1800.

(Courtesy of the St. Augustine Lighthouse & Maritime Museum)

~ The Chalupa *San Agustín* ~

Sam Turner

In 2007, the LAMP Heritage Boatworks was established at the St. Augustine Lighthouse & Maritime Museum to recover, preserve, and pass on the traditional art of boat carpentry as practiced in St. Augustine. After 10 years of work, volunteer boat builders have fabricated a total of 13 watercraft, with three more under construction. Two of these vessels are historic reproductions: a 1760s English yawl boat used in St. Augustine during the British Period (1763–1783) and an 1870s Florida skipjack such as those built on the St. Johns River. Other craft include three traditional flatboats known as *barca chatas* in Spanish as well as rowing or sailing craft that are given away as prizes in the annual boat raffle drawing. The boat drawing program brings in necessary funding to keep heritage wooden boat building alive and well in St. Augustine.

Of particular importance and a point of pride was the construction of an authentic replica of a sixteenth-century Spanish watercraft called a *chalupa*. This type of craft evolved on the north coast of Spain, where it was used by the Spanish and Basque fishing industry as well as for general transportation and as ship's boats. St. Augustine's founder, Pedro Menéndez de Avilés, and many of his soldiers and settlers were from the port of Avilés in Asturias on the northern coast of Spain. When they settled in St. Augustine in 1565, they brought their maritime culture along with them, including naval architecture and boat-building techniques.

A 2008 LAMP research trip to the Archive of the Indies in Seville, Spain, yielded a bundle of documents called the *Caja de San Agustín de Florida, cuentas de bastamientos* ("the St. Augustine box, supply accounts"). These documents detailed the king's property in St. Augustine between 1597 and 1601. Entry number 27 states "In addition add to his charge [the King's official] one chalupa that serves this presidio that was made in it for service with its masts, yards, and rudder with its irons and ten wooden oars for the service of said chalupa."

In addition to this documentation, archaeological evidence of a *chalupa* was obtained by Parks Canada in Red Bay, Labrador. A Basque whaling galleon called *San Juan* was wrecked in Red Bay 1565—the very year St. Augustine was founded. Crushed

Chalupa *San Agustín*, constructed by the St. Augustine Maritime Heritage Foundation, is equipped with 10 oars, a rudder, and two masts.

(Courtesy of the St. Augustine Lighthouse & Maritime Museum)

San Agustín, manned by Maritime Heritage Foundations volunteers conducting early rowing trials after being launched in 2015. *(Courtesy of the St. Augustine Lighthouse & Maritime Museum)*

beneath that galleon was one of her boats, a *chalupa*. Both galleon and *chalupa* were well preserved in the cold water, so information on their dimensions, planking, framing, and thwarts served to inform the St. Augustine replica project.

The *chalupa* replica project was a grass-roots community effort spearheaded by partnerships among the St. Augustine Maritime Heritage Foundation (which undertook fundraising and construction), the St. Augustine Lighthouse & Maritime Museum (which provided historical and archaeological documentation), and the Fountain of Youth Archaeological Park (which provided space for the building and interpretation of a sixteenth-century boat yard and the *chalupa*). The project took three and a half years to complete, from the groundbreaking in November of 2011 to the launching and christening in March of 2015. The *chalupa* was named *San Agustín* in honor of the city of St. Augustine, and was used for the 450th commemoration and the September 8, 2015, re-enactment of the landing of Pedro Menéndez.

Today, *San Agustín* is operated, in both rowing and sailing configurations, by the St. Augustine Maritime Heritage Foundation. The *chalupa* is used in middle school education, the annual landing day event, and as part of a living exhibit on early St. Augustine at the Fountain of Youth Archaeological Park.

San Agustín under sail.
(Courtesy of the St. Augustine Lighthouse & Maritime Museum)

casks or barrels whose contents remain unknown at present. Numerous pewter plates and a cache of bronze shoe buckles also have been unearthed, along blocks of cut stone—possibly intended for building material—and a great number of broken pottery pieces. Many of these finds may be dateable; the analysis is preliminary, but we currently believe that this shipwreck dates from 1750 to 1800, perhaps around the same time as the Storm Wreck and possibly from the Second Spanish Period. This ship appears to have been an inbound merchant vessel that wrecked fully laden with cargo. As such, its further excavation has the potential to shed light on trade patterns and the material needs of St. Augustine's consumers toward the end of the colonial period.

Place, Partnerships, Programs, and the Public: A Model for Regional Maritime Archaeology

Many factors have contributed to our success at LAMP as a regional archaeological and historical research institute. Prominent among these is our location in St. Augustine, the nation's oldest city, which attracts millions of visitors each year. Heritage tourism drives an economic engine that supports archaeology and makes it a part of the everyday life of both residents and visitors. The city of St. Augustine has an active archaeology program and was one of the first local governments to pass an ordinance protecting archaeological resources.

St. Augustine's residents have widespread appreciation of its archaeology and history, and it is one of relatively few cities with such a vibrant and sizable community of professional and avocational archaeologists. Community groups such as the St. Augustine Archaeological Association and the St. Augustine Historical Society have provided volunteer labor and institutional and financial support for LAMP's research. The Florida Public Archaeology Network, whose Northeast Regional Center is located on the Flagler College campus in St. Augustine, is another regular partner with LAMP and has provided support and assistance, particularly for outreach programming. Local academic institutions include the college and also the Historic St. Augustine Research Institute, which has provided funding for archival research, most recently for Sam's colonial Spanish research in Cuba.

LAMP's most important partner is, of course, our parent organization, the St. Augustine Lighthouse & Maritime Museum; the two effectively act as one institution. The lighthouse is the second-most visited St. Augustine attraction, behind only the National Park Service's Castillo de San Marcos. The lighthouse sees more than 220,000 visitors each year. Admissions and gift shop sales fuel its mission to discover, preserve, present, and keep alive the stories of the nation's oldest port. There are, of course, major expenses associated with maintaining a lighthouse and other historic buildings while retaining a staff of almost 50, but this revenue is sufficient to provide the staff's salary and operational funding for LAMP.

Archaeology is expensive, especially fieldwork and conservation, and LAMP also regularly seeks additional sources of income. Additional revenue streams have been generated through the annual summer field school, remote sensing workshops, donations, the annual raffle of a wooden boat built by LAMP's Heritage Boatworks, and the archaeological contracts and grants, particularly those provided by the State of Florida's Division of Historical Resources. Partnerships in the community have been critical for providing student housing, research vessels, and dockage.

A robust public archaeology program is an integral component of the LAMP model. Hundreds of thousands of visitors have participated in archaeology tours at the lighthouse and have seen its shipwreck exhibits. LAMP has sponsored symposiums and regular speaking engagements in the community and across the region, and has used blogs and social media to spread the message to a broader online community. At every opportunity, LAMP has welcomed members of the public who want to be more directly involved with archaeology in the field or in the laboratory. Certified divers can undergo scientific diving training and dive alongside archaeologists, and non-divers can crew aboard the dive boat to help catalog artifacts or log dives, or they can work in the laboratory. LAMP has taught high school students how to dive so they can join the research team, and it has a strong college internship program that has attracted dozens of students locally and from as far away as India and Australia. This dedication to public engagement has paid off in financial and logistical support and has led to more effective stewardship of archaeological resources. Over the last 17 years our community has gained an understanding of and appreciation for the archaeological heritage that is hidden beneath the waves. With this attitude comes better protection for these sites through political advocacy and a widespread preservation ethic.

With its established heritage tourism industry and local archaeological community, the nation's oldest port is certainly an ideal setting for a maritime archaeology research program. However, there is no reason why the model that has proven so successful for LAMP cannot be modified for application in other areas of Florida or elsewhere in the world.

LAMP's operations and funding strategies have changed over time, adapting to shifting circumstances, but our vision has always focused on conducting high-quality, meaningful research and sharing that research with the local and visiting communities. This vision will carry on as LAMP's current leadership enters its second decade. Years of excavation at the Storm Wreck have led to the completion of that project and the opening of a new exhibit, and the discovery of a new shipwreck promises to be just as exciting.

LAMP's headquarters at the St. Augustine Lighthouse & Museum are undergoing a fundamental change as well. As I write this, construction crews have broken ground on a new Maritime Archaeology & Education Center, which will serve as the new LAMP office, laboratory, and dive locker facility. One of the most exciting features of the new building is an observation room built into the conservation laboratory so visitors can observe artifact treatment and speak directly with scientists at work. This will ensure that LAMP's mission endures as the organization continues to evolve, sharing with millions of visitors and local residents the maritime heritage of the nation's oldest port.

Charles T. "Chuck" Meide, director of the St. Augustine Lighthouse Archaeological Maritime Program, is an accomplished maritime archaeologist who has worked on scores of shipwrecks in Bermuda, Ireland, the Caribbean, and the United States.

Dr. Sam Turner is an archaeologist, historian, and director of Heritage Boatworks at the St. Augustine Lighthouse & Maritime Museum. He has worked on shipwrecks in Europe, the Middle East, the Caribbean, and the United States. Turner is experienced in Spanish paleography, which he uses for the study of sixteenth-century Spanish documents. He has written more than 60 columns on the lives of Ponce de León and Pedro Menéndez de Avilés for Florida newspapers.

For Additional Information

Websites

LAMP Archaeological Research, http://www.lampmaritime.org/LAMP/Research/research

St. Augustine Lighthouse & Maritime Museum, http://www.staugustinelighthouse.com/

St. Augustine Maritime Heritage Foundation, http://staugmaritimeheritage.org/

Videos

Lighthouse Archaeological Maritime Program, "The Storm Wreck: St. Augustine and the Loyalist Influx," August 12, 2013, https://www.youtube.com/watch?v=0sTRPP2dSnc

St. Augustine Lighthouse & Maritime Museum, "Get Wrecked! with Underwater Archaeologists, April 14, 2016, https://www.youtube.com/watch?v=f5OF8THZojw

St. Augustine Lighthouse & Maritime Museum, "Wrecked! Uncover the Secrets of Shipwreck Artifact Conservation," April 20, 2016, https://www.youtube.com/watch?v=g_2Vj2Csm8k

University of Florida, Florida Museum of Natural History, "First Colony: Our Spanish Origins," January 7, 2014, https://www.youtube.com/watch?v=EJseaXWbMqo

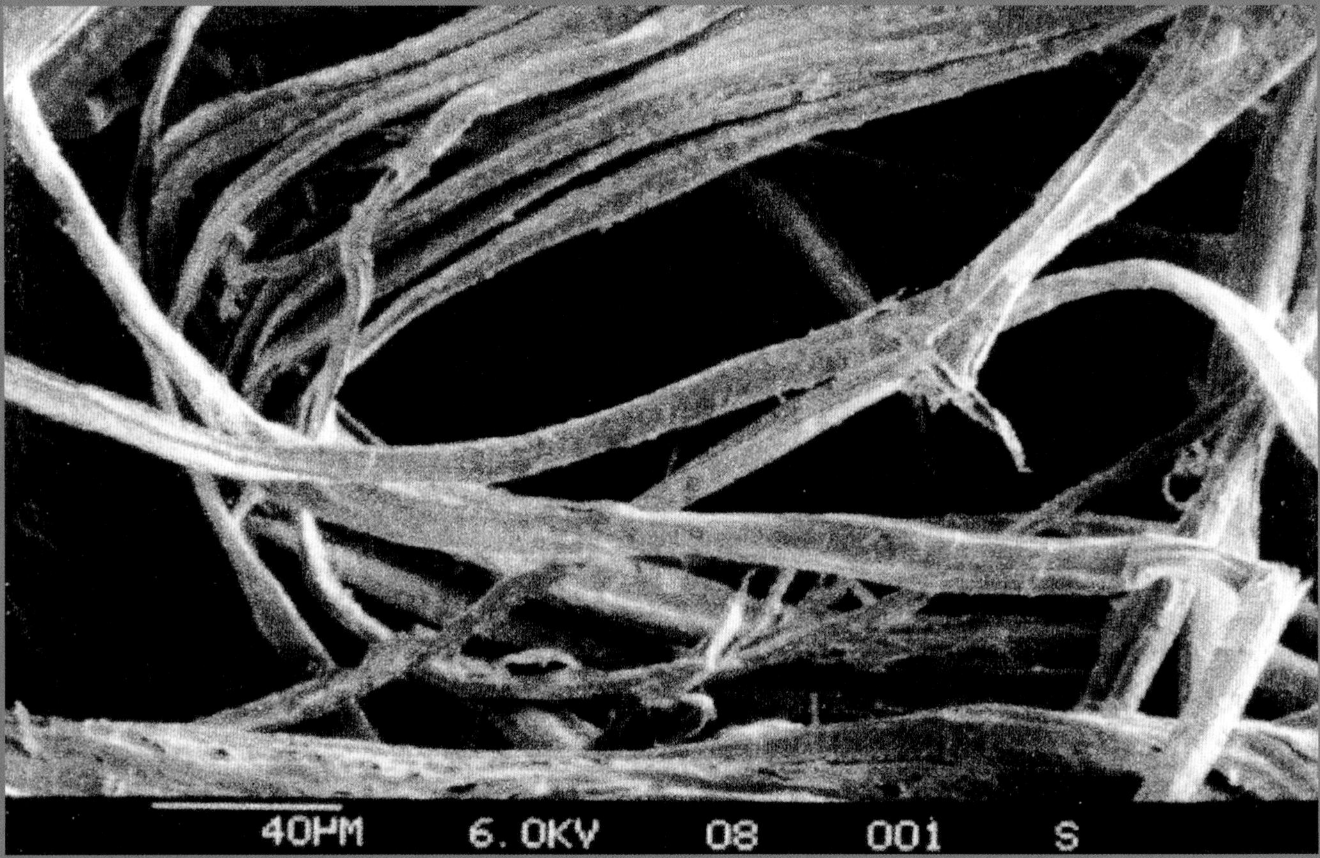
40ΜM 6.0KV 08 001 S

CHAPTER 10

Laboratory Archaeology: Conservation of Florida's Waterlogged Artifacts

JOHN R. BRATTEN

Waterlogged cultural and natural materials have an immediate need for conservation, and a number of factors can contribute to the degradation of objects once they have been removed from the water. For instance, wood allowed to dry without treatment will exhibit dramatic warping or cracking when the water-filled cells collapse. Untreated leather will be damaged by bacteria and molds. Caustic acids will form in salt-laden iron artifacts and cause irreversible damage. Even durable artifacts such as pottery, glass, or bones need treatment to remove soluble salts lest they crystallize on the surface and lift glazes or cause cracking. Insoluble salts (such as iron stains) may need to be removed carefully from artifacts to reveal diagnostic markings. Fragile items such as textiles, rope, or plant remains need to be "bulked up" with consolidants before they are dried.

To accomplish these preservation tasks, it is necessary to establish a conservation laboratory where the appropriate treatments can be performed. The laboratory also is the place where conservators and their assistants, whether they are students or volunteers, compile records, photograph objects, and begin the analysis of these objects. I have assembled two such conservation laboratories, the first at the Lake Champlain Maritime Museum and the second in Pensacola, to treat artifacts from the Emanuel

An iron cannon from the sea that has not received proper conservation treatment and is slowly disintegrating.

(Courtesy of the UWF Division of Anthropology and Archaeology)

An iron cannon from the sea that has just finished laboratory treatment and is ready for display.

(Courtesy of the Florida Division of Historical Resources)

A conserved iron cannon from a shipwreck displayed in the Museum of Florida History in Tallahassee.

(Courtesy of the Florida Division of Historical Resources)

Point Ship from the fleet of Tristán de Luna, wrecked in 1559. It has been my experience that for every two months an archaeologist spends in the field, one year will need to be spent in the laboratory. In fact, just as many, if not more, discoveries are made in the laboratory as are made in the field.

Becoming a Conservator

Archaeology and conservation are my second career—and I was not even familiar with the concept of artifact conservation until I was accepted into the Nautical Archaeology Program at Texas A&M University. While I was growing up in Missouri, I had aspirations of a career in marine biology, but Missouri was not the place to enroll in that type of program. Instead, I majored in biology and completed a number of chemistry courses. When an opportunity to receive an assistantship presented itself, I enrolled in a new master's program in science education, which required that I complete additional physics and chemistry courses.

After graduation, I was employed as a science teacher—in fact, for nine years I was the entire science department of a rural Nebraska school. Then, in 1989, I read the book *The Sea Remembers* by Peter Throckmorton, and this book about sunken ships inspired me to apply to Texas A&M's Nautical Archaeology Program. My science background led Donny Hamilton, a professor in the program, to offer me an assistantship in his conservation laboratory, where I worked for a number of years, mainly treating artifacts from the sunken city of Port Royal, Jamaica. In that laboratory I gained my first hands-on experience working with sea-encrusted iron and fragile organic artifacts.

The Port Royal artifacts were very similar to the kinds of items recovered from various shipwreck projects I have worked on in Florida. These include heavily concreted metal objects fashioned from iron and copper, waterlogged wood, ceramic fragments, glass, rope, and faunal remains. Among these have been a wealth of iron spikes and bolts, an iron breastplate, wooden rosary beads, bone dice, an ivory manicure set, a few silver coins, and far tinier items—no less interesting, and equally important—such as olive pits, rat bones, and cockroach wing fragments.

Although anyone could buy an old copy of *The Conservator's Cookbook*, the treatment of waterlogged and salt-laden artifacts is not something that should be approached using a recipe from a manual. Training and firsthand experience working in a laboratory are essential. There are also professional and ethical responsibilities that a conservator should observe. One of these is the *principal of reversibility*. Every attempt should be made to apply a treatment that can be reversed, should retreatment become necessary. For example, glues should be chosen that do not crosslink (become insoluble) or yellow over time. In addition, conservators should attend conferences to stay up to date on new techniques, and they should participate in additional conservation training courses or workshops. And if an artifact requires a conservation treatment that is beyond a conservator's training or laboratory's capabilities, it should not be given a second-rate treatment. Much like the medical doctors' adage, we should do no harm.

Equipping the Laboratory

Although conservation can begin in the field by ensuring that wet artifacts stay wet and are packaged for transport in the safest manner, the real work begins in the laboratory. The steps include accessioning (labeling and creating a record for each artifact), cleaning (mechanical or chemical, but mechanical is preferred), stabilization, note taking, artifact illustration, photo documentation (before and after), and preparations for long-term storage or exhibit. One of the real advantages of the conservation laboratory is that artifacts can be studied and documented in a controlled environment with no time limitations (unlike underwater).

So it is essential to establish the conservation laboratory long before the fieldwork begins and make it ready to receive the artifacts. With regard to a space for processing waterlogged artifacts, a wet area and a dry area should be established, if possible. Although many kinds of spaces can be used, one with access to lots of fresh water, floor drains, and a fume hood is ideal. Electrolytic cleaning vats can be placed outside if they are protected from the weather. In good weather, messy cleaning also can take place outside as long as fresh water is available. Good lighting and plenty of electrical power also are ideal. Laboratory ovens for heating solutions may require a 240-volt power supply.

As with most archaeology projects, I have never had an unlimited budget to buy new equipment, so in constructing my laboratories I have needed to be inventive. My search began with looking for containers to serve as freshwater baths into which I could place newly recovered artifacts to begin the desalination process. To this end, I

A well-appointed conservation laboratory, which includes a first-aid kit, refrigerator, and a mechanical cleaning station with fume hood (left), an electrolytic cleaning station (center), and a freeze drying station (right). Behind the closed door is an X-ray machine.

(Courtesy of the UWF Division of Anthropology and Archaeology)

obtained several stainless steel vats for free from a photo-developing company that recently had gone out of business. I also converted old display case bonnets into clear Plexiglas vats by reinforcing their sides with epoxy. Plastic 55-gallon drums cut in half also have made good storage containers, as have a variety of other, smaller plastic containers. The process of desalination itself is easily monitored with a handheld conductivity monitor.

An X-ray machine is extremely useful for documenting and identifying concreted iron objects, but before I had my own machine I found that many dentists, chiropractors, physicians, and veterinarians were happy to X-ray our artifacts out of sheer interest in the projects. The first X-ray machine I eventually obtained for my laboratory was an older model that had been reclaimed from a dentist's office and used as a display item in a dental exhibit at the T. T. Wentworth Jr. State Museum in Pensacola. One quick phone call to a local X-ray company later, a salesman not only came to inspect my machine for safety, but also donated a large amount outdated X-ray film that we could use for conservation purposes. After this first machine was relegated to its own artifact status, I acquired a portable military unit, which I used for several years. Today, I use a fully digital model that was designed for a veterinarian: its large examination table makes it absolutely ideal for a conservation laboratory, and the resulting digital radiographs can be saved on a computer hard drive, thus eliminating the need for a darkroom to develop films.

A dental X-ray machine that was kindly loaned to us for use at the first Pensacola laboratory in the T. T. Wentworth Jr. State Museum. *(Courtesy of the Florida Division of Historical Resources)*

Conservation students Andrew Willard (left) and Stephen Atkinson (right) cleaning a wooden cannon carriage wheel. *(Courtesy of the UWF Division of Anthropology and Archaeology)*

Staffing the Laboratory

A conservation laboratory is not complete without staff, and mine have been filled with numerous volunteers and students. For the last 20 years, I have taught an artifact conservation class that provides students with hands-on laboratory experience. The course begins with safety considerations, then moves to the use of adhesives and consolidants. From there, the students practice their newly acquired textbook skills on ceramics, glass, stone, leather, rope, wood, and all types of metals.

Of the many useful conservation manuals, journals, and reports that are available, the laboratory manual I use with my students is *Methods of Conserving Archaeological Material from Underwater Sites* by Donny L. Hamilton of Texas A&M University. This is the same conservation manual that I used as a student; it has been updated numerous times and is available online for download.

In the course of our work, many of these people have revealed unanticipated talents for artifact drawing or photography, while others have turned out to be proficient with the use of computers, and they have created the databases that are so essential for report writing. Many of these same students continue to volunteer in the laboratory or enroll in a directed study course to learn advanced conservation techniques and work on larger or composite artifacts. Often, this conservation experience has helped these students find their first employment or gain entry into a graduate program in conservation.

Techniques of Conservation

Many conservation treatments can be performed with a modest budget, although costs will increase when paid assistants are used because conservation can be very time-consuming. Although the limited space prevents me from describing actual treatments in detail, I can offer a few general examples. Some objects, such as coarse earthenware fragments, may require little treatment—simple washing and desalination. But other objects, such organic artifacts like wood, leather, or rope, require more complex treatments: in this case, a freeze dryer is used to remove water so that cellular collapse is prevented. After a pretreatment with a 30 percent polyethylene glycol solution, the artifact is placed in the freeze dryer and flash frozen; then the water is removed by sublimation—it goes directly from solid form to gas.

Numerous pieces of equipment and chemicals associated with analysis and preservation treatments can be purchased cheaply and locally, but others must be purchased from specialized companies. Larger items such as X-ray machines or freeze dryers can be very expensive ($30,000 to $80,000 and up). The items required for safety also can be expensive, such as fume hoods or safety showers. The common laboratory chemicals range from baking soda (sodium bicarbonate, used as a soft polishing agent) and alcohol (a dehydration agent) to polyethylene glycol (a wood consolidant) and Acryloid B-72 (a reversible glue and consolidant). The typical equipment also includes photo copy stands, plastic containers, dental picks, and DC power supplies.

Electrolytic Reduction

Metal artifacts, such as a concreted iron gudgeon (one of the large iron straps used to secure the rudder to the stern of a ship), may require months of effort. After detailed drawings and photographs of the object have been obtained, hours of work

Chuck Hughson mechanically cleaning a large iron conglomerate with a pneumatic chisel.

(Courtesy of the Florida Division of Historical Resources)

can ensue carefully removing the adhering concretion from the iron with a pneumatic air scribe. Then a treatment known as electrolytic reduction is applied to remove the chloride compounds from metal objects that have been immersed in salt water for hundreds of years. Larger objects such as anchors or cannons may require several years of conservation efforts to ensure that they are free of the presence of chlorides.

Electrolytic reduction involves a tank filled with a large volume of electrolyte solution, which may need to be changed several times during the process. First the metal artifact is attached to the negative terminal of a DC power supply, and the tank (if it is made of metal—stainless steel is ideal, but mild steel will work) is connected to the positive terminal. Chlorides, the negative ions contained in salt, are drawn from the artifact (the cathode) by the attraction of the positively charged tank (the anode). Hydrogen is released from the artifact, and oxygen from the tank walls. These hydrogen bubbles loosen any final corrosion on the metal, thereby performing a mechanical cleaning process as the chlorides are removed. The negative flow of electrons to the artifact also will "reduce" some of the corrosion products on the artifact's surface, resulting in a smoother finish. This relatively straightforward treatment can be performed in most laboratories efficiently and relatively cheaply.

Conservation of an Iron Anchor

In March 2014, the University of West Florida received an iron anchor for conservation. Heavily laden in concretion, the anchor had been raised from its location in the Gulf of Mexico by a trawler. Unfortunately, it was allowed to sit outside for almost a year and had begun to deteriorate at an increasingly rapid rate. To preserve as much detail as possible, UWF agreed to conserve the anchor. The first steps in the conservation process were photographic documentation, three-dimensional (3D) scanning, and precise recording of anchor's dimensions.

The next step was to remove the bulk of the adhering marine concretion from the surface of the anchor by mechanical means. This task was completed with the use of a handheld pneumatic chisel (an air scribe) as well as a hammer and chisel. Care was taken to remove the concretion with as little damage as possible to its original surface. After the mechanical cleaning process, the anchor was placed in a large stainless steel tank for an electrolysis treatment.

The anchor was carefully lowered onto stacked cinder and wooden blocks to prevent it from touching the tank, then it was submerged in approximately 2,000 gallons of fresh water. For several months, conservators periodically measured the percentage of chlorides that had migrated into the anchor over its centuries of immersion in the salty sea water.

The primary conservation treatment used for the anchor was electrolytic reduction cleaning, also known as electrolysis, which relies on a DC power source, an alkaline electrolyte, and an anode (the stainless steel tank). By passing an electric current between the tank and the anchor, cleaning is performed by the liberation of hydrogen bubbles at the cathode (the anchor and negative terminal). Negatively charged chloride ions are removed by attraction to the positive tank (the anode), and reduction is possible because of the addition of electrons to the corroded iron.

Two views of a pre-conserved anchor with a concreted surface that were produced by measurements, photo documentation, and three-dimensional scanning.

(Courtesy of the UWF Division of Anthropology and Archaeology)

The anchor being lowered into a stainless steel tank with the help of a forklift.

(Courtesy of the UWF Division of Anthropology and Archaeology)

Stephen Atkinson preparing the anchor and tank for electrolysis by connecting electrical leads to both.

(Courtesy of the UWF Division of Anthropology and Archaeology)

Once the electrical leads were properly attached and the tank prepped for solution, conservators filled the tank again with fresh water, then added

The cleaned anchor receiving a final tannic acid coating.

(Courtesy of the UWF Division of Anthropology and Archaeology)

approximately 758 pounds of sodium sesquicarbonate to create a 5 percent electrolyte solution. Once electrolysis had commenced, conservators closely observed the anchor in the following weeks and months to ensure that the conservation process was working well and to monitor the chloride level in the solution. Electrolysis began in October 2014 and concluded in December 2015. At that time, it was determined that chlorides were not present to a degree that might damage the anchor (less than 100 parts per million). The remaining concretion was sufficiently loosened so that the final mechanical cleaning could be accomplished.

After removal of the electrolyte solution, the anchor was given three full-tank rinses in fresh water to remove any residual electrolyte from the iron. Finally, three coats of protective tannic acid were applied to inhibit rusting of the anchor.

Artifact Analysis

The science of conservation has changed considerably during the last 20 years. One striking improvement has been the application of recent advances in physical and chemical sciences to artifact studies. Some of the specialized analyses conducted or contracted through the Emanuel Point Ship Conservation Laboratory have included computerized axial tomography (CAT) scans, ballast analysis, lead isotope ratio analysis, and botanical and faunal species verification, all of

This iron breastplate, recovered from the Emanuel Point Ship, consisted of a heavy encrustation with almost no parent metal inside.

(Courtesy of the Florida Division of Historical Resources)

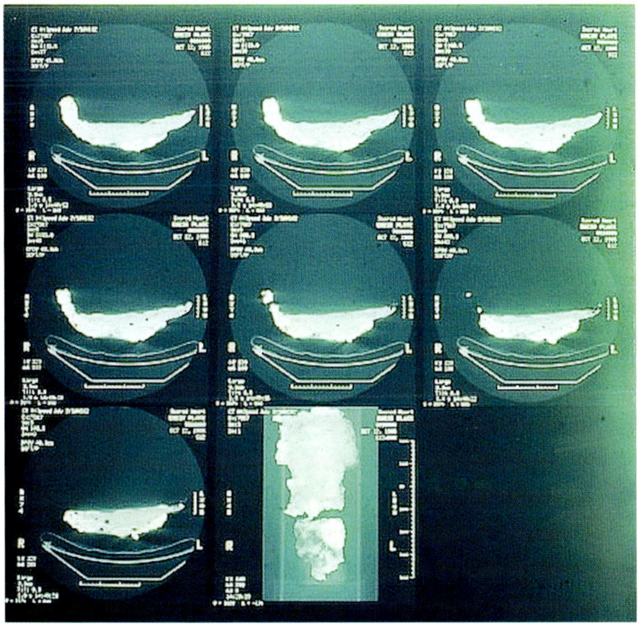

These cross sectional views of the iron breastplate were produced by CAT-scanning.

(Courtesy of the Florida Division of Historical Resources)

which have provided additional clues to the identification and interpretation of the various shipwrecks we have investigated.

Computed Axial Tomography

The use of CAT scans to examine a concreted piece of armor provides an excellent illustration of the collaboration between other sciences and archaeology. The breastplate was recovered from the Emanuel Point Ship adjacent to the after edge of the rudder in the starboard stern area. Heavily encrusted, the plate was recorded carefully in situ and removed from its context for transit to the laboratory. However, due to its extreme weight and fragile condition, the plate cracked upon recovery and arrived in the three pieces. After an examination in the laboratory, we determined that almost none of the original metal remained in the heavy concretion.

This armor, like most iron artifacts recovered from a marine environment, was completely

This replica of the iron breastplate from the Emanuel Point Ship was based on CAT-scan images of the original.

(Courtesy of the Florida Division of Historical Resources)

encased in a heavy coating of mineral deposits. Before any attempt was made to conserve the concreted armor, we thought it would be prudent to determine the original shape and the extent of corrosion. A series of high-quality X-rays was taken of the breastplate at Sacred Heart Hospital in Pensacola. The CAT scanning procedure employs a spinning X-ray head that allows a person to view a human organ (or an artifact) on a computer monitor in real time. The device can rotate or slice the image in any direction or thickness. In the case of the breastplate, cross sections were made across the longitudinal axis at 1-centimeter intervals. Overhead views and close-ups of the arm and neck openings provided additional details of the overall construction and degree of preservation.

Not surprisingly, the radiographs of the breastplate revealed that no original iron was left within the encrustation. The images clearly showed a detailed mold of the object, although cracked and broken in several places. The information derived from the cross sections was sufficient to enable measured drawings of the breastplate to be prepared from which a replica could be made. Although the left side of the breastplate is broken, slightly deformed, and incomplete, it was possible to reconstruct it by comparison with the almost perfectly preserved right side. From the features visible in the images, we ascertained that the breastplate was made in Italy or Spain around 1510.

Because all the original metal in the breastplate had been converted into very soft iron corrosion products (mostly iron sulfide), we decided that the best conservation treatment would be to make a cast of the plate by filling the cleaned concretion mold with epoxy. With this technique, a close copy of the front side of the breastplate was fashioned. Based on the CAT scan procedure, a very detailed drawing was made by Ian Eaves, the former Keeper of Armour for the Tower of London. From that, we commissioned a replica from a firm in England, that now is on display in our Archaeology Institute.

Metallurgical Analyses

Several large metallic containers were recovered from the bow of the Emanuel Point Ship that we believed were associated with the ship's galley. A few of these were corroded to such an extent that the composition of the parent metal was in question. To learn more about the metal, we sent samples from the bottom of one large pitcher to the Chemistry Centre of the Western Australia Maritime Museum, where an elemental analysis was conducted with a scanning electron microscope equipped with an energy dispersive X-ray analyzer (SEM/EDXRA). The results indicated that the samples were mainly composed of copper sulfide, suggesting that the vessel was made of copper. However, the corrosion pattern was not entirely consistent with that of an anaerobic attack on pure copper.

We requested a second analysis of the metal from the Winterthur Museum Analytical Labo-

Chuck Hughson displays the large copper pitcher that was found to be lined with tin. It was used aboard the Emanuel Point Ship to heat liquids on the firebox.

(Courtesy of the Florida Division of Historical Resources)

ratory in Winterthur, Delaware. Technicians at that laboratory subjected samples from the bottom, interior, and exterior walls of the vessel to qualitative energy dispersive X-ray fluorescence. Once again, the major component of each sample was copper, but small concentrations of tin, antimony, silver, and lead also were detected in each part. Comparison with a reference standard indicated that copper was present in concentrations of 98+ percent, whereas the other components appeared in concentrations of less than 1 percent.

Based on these data, we concluded that the pitcher was made primarily of copper alloyed with small amounts of several other elements. However, the tin content of the sample from the interior of the pitcher was about three times as high as that found in any other sample. This finding suggested that the pitcher's interior may have been tin-lined, a common practice with copper vessels.

The object was conserved by washing it in a weak solution of sodium sesquicarbonate at 2 percent concentration. This process helped to wash out the chlorides formed from contact with sea water, but caused minimal disruption of the sulfides—had those corrosion products been removed, there would have been nothing left of the vessel.

One other vessel from the Emanuel Point Ship was subjected to metallurgical analysis. A two-handled, round-bottomed cauldron composed of riveted copper plates was found to contain an extremely heavy, dense residue within its bottom. This residue was tested at Duquesne University in Pittsburgh, Pennsylvania. The chemists at that laboratory identified the substance as pine tar, suggesting that the cauldron had contained pitch. The pitch may have been heated in the cauldron and then used for caulking the deck seams of the ship.

Isotope Analysis

Lead isotope analysis is a geological dating process that can be applied to shipwreck archaeology. Like carbon-14 dating, lead isotope dating is based on the predictable disintegration rate of radioactive elements. Lead has four principal isotopes, and their radioactive decay ratios will vary according to the age of the lead. The isotopic composition of the lead is determined by mass spectrometry, and the ratios are plotted against each other to produce a growth curve. The determination of proveniences by lead isotope studies can provide additional clues to the original building site of ships, the regions where the vessels may have undergone repair, or the geographical location of the mines from which the lead was obtained.

Isotope determinations were made for lead samples recovered from the Emanuel Point Ship and a second shipwreck from the Luna fleet (EPII) located nearby (see Chapter 8). To our surprise, all 30 samples were sourced to a single mine in Spain.

Organic Materials Analyses

Survival of organic materials at an archaeological site is determined largely by the matrix (the surrounding material), which usually is some kind of sediment or soil. These vary in their effects on organic materials. Extremely acidic or alkaline matrices, or those with bacteria or other microorganisms, can be very destructive. Fortunately, the survival of organic materials from both Emanuel

Point vessels is extremely good. The high degree of preservation is due primarily to the exclusion of oxygen by waterlogging and the rapid silt deposition onto the wreck sites because of their proximity to a bayou.

Fibers

The discovery of a fabric sample from the first Emanuel Point Ship was fortuitous because textiles do not tend to survive for any length of time in the archaeological record except in extremely dry or frozen environments. The textile sample was discovered in the stern area, between a lead sheet and an iron strap (gudgeon) used to secure the rudder to the ship. The textile originally was placed under the lead sheet to act as a gasket or caulking.

The fiber sample was identified at the U.S. Department of Agriculture's Southern Regional Research Center in New Orleans. Technicians at that laboratory carefully teased individual fibers from the sample to examine them with an ordinary light microscope and a scanning electron microscope. The analysis indicated that the fibers probably are hemp, especially since the fibers twisted counterclockwise after drying, which is consistent with hemp.

It is likely that the hemp fabric is discarded sail cloth. Standard Spanish naval practice called for collecting rigging and sails from ships on returning voyages and distributing them for use

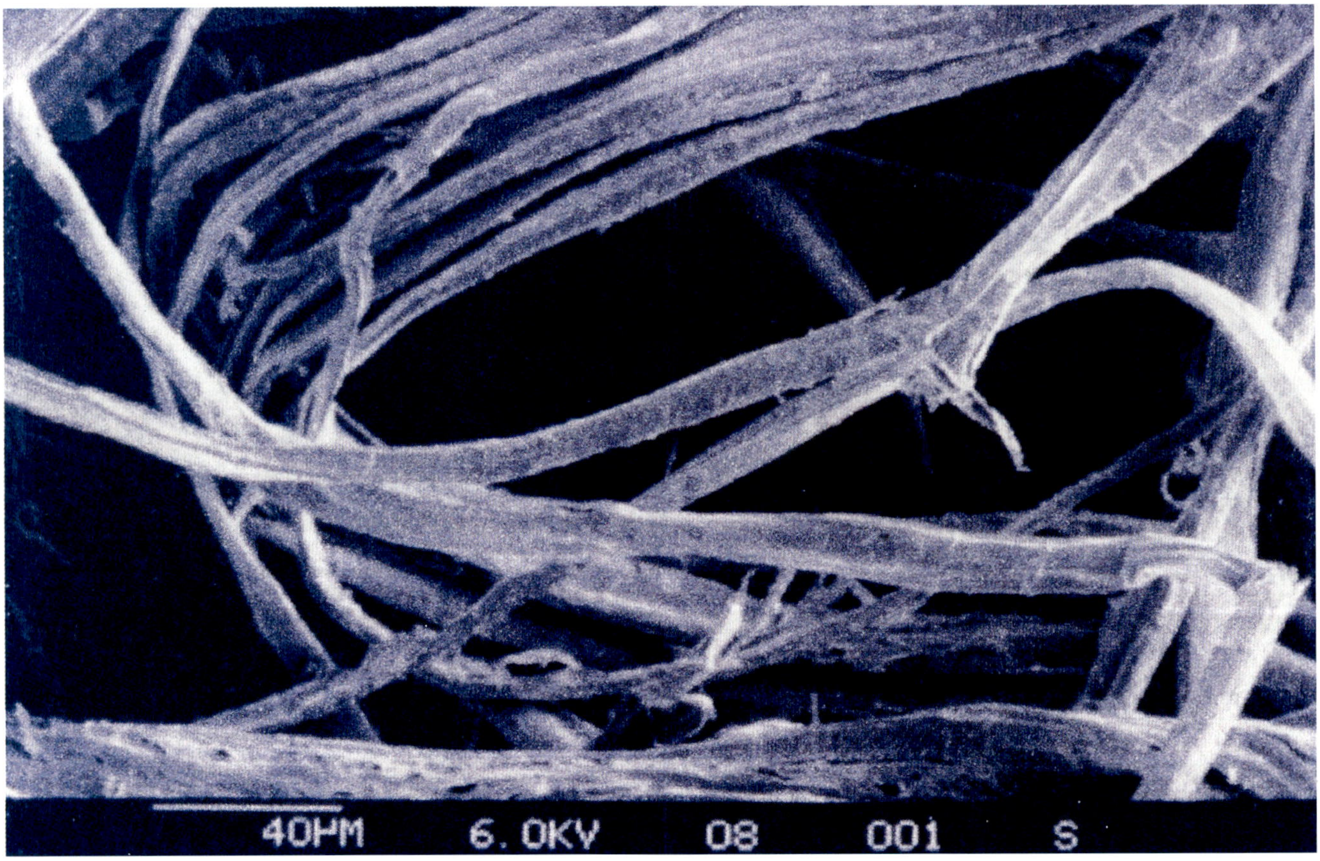

A scanning electron microscope view of the fabric thought to be hemp that was used as a caulking between a lead sheet and the wooden hull of the Emanuel Point Ship. *(Courtesy of the Florida Division of Historical Resources)*

in one fleet while another underwent careening. Some would be used to cover stored boxes of biscuit and gunpowder to protect them from rats, and others, such as this sample, ended up as caulking material.

Dunnage

Below midships ballast and between frames in the stern, the first Emanuel Point Ship's bilge sediments preserved a surprising array of other organic debris that accumulated during the vessel's sailing career. Materials recovered in these deposits include wooden packing materials (dunnage), leather, rope and cordage, animal remains, and a variety of botanical specimens, such as leaves, nuts, and seeds.

Intermixed in the ship's ballast were examples of rough-hewn wood that may constitute a portion of the ship's dunnage, used to pack and cushion cargo in the ship's lower hold atop the ballast stones. The small wooden branches occur in various lengths and diameters, and many retain a golden-colored bark. Two species of the dunnage wood have been identified—persimmon and hornbeam. Both types are native to the New World, which implies that the vessel was provisioned (or reprovisioned) in Mexico or elsewhere in the New World before its voyage to Florida.

Leather

Several leather fragments were recovered during excavation of the main mast step. The largest pieces are the remains of shoes that exhibit stitching holes on the outer edges. Many of the holes retain traces of the original thread that secured individual parts of the shoes. The leather fragments have been identified tentatively as cow hide that probably was tannin treated. Two of the largest leather fragments may have belonged to a woman's or girl's platform shoe, known as a *chapin*, of typical Spanish style, and a man's boot.

Faunal Remains

A large number of complete or fragmented bones and teeth (non-human) were identified from the excavation campaigns at both Emanuel Point Ships. Faunal specimens were collected from all test and excavation units inside and outside the surviving ship structure. Information such as sex, age criteria, and taphonomic processes (burning, cut marks, rodent gnawing, and breakage) was noted for all materials, along with limited morphometric data. Faunal specimens collected from the ships' bilges appear to represent deposits of discarded bones from shipboard provisions as well as the remains of animals that died in or near the ship. The specimens include the bones of domestic pigs, cows, sheep or goats, and domestic chickens. Several specimens exhibit cut or saw marks that indicate butchering practices.

The largest collection of faunal remains comes from stowaway rats that bred and died in the ships during their careers at sea—most notably bones from black rats (*Rattus rattus*). Analysis of the mandible and maxilla specimens revealed ancient evidence of moderate to severe abscesses and infections in the rat population. In addition, six limb bones from very young (immature) rats were noticeably stunted and have a distinctive, abnormally flaring or cuplike outgrowth of the end of the shafts. These pathological changes typically are associated with rickets.

Considering the large population of rats on board, the discovery of two left tibiae (lower rear

These large animal bones were part of the food stores carried aboard the ships. *(Courtesy of the Florida Division of Historical Resources)*

limb bones) of the European house mouse (*Mus musculus L.*, or more properly *Mus domesticus*) was unexpected. The mice probably thrived in another niche aboard the ship—perhaps above the waterline, closer to the human occupational zones; in this case, they more appropriately might be called "ship mice." The remains of a cat discovered on the second Emanuel Point Ship suggest that there was an attempt by the Spanish to keep these vermin under control.

A number of insect parts were uncovered in situ from deposits containing olive pits and other organic materials in the ballast. Examination of these remains revealed the presence of the wing, pronotum (a thoracic segment), and ootheca (egg case) of the American cockroach (*Periplaneta americana*). The remainder of the sample consisted of elytra (wing covers) from a species of *Dermestes*, most likely *Dermestes maculatus* De Geer, commonly known at the hide beetle.

Undoubtedly, hide beetles were an even greater shipboard pest than the cockroach. Hide beetle larvae bore into hard and soft woods, and they have been known to damage cork, books, tobacco, tea, linen, cotton, woolens, salt, and even lead. Most frequently noted is the beetle's indiscriminate boring into various materials that are not used as food. Both larvae and adult hide beetles feed on a variety of substances with high protein content (such as bones, carcasses, skins, meats, or cheese). Their presence aboard the first Emanuel Point Ship suggests that they may have been brought aboard with a cargo, possibly leather hides.

Botanical Remains

Archaeobotanical analyses from this shipwreck show diverse examples of plant remains that help establish the ship's cultural association, its original region of embarkation, and its subsequent travels. Most archaeobotanical remains from the shipwreck consist of seeds and nuts from both tropical and temperate trees. Edible soft fruits from three American species and three European domesticates have been identified. The American taxa are the common persimmon, sapote, and (tentatively identified) papaya. Each species has a long history of use by different Native American peoples throughout the circum-Caribbean. The three European fruit trees represented in the ship remains include olive, plum/prune, and cherry. More than 400 olive pits from two distinct varieties have been identified as "Gordal" and "Mission" olives. Both types were, and still are, grown in the Andalusia region of Spain and are morphologically distinct from African and Portuguese varieties.

Several edible nut species appear in the Emanuel Point assemblage, including European almond and hazelnut. Two American nut-producing genera are identified as hickory and oak. A single fragment of coconut shell was recovered. Coconut is considered pantropical, but it is uncertain whether it was present in the Atlantic Ocean and Caribbean before the European presence in the Americas. Two fragments of bottle gourd rind were recovered as well; the hard-shelled fruits may have served as containers aboard the vessel. Other seeds, leaves, and twigs, the presence of

These olive pits represent the staple Spanish food fare that came with colonists to the Americas.

(Courtesy of the Florida Division of Historical Resources)

which may be the result of sediment deposition after the wreck, include magnolia, swamp tupelo, red maple, and live oak.

Similar trends are seen in the plant foods found aboard the second Emanuel Point Ship, providing further evidence that these vessels were indeed from the same fleet, but they display subtle differences as well. Olive pits again represent the most commonly recovered food item. This is not surprising, because olives were an important part of Spanish diets. Plum, cherry, hazelnut, persimmon, hickory, and acorn were also found on the second Emanuel Point Ship.

The absence of European wine grape specimens is curious, considering their presence on other early shipwrecks and their frequent mention in documentary records, but wine residues or grape seeds may have been missed by the sampling thus far.

To test the feasibility of recovering pollen from the shipwreck, several sediment samples were collected from bilge debris in the pump wells, mast step mortise, and between the floors and buttresses of the first Emanuel Point Ship. Four sediment samples were sent to the Palynology Laboratory at Texas A&M University for pollen processing and a presence/absence analysis.

Preservation of pollen in the samples ranged from fair to good. Each sample contained a large amount of pollen, a variety of taxa, few indeterminate grains, and high concentration values. The fossil pollen recovered in the samples was dominated by pine, with lesser contributions of pecan, walnut, maple, oak, ragweed, sunflower, and corn or maize grasses. These pollen types reflect the contributions of floral types that are indigenous to the areas bordering Pensacola Bay. The initial presence/absence analysis confirmed that sufficient quantities of identifiable pollen are preserved in the bilge sediments to warrant statistically valid counts. A complete analysis of these samples and future samples taken from the wreck may yield more specific information pertaining to the environment at the time the wreck occurred, the shipboard diet, and the cargo.

We have not undertaken an extensive pollen analysis yet, but I hope to encourage one of my students to do this. One student did write an excellent thesis about the foodways of the first Emanuel Point Ship that discussed the Spanish diet and its parallels with the artifacts found on the ship. Other students have written theses related to the floral and faunal assemblages of both wrecks at the time of this writing.

✳ ✳ ✳

The conservation and analysis of the artifacts recovered from a shipwreck are essential to completing the story behind the people who sailed the ships. Just as archaeology fills in the gaps that the historical record leaves out, archaeology will never be complete without the complete laboratory analysis. The bulk of the conservation work for the first Emanuel Point Ship has been completed (a 25-year undertaking!). However, analysis of the material is ongoing. Now that we have found additional wrecks associated with Tristán de Luna's fleet, comparisons can be made and new analyses conducted, and much of this work will be undertaken by students.

Dr. John R. Bratten, chair and associate professor of the Department of Anthropology at the University of West Florida, has taught nautical archaeology and artifact conservation to scores of undergraduate and graduate students over the years. Bratten is the author of *The Gondola* Philadelphia *and the Battle of Lake Champlain* (Texas A&M University Press, 2002).

For Additional Information

Publications

"About Conservation: What Is Conservation?" American Institute for Conservation of Historic and Artistic Works, http://www.conservation-us.org/about-conservation

Colleen Reese, "After the Dive, What Happens to All Those Artifacts?" University of West Florida Maritime Field School 2008, October 7, 2008, Museum of Underwater Archaeology, http://mua.apps.uri.edu/project_journals/wf/wf_10-7.shtml

Andrew Thomson, "18th Century Cannon Conservation—The Next Step," October 6, 2015, St. Augustine Lighthouse and Maritime Museum Keeper's Blog, http://www.blogstaugustinelighthouse.org/tag/artifact-conservation/

Websites

Florida Division of Historical Resources: Collections and Conservation, http://dos.myflorida.com/historical/archaeology/collections-and-conservation/

Mel Fisher Maritime Museum, Conservation, http://melfisher.org/conservation.htm

Smithsonian Museum Conservation Institute, https://www.si.edu/mci/english/research/index.html

Videos and Recordings

Judy Bense, "Unearthing Florida: Conservation" (audio presentations), WUWF Public Media, http://unearthingflorida.org/inside/listen6.htm

"The St. Johns Wreck: Solving a Sunken Mystery, Part II—Artifact Conservation," Mel Fisher Maritime Museum, https://www.youtube.com/watch?v=H2cu_PMwu2s Short documentary on metal artifact preservation in the laboratory

CHAPTER 11

Museums in the Sea and Time Capsule Trails: Public Outreach and Partnerships to Preserve Florida's Maritime Heritage

DELLA A. SCOTT-IRETON

Florida's amazing variety of submerged archaeological sites is a lure for scuba divers from all over the world. Our state's warm, generally clear water, vibrant artificial and natural reefs, and plethora of marine life increase its attraction, but the added mystery of sunken ships creates a more compelling allure. Florida is considered one of the top diving locations in the world, and definitely is the leader in the continental United States. The diving industry in the state, including dive shops, instruction, referral training, gear sales and maintenance, and charter boat operators, annually caters to tens of thousands of local and visiting divers while contributing millions of dollars to Florida's economy. The pressure of all these visitors can negatively affect the fragile, nonrenewable submerged historic sites. Further, media-induced misinformation about Florida's shipwrecks has resulted in gullible divers believing that every wreck around the state contains treasure for the taking. When they do not find gold and silver, these ill-informed divers sometimes settle for taking other "souvenirs" of their visit, damaging both the wreck site and the ecosystem formed around it.

As archaeologists working for the State of Florida figured out years ago, even though all historic shipwrecks in Florida are protected under state or federal law,

Logo of Florida's state underwater archaeology team in the Bureau of Archaeological Research.

(Courtesy of the Florida Division of Historical Resources)

Bronze plaque designating *Urca de Lima* as a State Underwater Archaeological Preserve.

(Courtesy of the Florida Division of Historical Resources)

the best way to safeguard our underwater cultural sites is to educate divers about the place these sites occupy in our heritage and their value as a tangible part of our common past. Toward this end, an array of strategies, programs, and partnerships has been developed to educate and inform the public—both diving and landlubber—and to engage them in Florida's maritime heritage and underwater archaeology. Let's explore them!

Underwater Archaeological Preserves

The first concerted effort to provide public information about Florida's historic shipwrecks was the state's Underwater Archaeological Preserve system. These "museums in the sea" are historic shipwrecks around the state that are interpreted especially for divers and snorkelers. The ships' histories and archaeology are presented through printed brochures and a poster, and a comprehensive website also enables virtual visits to the ship sites via photos and videos. A laminated underwater guide helps diving visitors navigate the wrecks and distinguish what they are seeing. The first of these "shipwreck parks" was created in 1987 at the wreck of *Urca de Lima*, one of the casualties of the 1715 Spanish plate fleet that was cast ashore in a hurricane on Florida's east coast. The ship had grounded in about 20 feet of water, and much of her cargo was salvaged soon after the disaster. Because the site was known to local divers, officials of St. Lucie County where the shipwreck is located asked the state's Bureau of Archaeological Research (BAR) to make the site a park to deter the continued treasure hunting and unlawful looting. The successful creation of the *Urca de Lima* Underwater Archaeological Preserve sparked interest in other areas of the state, where local diving operators wanted their own shipwreck parks.

To respond to these requests, BAR archaeologists developed a process for establishing additional Preserves, which has proven effective and efficient. The process begins with a nomination from the public, which sets in motion an inspection by BAR archaeologists to ensure that the shipwreck meets certain criteria. The ship does not need to be famous, but it does need to be located in state waters and have something interesting to

Poster for Florida's Underwater Archaeological Preserves.
(Courtesy of the Florida Division of Historical Resources)

Friends of *Regina* recording the shipwreck to create a site plan for interpretation.
(Photo courtesy of the Florida Division of Historical Resources)

see, offer safe diving conditions, and have a verifiable history. If the site meets these basic guidelines, an official proposal is produced that contains the site's history, a biological assessment, and an archaeological site plan. The proposal is presented to the public at an open meeting held near the shipwreck site. If the community accepts the proposal, the project continues toward official establishment. If the locals reject a proposal, the state will not pursue the nomination—but to date, this has never happened. The information produced by the project is used to create interpretive materials, and the new Preserve is presented to the public in a grand opening ceremony. Part of the ceremony is placing a bronze marker at the shipwreck site to identify its status as an Underwater Archaeological Preserve and Florida Heritage Site. The ship also is nominated to the National Register of Historic Places; at this writing, all 12 of Florida's Preserves have been listed successfully on the national register.

One of the most important elements of the preserve process is the creation of a "Friends" group for the shipwreck. Composed of local people who want to get involved, Friends groups generally include divers, charter boat operators, a local historical society, and sometimes school children, politicians, and others with a vested interest in boosting heritage tourism in their community. The Friends groups help to promote the Preserve proposal, organize meetings, raise funds, design the brochure, create a shore-based exhibit, and address other needs. Diving Friends who want to help with fieldwork to record the wreck are an important source of assistance. To train these divers in archaeological methods, BAR developed the Orientation to Underwater Archaeology for Sport Divers course. This hands-on workshop teaches methods of nonintrusive recording and monitoring so divers effectively can help archaeologists to produce the site plan and can continue their assistance with ongoing Preserve management. The bureau relies on these trained and interested individuals to inspect the Preserves periodically and report any evidence of vandalism or looting.

This proven systematic process has enabled BAR archaeologists to make the Preserve program a successful, continuing effort. To date, 12 shipwrecks are Preserves, and additional nominations are received constantly at the bureau office in Tallahassee. After *Urca*, another galleon—*San Pedro* of the 1733 fleet wrecked in the Florida Keys—became a Preserve, and it subsequently also became a Florida state park. *City of Hawkinsville* near Old Town, the last and largest steamboat on the Suwannee River, was the third, followed by USS *Massachusetts* (BB-2), the nation's oldest surviving battleship, which was sunk for target practice off Pensacola, and then SS *Copenhagen*, a steamer wrecked on the reef off Pompano Beach. SS *Tarpon*, wrecked in a gale offshore of Panama City, was the sixth, then the German racing yacht *Half Moon* (formerly *Germania*) near Miami. Following in quick succession were the Norwegian lumber bark *Lofthus*, wrecked in a storm off Boynton Beach; the steamer *Vamar*, sunk under mysterious circumstances at Port St. Joe; the molasses barge *Regina*, lost while under tow during a storm at Bradenton Beach; and the Italian lumber ship *Georges Valentine*, cast ashore near Stuart. After a gap of a few years, the Civil War tugboat-turned-gunship USS *Narcissus*, sunk by boiler explosion in a storm off Tampa just after the war, became the twelfth Preserve.

Each of the Preserve projects has become an exercise in learning the intimate secrets of the shipwreck. The cavernous hull of USS *Massachusetts* hid surprises—the ship's dynamo, which produced its electricity, was installed on the wrong side based on the official ship blueprints. But an even bigger surprise was the enormous goliath grouper that lived on the port side under the forward 13-inch gun turret. We discovered it after a member of our team accidentally dropped his recording slate; descending after it, he came face to face with the grouper as it charged out of its hidey-hole to investigate the shiny falling object,

A T-shirt created by Friends of *Vamar* reflecting the ship's different names over time, displayed by the author.

(Photo courtesy of the Florida Division of Historical Resources)

and they frightened each other thoroughly, each squawking and fleeing in opposite directions. *Copenhagen* was the biggest underwater mess I had ever seen, but after three months of careful mapping I knew every hull plate. Twenty years later, when I visit the ship I still recognize the features I mapped. *Half Moon* produced a dumpster's worth of old polypro trap line and nets that had become wrapped around her broken hull, all of which had to be removed before we could map it.

One of the most rewarding aspects of the Preserve projects has been finding people with personal connections to the more recent shipwrecks. For instance, we spoke with Russ Smiley, the son of *Half Moon*'s captain, and he remembered the night she sank in Bear Cut and being rescued along with his parents from the drifting hulk by the U.S. Coast Guard. Clayton Adams, a lifelong Cortez resident, told us about his part in rescuing the crew of *Regina* after she went aground on Anna Maria Island in a storm in 1940.

Only 18 years old at the time, he volunteered to swim toward the wreck with a line around his waist, and he saved two crewmen. Former Chief Petty Officer Charles Brems, in his 90s when we interviewed him, told amazing tales of his time on USS *Massachusetts* and provided unique photographs and detailed information. All these gentlemen have passed away now, but how fortunate we were to have been able to meet and chat with them!

The successes of Florida's Preserves inspired other states to establish shipwreck parks, and submerged shipwreck attractions now exist in Maryland, Wisconsin, California, and North Carolina, as well as in other countries around the world. Very popular at home, the Preserve poster is reprinted regularly, with dive shops clamoring for the update whenever another Preserve is added. The associated Museums in the Sea website (www.museumsinthesea.com) generates hundreds of thousands of hits annually from around the world. The overwhelming achievement of educating the public, engaging divers, and motivating citizen participation has inspired state archaeologists to consider other, similar strategies to reach additional Florida divers and the non-diving public.

Florida's Heritage Trails

The Florida Maritime Heritage Trail grew out of the success of the Preserve program and answered a need to provide information about Florida's maritime past to all interested citizens and visitors. Rather than focusing only on underwater sites, the trail was envisioned as including all aspects of Florida's maritime history and legacy, thereby making it appealing to non-divers as well as those more connected with "innerspace." Because Florida is such a large geographical area with many maritime-related places to explore, the Maritime Heritage Trail was designed to be more of an information trail than a physical trail with stops that a visitor can complete in a few hours, although the featured places certainly can be visited.

The trail was organized into six themes, each designed to highlight the state's maritime past: Coastal Communities, Environments, Forts, Lighthouses, Ports, and Shipwrecks. The posters designed for each theme feature striking images on the front, and information about destinations to experience the theme on the back. Because the posters sometimes are out of print, a website also provides more extensive descriptions and images than can fit on the poster.

The idea of the statewide Maritime Heritage Trail proved intriguing, and encouraging feedback from the public steered archaeologists toward developing additional trails on a more local scale. As part of its maritime heritage program, the Florida Keys National Marine Sanctuary selected nine of the most historically and visually interesting wreck sites in its waters to create a Shipwreck Trail. These sites—ranging from sailing vessels that ran aground on the reef to modern ships that were sunk intentionally to serve as artificial reefs—provide snorkelers and divers a chance to explore a variety of ship types in clear water surrounded by vibrant tropical marine life. The state of Florida's Underwater Archaeological Preserve *San Pedro* also is included on the trail, an example of cross-marketing that has made the galleon one of the most visited shipwrecks in the Keys.

The popularity of the sanctuary's trail and the popular draw of the Keys as a diving destination inspired BAR archaeologists to create another trail with wreck divers in mind, this one focusing on the ships of the 1733 Spanish plate fleet. These ships, which had been strewn in a violent hurricane along 80 miles of the Keys, were salvaged thoroughly by the Spaniards soon after the disaster. The increasing use of scuba equipment in the 1950s and 1960s also inspired modern treasure hunting after the ships were rediscovered. Despite the heavy damage they have sustained from modern salvors, these shipwrecks remain some of the oldest artificial reefs in the Keys, and they are home to an amazing array of fish, corals, crustaceans, and mollusks.

Dodging hurricanes themselves in the summer of 2004, BAR archaeologists produced site plans, ship histories, biological inventories, and site descriptions, which were presented to the public as a booklet and a website. The additional information available via these resources describes the development and history of the Spanish fleet system and explains why the iron cannons and anchors salvaged from the wrecks by the early treasure hunters are rusting away because they were not conserved properly.

Bureau archaeologists also have examined other areas of Florida to find a variety of interesting shipwrecks in close proximity that could be linked as a trail. The Panhandle proved to be an inspired location, with its dependence on beach tourism and thriving diving industry that accommodates a large number of local and visiting divers. The Panhandle Shipwreck Trail grew out of discussions with diving community representatives from Pensacola to Port St. Joe, including dive shop owners, charter boat captains, and divemasters. The 12 shipwrecks chosen for the trail are among the most visited in the area, with divers often requesting more information about their histories and how they sank.

Cover of the booklet guide to the 1733 Spanish Galleon Trail.
(Courtesy of the Florida Division of Historical Resources)

Although some wrecks are quite famous among divers, such as the "great carrier reef" USS *Oriskany* and the nearly intact *Black Bart*, others are more obscure; relating their stories helps to stimulate visitation and boost their economic potential for the local tourist industry. For a nominal fee, participating dive shops and charter boats provide divers with a passport for the trail—a dedicated log book to record their dives on the trail's shipwrecks. Upon completing the entire trail, divers can request a prize from BAR: a limited-edition T-shirt proclaiming the accomplishment! The

The limited-edition Panhandle Shipwreck Trail T-shirt, an exclusive collector's item for those who have dived all the trail wrecks. *(Photo courtesy of the Florida Division of Historical Resources)*

small fee goes into reprinting the passports when needed, and the collectible nature of the passport promotes the trail as a travel destination and a heritage tourism attraction.

Recognizing the popularity of historic shipwrecks trails tied together through interpretation, the cultural resource managers at Biscayne National Park developed a Maritime Heritage Trail featuring the wrecks in their park's inviting waters. Six shipwrecks spanning more than 100 years of technological development—all lying in shallow, easily accessible, clear water—are interpreted with an informative brochure and a website. Ideal for snorkelers and new divers, these wrecks have long been known and visited; providing their names, histories, and ill-fated stories adds a new dimension for visitors. One of the Key's iconic reef lighthouses, Fowey Rocks, was added later to the trail to reflect the park's goal of including all types of maritime resources. Its inclusion is an example of how new sites can be added to heritage attractions, enabling them to grow and entice visitors for new experiences.

Educational Programs

Visiting historic shipwrecks satisfies many divers' desires to engage with their maritime history, but others want to get more involved. To provide training and ethics information, BAR and the Florida Public Archaeology Network (FPAN) developed two workshops targeted to sport divers—the Heritage Awareness Diving Seminar (HADS) for diving leadership and the Submerged Sites Education & Archaeological Stewardship (SSEAS) for general divers.

Although the programs have similar content, with presentations about underwater archaeology, maritime artifacts, conservation, and ethics, the purpose and audience for each is different. HADS enables diving instructors to teach the Heritage Awareness Diving specialty course by providing information, instruction modules, and teaching outlines. It serves as a course in underwater historic preservation that ties conservation of the cultural environment to conservation of the natural environment. SSEAS is tailored to sport divers who want to learn the basics of nonintrusive archaeological techniques so they can volunteer on underwater archaeological projects and contribute to preservation, research, and site monitoring.

Hundreds of divers have participated in these programs, and they probably are some of the most fun I've ever had underwater. Watching divers tangle with measuring tapes and get the hang of controlling them, or chase after a current-propelled slate before remembering to weight it in place, always reminds me that I'm watching novice divers becoming avocational archaeologists and citizen scientists.

Partnerships that involve organizations with similar goals of education, public engagement,

Divers in a SSEAS class practicing archaeological recording skills at the wreck of *Lugano*, a site in Biscayne National Park's Maritime Heritage Trail. *(Photo courtesy of the Florida Public Archaeology Network)*

and site protection are among the most important developments in promoting underwater archaeology and submerged site preservation. The BAR is the leader in Florida, spearheading Preserves, trails, and diver training programs. The Florida Public Archaeology Network (FPAN) promotes and enables public involvement in our state's heritage, both on land and under water. FPAN offers training courses and workshops for law enforcement, park rangers, teachers, cemetery preservation groups, forestry professionals, and scuba divers. Employing the trickle-down strategy of instructing teachers and managers who then share what they have learned, these programs have had a dramatic impact on site preservation and appreciation. Fortunately, Florida has a variety of organizations dedicated to educating and involving the public in the study of our state's maritime past.

The Lighthouse Archaeological Maritime Program, with the fitting acronym of LAMP, is the St. Augustine Lighthouse & Maritime Museum's underwater archaeology branch, dedicated to investigating and understanding the unique maritime heritage of our nation's oldest continually inhabited city (see Chapter 9). LAMP

Logo of the Lighthouse Archaeological Maritime Program, one of the premier independent maritime archaeology programs in the United States.

archaeologists persistently search for and locate sunken vessels as well as the remains of harbor facilities and other maritime infrastructure that made St. Augustine an important colonial port. Lighthouse Museum interpreters and LAMP staff incorporate this information into exhibits and programs that reveal the daily lives and activities of the people who have called St. Augustine home over the centuries.

LAMP archaeologists have discovered and investigated some fascinating shipwrecks. One ship, known as the Storm Wreck, sank while trying to get over the treacherous sandbar into the harbor. The ship appears to have been carrying people loyal to Great Britain away from war-ravaged Charleston during the American Revolution—when those who did not want to become Americans were fleeing the invasion of their city by soldiers they considered treasonous rebels and insurgents. We don't learn about that part of our nation's past in the history books or in school, but this shipwreck is filling in the gap.

Another organization, Marine Archaeological Research and Conservation, Inc. (MARC), consists primarily of avocationals and researchers whose initial training was not in underwater archaeology, but who have acquired the skills and knowledge to become thoroughly proficient. MARC is a Florida-based nonprofit dedicated to "increasing public awareness and protection of our submerged cultural resources," as its website states. MARC teams have assisted with Underwater Archaeological Preserve projects, discovered missing parts of known wrecks, conducted cultural and biological surveys in support of research, produced amazing site plans and photomosaics of shipwrecks, and shared their findings with the public. Working with MARC divers, who are passionate, enthusiastic, and professional, is a lesson in how much skilled avocationals can contribute to learning about and, most importantly, protecting fragile submerged sites. Their voices among the diving community are powerful tools for preservation.

Logo of the Marine Archaeological Research and Conservation (MARC) avocational group, which specializes in shipwreck mapping, photomosaic site plans, and video documentaries.

Members of the Maritime Archaeological and Historical Society (MAHS) mapping an as yet unidentified shipwreck in the Florida Keys. *(Photo courtesy of MAHS)*

Groups from outside Florida also like to come to our state to take advantage of our inviting environment and amazing shipwrecks and cultural sites. The Maritime Archaeological and Historical Society (MAHS) is a group of avocational archaeologists hailing from various states. Their purpose is to "enhance public awareness and foster appreciation" for historic shipwrecks and other types of submerged heritage. Although the group is based in Washington, DC, MAHS divers participate in research and monitoring projects all over the world, and they have assisted resource managers in Florida for many years.

Organizations such as Diving with a Purpose, Junior Scientists in the Sea, and the PAST Foundation also provide archaeology students of all ages and skill levels with the opportunity to conduct shipwreck research and obtain information that assists state and federal agencies in their management and outreach responsibilities. Partnerships such as these result in hands-on experience and engagement for the participants while providing needed data for long-term site preservation and promotion. It's a win for everyone!

The story of public education and engagement with Florida's submerged heritage sites is ongoing and ever-changing. From the early days of monthly articles in *Scuba News* magazine to current strategies of live excavation Internet feeds and real-time updates of field discoveries, Florida's maritime archaeologists strive to connect citizens and visitors with our state's amazing maritime past. Shipwrecks often are out of sight and therefore out of mind for people who do not scuba dive or who live far from the sea, so developing methods for bringing the shipwrecks to these people, instead of the people to the shipwrecks, is the future of public engagement with maritime sites. And for those lucky enough to visit our underwater heritage in person, archaeological training classes and monitoring programs enable them to be producers of information, rather than just consumers. These new citizen-scientists will help to pass on the concepts of site appreciation and preservation to future generations.

Dr. Della A. Scott-Ireton is Associate Director of the Florida Public Archaeology Network. As a tireless proponent of public outreach and participation in archaeology, Scott-Ireton is co-editor of *Submerged Cultural Resource Management: Preserving and Interpreting Our Maritime Heritage* (Kluwer, 2003), and *Out of the Blue: Public Interpretation of Maritime Cultural Resources* (Springer, 2007) and is editor of *Between the Devil and the Deep: Meeting Challenges in the Public Interpretation of Maritime Cultural Heritage* (Springer, 2014).

For Additional Information

Organizations

Diving with a Purpose, http://www.divingwithapurpose.org/

Florida Bureau of Archaeological Research, http://dos.myflorida.com/historical/archaeology/underwater/

Florida Public Archaeology Network, http://www.fpan.us

Junior Scientists in the Sea, http://jrscientistsinthesea.com/

Maritime Archaeological and Historical Society, http://www.mahsnet.org

The PAST Foundation, https://pastfoundation.org

St. Augustine Lighthouse and Maritime Museum, http://www.staugustinelighthouse.com

Interpreted Attractions

1733 Spanish Galleon Trail, http://info.flheritage.com/galleon-trail/

Biscayne National Park Maritime Heritage Trail, https://www.nps.gov/bisc/learn/historyculture/maritime-heritage-trail.htm

Florida Keys National Marine Sanctuary Shipwreck Trail, https://floridakeys.noaa.gov/shipwrecktrail/welcome.html

Florida Panhandle Shipwreck Trail, http://www.floridapanhandledivetrail.com

Florida's Maritime Heritage Trail, http://info.flheritage.com/maritime-trail/

Florida's Underwater Archaeological Preserves, http://www.museumsinthesea.com

CHAPTER 12

Preserving the Past for Future Generations: Conclusion

ROGER C. SMITH

The archaeological sites featured in this book were discovered in many different ways. Initially, most of the people on the water were fishermen, and they discovered the places where fish congregate, which often are sunken sites that became artificial reefs. Spear fishermen, mainly sport hobbyists who fished in and under the water, also became familiar with these artificial reefs. Once scuba diving became popular, recreational divers began to explore the natural and cultural resources they encountered as well. As with fishermen and their catches, the divers would tend to take home the things they found underwater, and the hobby of collecting artifacts gradually became a routine part of the recreational experience. Divers quickly learned that some of these artifacts, such as stone projectile points lying on riverbeds or silver coins buried in offshore shipwrecks, not only were valuable as souvenirs but also had monetary worth. As the divers compared, traded, or sold the artifacts they found—which they viewed as proprietary "finders keepers" items—their collector mindset was reinforced.

Unlike prehistoric tools or fossils found underwater, with which few people readily could identify, the silver and gold artifacts discovered on old Spanish galleons immediately made the news. These items caught everyone's attention, particularly those who already were familiar with the underwater world. For some, the idea that one could get rich pursuing a hobby left them lying awake at night. For those who had actually found underwater treasures, the realization that others wanted to find them too left them

Florida Treasures and More. (Photo by the author)

lying awake as well—and led to the desire for proprietary protection. Thus, what started as just a hobby became a small business enterprise that sought validation and state sanction. A small cottage industry of sunken treasure hunters obtained leases for the state's submerged bottomlands. These leases were similar to the upland mining leases granted by the state department of agriculture for a nominal annual fee.

Meanwhile, the divers collecting artifacts in Florida's rivers and springs began to realize that there were fruitful areas containing assemblages of artifacts and bones. When these materials were shown to university archaeologists, for the first time they became aware of the potential of underwater sites—but they lacked the requisite skills to explore the sources of these discoveries. Although a few academic archaeologists eventually learned to dive, their focus was on objects that had fallen into the water from land sites.

State management of archaeological sites on public lands evolved in the early 1960s with the appointment of the first state archaeologist, who served a board of antiquities. The first state underwater archaeologist, Carl Clausen, was an archaeology graduate student, and his assignment was to monitor and manage the east-coast leases to treasure hunters who were diving the shipwrecks of the 1715 Spanish fleet. He began to map some of the sites and helped to establish a conservation laboratory in Tallahassee. The Florida legislature passed the Historical Resources Act in 1967 to protect historical and archaeological sites on state-owned lands including the submerged bottomlands, which included all navigable waterways offshore and in the interior of the state.

While hobby divers and treasure hunters continued to make discoveries, a growing number of archaeologists learned that underwater sites also could help to answer questions about prehistoric and historic human behavior. State and federal management agencies began to protect submerged sites as they already did upland sites, with permit requirements for activities that would impact resources and penalties for violations. Archaeological surveys were required of submerged areas that could be affected by development, which resulted in new discoveries. These same agencies were tasked with making inventories of underwater resources, and the inventories were conducted by archaeologists who worked with waterfront communities, amateur organizations, university field schools, and diving volunteers to locate and record new sites.

Management of underwater archaeological sites in Florida is administered by the Florida Department of State (FDOS), the National Park Service (NPS), and the National Oceanic and Atmospheric Administration (NOAA). State-managed areas encompass all navigable bodies of water, including rivers and bays, out to three miles on the Atlantic coast and 10 miles on the Gulf coast. Archaeological sites and cultural materials older than 50 years in these areas are publicly owned, with title vested in the Florida Department of State's Division of Historical Resources. The division includes the Bureau of Archaeological Research, which employs a team of underwater archaeologists.

NPS jurisdiction includes the waters of Biscayne National Park, Everglades National Park, Dry Tortugas National Park, and one-half mile offshore of Canaveral National Seashore. Archaeological and collections management services are provided by the Southeast Archeological Center in Tallahassee; underwater surveys and assessments are provided by staff of the NPS Submerged Resources Center in Lakewood, Colorado. NOAA jurisdiction includes the Florida Keys National Marine Sanctuary (FKNMS), which extends offshore to the 300-foot-depth contour of the Florida Straits. FKNMS offices are located in Key West and Key Largo. Each of these state and federal agencies requires permits to conduct activities focused on underwater archaeological sites.

The state laws that protect Florida's submerged history include the Florida Historical Resources Act (1967) that governs the use of publicly owned archaeological and historical resources on land and underwater. Divers are encouraged to participate in the identification, recording, and reporting of underwater sites to preserve them, but disturbing or digging on publicly owned sites is illegal unless permission is obtained in advance from the Division of Historical Resources. Intentional excavation of underwater sites without written authorization is considered a third-degree felony, so it is best to record and report one's discoveries and to seek help before proceeding with further investigation.

Florida passed laws protecting unmarked human burials in the late 1980s. Chapter 872 of the Florida Statutes made it illegal to willfully and knowingly disturb human remains, whether on public or private lands. Under these provisions, the state archaeologist may take jurisdiction and control of the remains of humans who have been dead for at least seventy-five years. Later, the federal Native American Graves Protection and Repatriation Act was passed by Congress in 1990, which added additional weight to the state law.

Another pertinent federal law is the Archaeological Resources Protection Act, enacted by Congress in 1979. This law provides stiff penalties for intentionally looting or vandalizing archaeological sites. Although the law does not apply to state lands, its passage paved the way for states to enact similar laws for the protection of cultural resources located on state lands. The federal Abandoned Shipwreck Act of 1988 reaffirmed that the title and management authority of abandoned shipwrecks belonged to the states in which they are located and provided guidelines for administering preservation programs. The Marine Protection, Research, and Sanctuaries Act of 1972 gave NOAA the authority to designate sanctuaries in U.S. waters to protect natural and historical resources. Designated in 1990, the Florida Keys National Marine Sanctuary covers 2,800 nautical square miles and includes the Florida Reef and numerous shipwrecks. Cultural resource management in the sanctuary is conducted in partnership and cooperation with the Florida Department of State. The Sunken Military Craft Act of 2004 was intended to protect all sunken military craft owned by the federal government and all foreign military craft that lie in U.S. waters from unauthorized disturbance. Protection under this law is given to sunken military watercraft, aircraft, and spacecraft as well as their associated contents.

The continued existence and protection of submerged cultural resources depends on Florida's residents and visitors. We all should be concerned about the preservation of these resources for the benefit of ourselves and future generations. Once these nonrenewable time capsules are disturbed or destroyed, they are gone forever. Even the careful scientific methods of archaeology are controlled destruction, so most archaeologists will only excavate portions of sites, conserving the remainder for future research and better investigative tools.

Our endangered coral reefs and manatees hopefully will recover with our help, but archaeological sites will never grow back. New shipwrecks may be made, but there will never be another wrecked Spanish galleon or sunken Civil War gunboat. And the study of these microcosms of history is vital to our understanding of the people who used Florida's waters before us.

Underwater archaeology is alive and well in Florida. In a state that has a large and varied number of submerged cultural resources, an active regimen of survey and planning, inventory and assessment, and interpretation and exhibition has greatly expanded the archaeological and historical record during the last 30 years. Increased cooperation between professional and amateur investigators has made possible several important surveys and excavations, providing tantalizing glimpses of Florida's enormous resource base. The general public's growing interest in historic preservation is demonstrated by its active participation at every step in the establishment of underwater archaeological preserves and heritage trails, and in the survey and investigation of numerous archaeological sites. Close coordination among regulatory agencies, private and public entities, and the media has served to protect and preserve Florida's heritage and to bring it to the public's attention. The growing commitment by academic institutions to training students in underwater archaeology—as demonstrated by the University of West Florida, Florida State University, University of Miami, East Carolina University, Indiana University, Flinders University, and Texas A&M University—has emerged in large part due to the tremendous potential for research in Florida's waters. Hopefully, these trends in resource assessment and management will continue well into the future.

For Additional Information

Websites

Florida Bureau of Archaeological Research, http://dos.myflorida.com/historical/archaeology/

Florida Keys National Marine Sanctuary, https://floridakeys.noaa.gov/welcome.html

Florida Public Archaeology Network, http://flpublicarchaeology.org/

National Park Service Southeast Archeological Center, https://www.nps.gov/seac/index.htm

National Park Service Submerged Resources Center, https://www.nps.gov/orgs/1635/index.htm

Index

(Page numbers in italics refer to illustrations)